GRAMMATICALIZATION

AMSTERDAM STUDIES IN THE THEORY AND HISTORY OF LINGUISTIC SCIENCE

General Editor

E. F. KONRAD KOERNER
(University of Ottawa)

Series IV – CURRENT ISSUES IN LINGUISTIC THEORY

Advisory Editorial Board

Raimo Anttila (Los Angeles); Lyle Campbell (Christchurch, N.Z.)
Sheila Embleton (Toronto); John E. Joseph (Edinburgh)
Manfred Krifka (Austin, Tex.); Hans-Heinrich Lieb (Berlin)
E. Wyn Roberts (Vancouver, B.C.); Hans-Jürgen Sasse (Köln)

Volume 193

Jurgen Klausenburger

Grammaticalization
Studies in Latin and Romance morphosyntax

GRAMMATICALIZATION

STUDIES IN LATIN AND ROMANCE MORPHOSYNTAX

JURGEN KLAUSENBURGER
University of Washington, Seattle

JOHN BENJAMINS PUBLISHING COMPANY
AMSTERDAM/PHILADELPHIA

The paper used in this publication meets the minimum requirements of American National Standard for Information Sciences — Permanence of Paper for Printed Library Materials, ANSI Z39.48-1984.

Library of Congress Cataloging-in-Publication Data

Klausenburger, Jurgen.
 Grammaticalization : studies in Latin and Romance morphosyntax / Klausenburger, Jurgen.
    p.   cm. -- (Amsterdam studies in the theory and history of linguistic science. Series IV, Current issues in linguistic theory, ISSN 0304-0763 ; v. 193)
 Includes bibliographical references (p.) and indexes.
 1. Latin language--Morphology. 2. Romance languages--Morphology. 3. Romance languages--Syntax. 4. Latin language--Syntax. I. Title. II. Series.
PA2133 .K58   2000
475--dc21   99-058275
ISBN 90 272 3700 X (Eur.) / 1 55619 971 6 (US) (Hb; alk. paper)   CIP

© 2000 – John Benjamins B.V.
No part of this book may be reproduced in any form, by print, photoprint, microfilm, or any other means, without written permission from the publisher.

John Benjamins Publishing Co. • P.O.Box 75577 • 1070 AN Amsterdam • The Netherlands
John Benjamins North America • P.O.Box 27519 • Philadelphia PA 19118-0519 • USA

To the memory of my parents

Table of Contents

Preface xi

CHAPTER 1
Introduction: Theoretical Foundations 1
1.1 Natural Morphology 1
    1.1.1 System-independent naturalness 1
    1.1.2 System-dependent naturalness 5
    1.1.3 The role of typology 9
1.2 Approaches related to Natural Morphology 11
    1.2.1 Inflectional organization 11
    1.2.2 Paradigmatic structure 14
1.3 Grammaticalization 18
    1.3.1 The metonymic-metaphorical model 18
    1.3.2 Paths of grammar 21
1.4 Studies related to grammaticalization 24
    1.4.1 The synthesis/analysis cycle 24
    1.4.2 Perception and processing issues 27
    1.4.3 Syntactic branching 29

CHAPTER 2
Verbal Inflection 37
2.1 Overview 37
2.2 Latin system 37
2.3 French and Italian results 42
    2.3.1 Data and segmentation 42
    2.3.2 Comparison of differences 44

2.4	Individual analogies	46
	2.4.1 Outline	46
	2.4.2 French	48
	2.4.2.1 Schwa	48
	2.4.2.2 *-ons*	51
	2.4.2.3 Imperfect indicative	53
	2.4.3 Italian	56
	2.4.3.1 Final *-i*	56
	2.4.3.2 *-iamo*	59
	2.4.3.3 Final *-o*	61
2.5	"Minimal" inflections in Modern French	63

CHAPTER 3
Grammaticalization Processes Involving the Verb 67

3.1	Synthesis and analysis in Romance verbs	67
	3.1.1 The rise of analyticity	67
	3.1.2 The motivation for synthesis	71
	3.1.3 The grammaticalization of auxiliaries	74
3.2	The grammaticalization of Romance personal pronouns	81
	3.2.1 Subject proclitics or prefixes in French?	81
	3.2.2 Pro-drop in Old French and Modern (Spoken) French	92
	3.2.3 Object clitics	97
3.3	The (un)likelihood of Romance inflectional prefixation	101

CHAPTER 4
Nominal Inflection and Grammaticalization 107

4.1	Rumanian noun inflection	107
	4.1.1 Data and synchronic analysis	107
	4.1.2 Historical evolution	110
	4.1.2.1 Inflectional endings	110
	4.1.2.2 Synthesis	112
4.2	The Old French case system	114
	4.2.1 Noun and adjective data	114
	4.2.2 A natural morphological analysis	117
	4.2.2.1 Old French synchrony	117
	4.2.2.2 Diachrony: Before and after Old French	119
4.3	Life cycle of (other) Romance case structures	122
	4.3.1 Spanish and Italian developments	122
	4.3.2 The definite article and Romance nouns	127

CHAPTER 5
Theoretical Issues in Grammaticalization 131
5.1 Grammaticalization and the 'invisible hand' in language change 131
    5.1.1 From Mandeville's paradox to 'invisible hand' explanations .. 131
    5.1.2 Can grammaticalization be explained invisible-handedly? ... 135
5.2 The explanatory potential of grammaticalization 137
    5.2.1 On the importance of irreversibility (unidirectionality) 137
    5.2.2 Morphocentricity 142
    5.2.3 Exaptation, regrammaticalization, degrammaticalization 145
    5.2.4 Are grammatical categories discrete? 147

CHAPTER 6
Conclusions 151
6.1 Results of this study 151
    6.1.1 Inflectional morphology 151
        6.1.1.1 Verbal inflections 151
        6.1.1.2 Nominal inflections 151
    6.1.2 Grammaticalization 152
6.2 Grammaticalization and naturalness 153

Appendix 157

References 163

Subject Index 173

Name Index 175

Preface

This study began more than a decade ago, intended as a contribution to a natural morphological analysis of Latin and Romance inflection, with the tentative title of *Parameters of naturalness in Romance inflectional morphology*. The major dichotomy in natural morphology developed in the 1980's was that between Mayerthaler (1981) (English translation 1988), representing 'universal', or 'language independent' naturalness, and Wurzel (1984) (English translation 1989), cast within a 'language dependent' framework. Both approaches were presented and examined in Dressler (1985b) and Dressler (1987), along with Kilani-Schoch (1988), with additional insights found in Wheeler (1993). In papers read at various national and international Romance linguistics and morphology conferences between 1986 and 1994, I applied natural morphological themes to aspects of Latin, French (both Old and Modern), Italian, and Rumanian inflectional morphology, enlarging the relevant literature to include studies such as Bybee (1985) and Carstairs (1987), which, though not "officially" part of natural morphology, nevertheless manifest characteristics very compatible with naturalness. During this same period, I also conducted various seminars in Romance linguistics at the University of Washington which were based on these works,[1] in addition to writing reviews and review articles of some of them for journals. Although natural morphological theory contributed insightful and promising avenues for my research, it did not provide a satisfactory framework for a major section of historical Romance linguistics, the rise and evolution of periphrasis. For the latter, grammaticalization theory offered the necessary formal edifice, as it has evolved in studies such as Heine et al. (1991), Hopper & Traugott (1993), Heine (1993), Bybee et al. (1994), and Lehmann (1995 — already found in its essence in Lehmann 1985). I would also add Schwegler (1990) on this list, since, as an updated review of the (traditional) synthesis/ analysis cycle, it clearly announces and deals with core issues of grammaticalization.

---

1. Such forums produced comments and ideas that may have been incorporated into the body of this monograph without specific attribution on my part being possible.

During a sabbatical leave at the Camargo Foundation, Cassis, France, in the Autumn Quarter of 1995, I was offered the opportunity to construct a grammaticalization 'scenario' appropriate for issues in historical Romance morphosyntax, incorporating works outside of grammaticalization studies proper, such as Hall (1992) and Bauer (1995). It was then that the real focus of this monograph crystallized in my mind: grammaticalization and how inflectional morphology constitutes only a part of, and is 'subordinated to', clines or chains of grammaticalization. Intuitively, such has probably always been my understanding of historical Romance morphosyntax, but it took grammaticalization theory to formalize such conceptualizations. It also became clear that such a study, combining natural morphology and grammaticalization, applying them to the very rich material of the Romance field, would fill a *lacuna* in both synchronic and diachronic linguistics.

Consonant with the preceding suggestions, I incorporate and alternate both natural morphology and grammaticalization issues in the text of my book. It begins with an introduction to a broad range of theoretical work which served as a foundation for this study (Chapter 1). The body of the monograph then contains first a chapter on verbal morphology (Chapter 2), on Latin, French, and Italian, and their interrelationships. Here, I deal with Latin inflectional morphology becoming (remaining?) Romance inflection, material all of which falls within the reach of natural morphological theory. Chapter 3, on the other hand, requires grammaticalization concepts, revisiting the well-known Latin to Romance verbal restructurings, French subject pronouns, and Romance object clitics. Chapter 4 merges natural morphology and grammaticalization in the presentation of questions involving Romance nominal histories, making use of French, Rumanian, Spanish, Italian, and Provençal examples. Chapter 5, finally, thoroughly examines outstanding theoretical issues in grammaticalization, prominently featuring the relevance of 'invisible hand' explanations and the crucial and pervasive role played by unidirectionality, or irreversibility. The strong tie-in between natural morphology and grammaticalization is (re)emphasized in the conclusion (Chapter 6), which also attempts to connect directly specifics of Chapter 2–4 with the theoretical discussion of Chapter 5.

This study was written, over the past decade, in various stages. For the first part, essentially Chapter 2, I am grateful for sabbatical leave granted to me by the University of Washington for Spring Quarter 1989. The major section, Chapter 3, was completed during another sabbatical quarter, Autumn 1995, which I spent at the Camargo Foundation, Cassis, France. For this opportunity I would like to thank both the University of Washington and the Foundation, which provided an ideal atmosphere and accommodations for the work. The writing of the remaining chapters of the monograph took place during the academic years 1996–1999.

I would like to acknowledge gratefully the help and encouragement provided to me by Konrad Koerner. This work has been greatly improved as a result.

Jurgen Klausenburger
Seattle, August 1999

CHAPTER 1

Introduction
Theoretical Foundations

1.1 Natural Morphology

1.1.1 *System-independent naturalness*

A first version of Natural Morphology was the one proposed by Mayerthaler (1981), which has become known as 'system-independent' or 'universal'. It is based on the notion of *iconicity*, which in turn is defined by the concept of *markedness*, as outlined in what follows.

Four grades of iconicity are established by Mayerthaler (1981: 24–25):
1. maximally iconic
2. minimally iconic
3. non-iconic
4. counter-iconic

Such degrees of iconicity reflect different relationships between the *signans* (form) and *signatum* (meaning) in morphology. These equations hold for each degree.

1. Maximal iconicity is obtained if Signans A possesses an "additional" formal marker compared to Signans B and if, at the same time, Signatum A may be considered *marked* and Signatum B may be considered *unmarked*. The best illustration for this relationship is found in the "regular" English plural: Signans A, let us say, *boys*, manifests an extra -*s* compared to *boy*, Signans B. Maximal iconicity results because the formal contrast is matched by the semantic equations of (a) plural = marked and (b) singular = unmarked.

    Minimal iconicity can be seen in the English singular vs. plural *man/men, goose/geese*, and others. Here, a formal difference is overt, but only 'minimally' so, since no supplementary morpheme is found in the plural.

2. Non-iconicity in English plurals would be detectable in *sheep/sheep*, for which the markedness difference remains unmatched by a formal differentiation.
3. Counter-iconicity is also demonstrated in English plurals, as in *phenomenon/phenomena*. Better examples, perhaps, are French *oef*, pronounced [oef], vs. *oefs*, phonetically [ö], or Welsh *coeden/coed* "tree, trees". The grades of iconicity are also considered levels of 'naturalness', on a continuum.

Thus, maximally iconic would be most natural, counter-iconic, of course, least natural. The *leitmotif* of Mayerthaler's study refers to "the principle of constructional iconicity [as] one of the organizing principles of language" (1981: 30). In addition, he claims that iconicity, and thus markedness, resides in human perception and possesses a biological basis and motivation. For him, it is a "comparative perception metric" (p. 62). Such a point of view can be substantiated by the following markedness values (p. 12):

Unmarked	**Marked**
front	back
vertical	horizontal
right	left
up	down
there	here

Such characteristics derive from the biological/neurological features of the prototypical speaker, who is visually oriented toward the front, normally erect and right-handed. Of course, grammatical category markedness distinctions are not observable in this sense, and they are only theoretically interpretable, by additional criteria. Such will include frequency, order of acquisition by children, and general "principles of preference" (Wurzel 1994: 2591), or "evaluative nonequivalence" of oppositions (Battistella 1990: 1). The latter is specifically demonstrable for the singular vs. plural opposition, as explained in Matthews (1991: 235). He shows that the semantic opposition here is not symmetrical. Rather, the plural has a 'positive' meaning, i.e. 'more than one'. On the other hand, the singular has a 'negative' meaning, i.e., 'not plural'. The nonequivalence between the two numbers may also be uncovered by the fact that the plural always must mean 'more than one', while the singular, in so-called 'mass nouns', may capture both a singular and a plural meaning. Such a possibility makes the singular the 'default' number, or the *unmarked* value of the number category.

It is interesting to observe that Matthews considers the iconic relations based on markedness used in the context of the 'universal' approach within

Natural Morphology but one of the facets of iconicity, labeled by him as *paradigmatic* (Matthews 1991:234). The other type of iconicity claimed by Matthews is *syntagmatic* (Matthews 1991:226). This one involves the opposition between 'central' and 'peripheral' categories. For verbal inflection, aspect, tense, and mood are seen as central, while person and number qualify as peripheral. The concept of iconicity enters the picture when the claim is made that central categories tend to be closer to the root of the verb than peripheral ones. Thus, the structural or formal proximity vs. distance from the root defines this contrast. In addition, (more) central categories are said to 'condition' (more) peripheral ones[1] (Matthews 1991:233). This fact is corroborated by the (traditional) classification of verbal paradigms as tense/aspect/mood groups, not person/number collections: we typically list an 'imperfect paradigm', not a 'first person singular paradigm' of a verb. Matthews illustrates syntagmatic iconicity with examples from both Italian and Latin. The Italian imperfect verb form *mangiavano*, for instance, has the canonical structure:

ROOT + TENSE + PERSON/NUMBER
mangia + *va* + *no*

The four Latin perfect formations show that ASPECT marking is either next to the root or inside the root (Matthews 1991:231):

ama-v-i
man-s-i
mo-mord-i (reduplication)
ven-i [weːn]-(vowel lengthening)

In addition to iconicity, Mayerthaler's theory incorporates two other "universal" principles, of *uniform coding* and *transparency* (Mayerthaler 1981:34–35). The first relates one signatum to a unique signans, as in the English suffix *-ing*, which is the only way to express "progressive". The overgeneralization apparent in child morphology, when the past tense of *come* is formed as *comed*, instead of *came*, would be another instance of uniform coding (Carstairs-McCarthy 1992:219). On the level of the root, Lat. *amicus* is completely uniform, phonetically always [amik-]. However, in Italian, *amico* and *amici* show the root-final consonant alternation [k] vs. [č] (Wurzel 1994:2592). The second, however, stipulates one signans = unique signatum. Here, the example is the English

---

1. This issue is also considered at length by Carstairs (1987), under the rubric of the Peripherality Constraint (cf. below, 1.2.2).

suffix *-est*, which can only mean 'superlative'. It is interesting to note that the comparative suffix *-er* does not qualify as transparent, since this suffix can also code 'agent' (*writer*) and 'instrument' (*cooker*) (Carstairs-McCarthy 1992: 219). Similarly, the German preterit of *schlagen*, which is *schlugen* (PL), is transparent with regard to mood, since the subjunctive would be *schlügen*, while this does not hold in the verb *laufen*, for which both the indicative preterite and the subjunctive are *liefen* (Wurzel 1994: 2592). The two principles combined produce 'uniform transparent coding', or a *biunique relationship* between signans and signatum (cf. Dressler 1985a).

One controversial aspect of Mayerthaler's proposals on naturalness in morphology is found in what he calls "markedness reversal (or inversion)". This principle applies if the coding pattern is counter-iconic, as in (1) the Old French singular masculine subject case of nouns, i.e. the noun *murs* and the adjective *durs*, opposed to the object case which is 'markerless',[2] and in (2) the English 3rd person present indicative verb form with the singular *-s* suffix, opposed to a zero suffix in the 3rd person plural. Mayerthaler would claim that "the marked coding pattern itself constitutes a 'marked' context, in which the usual markedness relationship between (1) the subject case and the object case (subject = unmarked, object = marked) is inverted" (Carstairs-McCarthy 1992: 221), and (2) the singular vs. plural in English verbs is likewise inverted. The latter is due to a division of the category present into (a) generic and (b) non-generic. Prototypical characteristics require the marking (with a suffix) of [+ generic], e.g., *he comes* (Mayerthaler 1981: 53). Markedness reversal must be considered a weak link in this theory, a "technical trick" (Wurzel 1984: 25, n.23).

Mayerthaler (1981: 62) proposes a formal *morphologische Markiertheitstheorie*, consisting of the following three theorems:

1. In case of competition, the less marked form wins over the more marked one;
2. Decrease in markedness in a semantically more marked category occurs *before* that of a semantically less marked category;
3. Less marked material is acquired before more marked material.

Hypothesis (1), of course, is crucial for language change, and it will be tested in various changes from Latin to the Romance languages, especially in Chapters 2 and 4. Hypothesis (2) means that in a potential paradigm leveling case, where more and less marked forms are in competition, the less marked form will be

---

2. For more on the Old French case system, see below, 4.4.2.

adopted (Wurzel 1994: 2593). As to the third hypothesis, it is, of course, easy to determine that unmarked categories, such the indicative, are acquired first, before the 'corresponding' marked subjunctive, or the present tense before any other tense, or the singular before the plural.

1.1.2 System-dependent naturalness

Although Wurzel (1984) considers the language-specific aspect of morphological naturalness, his theory ultimately is based on the following *universal* principles (pp. 174–175):

I.   The principle of typological uniformity and systematic nature of morphological patterns;
II. The principle of implicative structuring in morphology;
III. The principle of strict linking of morphological classes to extra-morphological characteristics;
IV. The principle of the formal reflections of identity and distinctions of contents;
V.   The principle of the formal reflection of content markedness relations.

In Wurzel's study, principle I turns into the concept of *system congruity*, and it is then fleshed out by way of *system defining structural properties* (SDSP), i.e., *system-definierende Struktureigenschaften*. Principles II and III are contained in his *paradigm structure conditions* (PSC), *Paradigmenstrukturbedingungen*.

Wurzel makes use of the following SDSPs (1984: 82):

1. The inventory of morphosyntactic categories and the properties representing them;
2. The appearance of base form inflection or stem inflection;
3. The appearance of separate or cumulative symbolization of categories;
4. The number and manner of formal distinctions in the inflectional forms of a paradigm;
5. The marker types occurring and their relation to the individual morphosyntactic categories;
6. The presence or absence of inflectional classes.

Modern German noun declensions, for instance, may be characterized by these six SDSPs as follows (Wurzel 1984: 95):

a. The German noun illustrates number by singular and plural, and case is represented by nominative, genitive, dative, and accusative.
b. Base form inflection occurs in German: *Freund, Freund + es* (GEN.SG).

c. Number and case are signaled cumulatively in the German noun, as *Freund + e* would have a suffix marking both plural and (nominative) case. However, if the definite article is added, it would mark case separately: *der Freund, den Freund*.
d. Three equally important distinction types occur, determined by gender/number (MASC.SG, FEM.SG, NEUTER SG/PL).
e. The marker type of article inflection exists for case, as well as the marker type of suffixation for case.
f. German noun declension has a number of inflectional classes.

Further insights into how such SDSPs function in languages may be gained by a comparison of Modern Greek and English with respect to SDSP (2), stem vs. base inflection. Carstairs-McCarthy (1992: 229) gives the following data:

	Modern Greek	
	Singular	**Plural**
Stem inflection	*ánθrop-os* "person"	*ánθrop-i*
	élin-as "Greek"	*élin-es*
	mér-a "day"	*mér-es*
	vun-ó "mountain"	*vun-á*
	spít-i "house"	*spít-ja*
Base-form inflection	*pséma* "lie"	*pséma-ta*
	garáz "garage"	*garáz*
	English	
	Singular	**Plural**
Stem inflection	*cris-is*	*cris-es*
	formul-a	*formul-ae*
	radi-us	*radi-i*
Base-form inflection	*cat*	*cat-s*
	beach	*beach-es*

It is clear from the given examples that Greek and English manifest both stem and base inflection in their nouns. However, stem inflection would be considered the SDSP in Greek, while base inflection would qualify as such for English. How is this determined? According to Wurzel (1984: 86), SDSPs are selected statistically:

a. by the number and relative size of inflectional classes in which a certain property is realized, i.e., the number of paradigms in which it occurs *in toto*;

b. by the quantity in which in these cases a structural property is realized, i.e., the number of forms in which it is present.

We can also be sure that stem inflection is not *system congruent* in English by the fact that it "is vulnerable to erosion (cf. *formulas, radiuses*); in Greek, on the other hand, stem inflection is system congruent and therefore stable" (Carstairs-McCarthy 1992: 229).

The issue of 'erosion' leads to a more general question about SDSPs: Do they undergo changes? If so, how and why do they change?

SDSPs resist morphological change (Wurzel 1984: 89); they, in fact, determine it. However, the answer to the above question is not negative, nevertheless, since SDSPs may be subject to transformations due to phonological change, as Wurzel demonstrates (1984: 103–104) by data from Old Swedish to Modern Swedish. A sound change (the deletion of post-vocalic word-final /r/) led to the abandonment of the formal distinction between nominative and accusative. Likewise, the reduction of final vowels of Old High German to [ə] led to a shift from stem inflection in OHG to base inflection in Modern High German (1984: 105). Two steps are involved:

a. The changeover in SDSPs, a qualitative change, is conditioned extra-morphologically;
b. the later spread or possibly complete imposition of (new) SDSPs, a quantitative step, is morphologically conditioned.

Therefore, "Morphology itself is conservative. It reproduces only already extant SDSPs, but does not itself create new ones" (1984: 109).

It is perhaps important to mention at this point that the issue of *markedness* is paramount in Wurzel's version of natural morphology also. So far, SDSPs have been isolated as the crucial means of determining system congruity in a language, or in parts of individual morphologies. What has been uncovered by way of SDSPs are *dominant* structural features, patterns that regenerate themselves in historical change. Wurzel's theory now goes one step further and equates the dominance of a certain morphological architecture with its default, or *unmarked* nature. Therefore, markedness considerations enter, just like in the 'universal' conception of naturalness. However, SDSPs operate quite differently from the dimensions of iconicity or uniform coding, and the delimiting of markedness values is achieved in a radically different way. "Whether one coding pattern is more iconic than another can be settled just by reference to the immediate data; but whether one pattern is more system-congruent than another depends crucially on the system (hence the language) in question" (Carstairs-McCarthy 1992: 229). Put succinctly, system-independent natural morphology operates with semantic markedness, determined in the same manner for all languages, relating to formal morphological structure in arriving at various degrees of iconicity or other coding manifestations. System-dependent natural morphology, on the other hand, operates with 'system' markedness, as defined above. A continuum of natural structure is uncovered, from the most natural (= unmarked, dominant) to the least natural (= marked, not dominant) pattern in the system.

While SDSPs determine the overall inflectional system, individual paradigms are structured by implications, in the form of PSCs. Wurzel demonstrates, for instance, that a complex paradigm like the Latin 3rd declension could be learned easily only because of two implicative patterns (1984: 120):[3]

   a.   /im/ in ACC.SG > /i:/ in ABL.SG > /i:s/ in ACC.PL. > /ium/ in GEN.PL.
   b.   /um/ in GEN.PL. > /e:s/ in ACC.PL. > /e:/ in ABL.SG > /em/ in ACC.SG

Such implications would cover nouns like *puppis, ignis,* and *rex*. PSCs are generally not equally important; and dominating, or *unmarked*, ones can easily be found, purely on the basis of frequency (Wurzel 1984: 127). As an illustration, the German *-s* plural dominates over *-n* plural, as ungrammatical *Freskos (for correct *Fresken*) may be heard, while a plural like *Kinen (for *Kinos*) is inconceivable (p. 126). In addition, it is well known that in child language the *-s* suffix occurs with nouns almost exclusively.

Just as SDSPs create system congruity, PSCs determine the stability of various inflectional classes. There may be stable, unstable, and stability-neutral inflectional classes (cf. Wurzel 1984: 129–130), classified as to their function according to the dominating PSC, not in accordance with the dominating PSC, or when no PSC dominates, respectively. It can be ascertained that dominant PSCs establish a strict coupling of the morphological properties of the words with their phonological and/or semantic-syntactic properties (cf. Universal Principle III, above). It is also clear that dominant PSCs have a unifying and stabilizing effect, setting the direction of inflectional class changes and preventing the splitting into too many sub-classes. Thus, the changeover from an unstable to a stable class is expected and 'natural'. Yet, there can be a decrease in class stability as well, but it would have to be due to extra-morphological, typically phonological change (p. 145). The most natural inflectional system would be one with stable classes but this state can never be reached, as all synchronic phases are characterized by tendencies to increase and decrease class

---

3. The sign '>' in this context means "implies."

stability simultaneously (p. 152).

A definition of *productivity* falls out quite logically from the two principal forces of system-dependent naturalness, system congruity and class stability. Productivity, which derives from the interaction of the two forces, represents the direction of the leveling and adjustments that affect an inflectional system, and constitutes by itself a secondary, surface, phenomenon, receiving a complete definition necessarily in terms of both SDSPs and PSCs (pp. 159–160).

1.1.3 The role of typology

According to the parameters of system-independent, or universal, naturalness, Turkish can be considered to have 'ideal' morphological architecture, since, as a strictly agglutinating system, its forms and paradigms are built according to the principles of constructional iconicity, uniformity, and transparency. In addition, the language appears totally system congruous and has no unstable inflectional classes, thus being perfectly 'natural' according to the system-dependent theory of naturalness also. A clear mystery for proponents of universal natural morphology, however, must be the existence of fusional languages, such as Latin (and any Indo-European tongue). Here, iconicity and biuniqueness do not exist, as is made clear by the following contrasts (Dressler 1985c: 4):

Latin	*insul-i:s*	*nostr-i:s*
	"island"-ABL.PL	"our"- ABL.PL
Turkish	*ada-lar-ImIz-dan*	
	"island"-PL-"our"-ABL	

Dressler points out that Turkish may be ideal with respect to the parameters of universal theory, but it also has two decisive disadvantages. First, its words are very long, stringing together many morphemes. If one assumes a parameter of 'optimal word length', which, let us assume, is between two and three syllables, then the Turkish word no longer qualifies as ideal. In addition, it seems obvious that agglutinating structure forces some inflectional markers to be quite distant from the lexical root to which they belong, making their processing less than optimal as well. Another way of describing the latter is to say that Turkish lacks the parameter of *indexicality*.[4] In terms of the parameters of (1) optimal word

---

[4]. Linguistic *signs*, in the semiotic theory of Charles Sanders Peirce, are to be divided into *icons*, for which the signans directly resembles its signatum in some respect, and *symbols*, displaying an arbitrary and conventional relationship between form and meaning. Between these two extremes lies

size and (2) indexicality, Latin ranks as an ideal language. As a matter of fact, cumulative languages could be considered highly economical, "because fusional packing allows two or more signata to share one signans whereas pure agglutinative packing does not" (Carstairs-McCarthy 1992: 225).

It is clear that the parameters of universal naturalness and the two new ones introduced by Dressler cannot be both extant in a language, and one may speak of a 'conflict of naturalness'. Dressler assumes that the theory of natural morphology must contain the component of "typological adequacy" (Wurzel 1994: 2597). Accordingly, agglutinating and fusional types differ in which principles of naturalness are favored: in a language like Turkish, iconicity and biuniqueness count as parameters of naturalness, in a language like Latin, on the other hand, optimal word length and indexicality (cf. Kilani-Schoch 1988: 134–135).

Dressler (1985a) not only introduces a theory of typology to mediate naturalness conflicts, but he also expands the universal version by way of a finer distinction of parameters. Five parameters, hierarchically ordered, are proposed (Kilani-Schoch 1988: 114–126):

1. Diagrammaticity (a subtype of iconicity, although the two concepts are often used interchangeably);
2. Morphotactic transparency;
3. Morphosemantic transparency;
4. Biuniqueness;
5. Indexicality.

For Dressler, there exist really two filters: not only the typological one, but also the language specific one. The universal input of natural parameters given must pass through both of them, according to the following flow-chart (Dressler 1985a: 292, 1985b: 322):

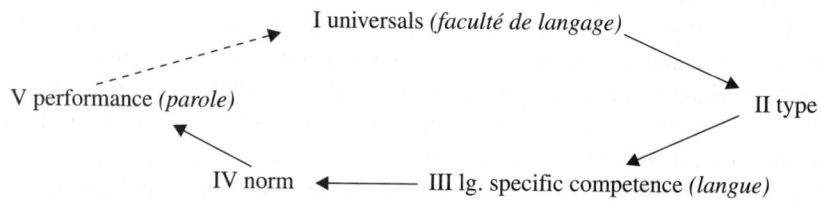

---

the *index*, which can be said to function like a 'signpost': A case suffix indicates that the root it belongs to is a noun (cf. Carstairs-McCarthy 1992: 224–225).

Such an inclusive diagram gives a complete view of the factors involved in a theory of natural morphology. It is interesting to establish a hierarchy of both system-independent and system-dependent naturalness principles, as has been done in Wheeler (1993). Although Dressler's chart would imply the dominance of universal parameters over the others, such is not the case. Wheeler (1993: 109) concludes

> that the evidence supports a reformulation and reordering of the hierarchy of naturalness principles as:
> I.   the principle of system congruity
> II. the principle of class stability
> III. the principle of avoidance of counter-iconicity
> IV. the principle of uniformity and transparency
> V.   the principle of markedness in syncretism
> VI. the principle of constructional iconicity
> VII. the principle of phonetic iconicity.

Principle VII has not been dealt with in our discussion, and, if accepted as part of iconicity, would rank at the bottom. Wheeler adds Principle III, and it is perhaps surprising to see it ahead of IV and VI. V is logically subordinate to IV.[5] It is striking that system-dependent parameters dominate system-independent ones so clearly. Although Wheeler offers his hierarchy "as an advance towards descriptive adequacy", he cautions that "we still lack an adequate overall theory from which the hierarchy of principles might be deductively derived" (Wheeler 1993: 109).[6]

1.2 Approaches related to Natural Morphology

1.2.1 *Inflectional organization*

Bybee (1985) represents an approach to morphological structure which, though not included in the literature on Natural Morphology, exhibits features closely allied to the latter and clearly participating in an effort to explain morphological

---

5. Syncretism will be discussed below, in 1.2.2, in the work of Carstairs (1987).

6. The recent theory of 'connectionism', which claims no 'rules' in morphology, seems to be able to handle aspects of structure covered by iconicity and other parameters. However, as Sánchez Miret, Koliadis, and Dressler claim, although its asset is "the explicitness of the account culminating in computer simulations", it cannot incorporate the concepts of markedness and productivity, so crucial within Natural Morphology (1998: 175).

structure in a spirit akin to natural theory. Morphology is characterized within the following global schema (Bybee 1985: 12, 24, 30, 31):

Hierarchical Continuum of Grammatical Expression					
	+	+	+	−	−
LEXICAL	degree of fusion	morphophonemic proximity	degree of relevance	degree of generality	degree of obligatoriness
DERIVATIONAL					
INFLECTIONAL — VALENCE					
INFLECTIONAL — VOICE					
INFLECTIONAL — ASPECT					
INFLECTIONAL — TENSE					
INFLECTIONAL — MOOD					
INFLECTIONAL — NUMBER					
INFLECTIONAL — PERSON					
INFLECTIONAL — GENDER					
FREE GRAMMATICAL					
SYNTACTICAL					
	−	−	−	+	+

In this scheme, morphology constitutes but one expression type, sandwiched between the two extremes, lexical and syntactic expression. Such a trichotomy is determined by *relevance* and *generality*. These two central parameters constitute opposites: the former parallels semantic fusion and morphemic proximity, the latter obligatoriness, as indicated by the + and − in the table. Relevance of one meaning element to another is established "if the semantic content of the first directly affects or modifies the semantic content of the second" (Bybee 1985: 13). The packaging of semantic elements highly relevant to each other is expressed by degrees of fusion, which is maximal in lexical expression, minimal in syntactic combinations. In order for a morphological category to manifest lexical generality, it must be "applicable to all items of the appropriate semantic and syntactic category and must obligatorily occur in the appropriate syntactic context" (p. 17). Inflectional morphology must maintain just the right balance between relevance and generality: it has to be general enough not to become lexically fused, yet relevant enough to remain morphological and not reach syntax. In addition, Bybee, basing herself on a wide corpus of languages, is able to establish a hierarchy among (verbal) inflectional categories, ranging from *valence* (highest in relevance) to *gender* (highest in generality). The most likely candidates for inflectional morphology are to be found in the center of the scale (p. 19). The following equations summarize the major aspects of Bybee's conception of morphological structure:

a. the more relevance, the more fusion;
b. the more relevance, the less generality;
c. the more relevance, the greater likelihood of derivational morphology;
d. the more generality, the greater likelihood of inflectional morphology;
e. the more relevance, the closer to the root; and
f. the more generality, the more obligatoriness.

What are the connections between Bybee's framework and Natural Morphology? One can find three pertinent areas.

1. In the presentation of grammatical expression, above, five parameters are used by Bybee. One may interpret the correlation of the two (semantic) parameters of relevance and fusion with that of morphemic (morphotactic) proximity as an *iconic* relation: the closeness of affixes that are *relevant* to the root 'diagrams' this rapport.[7]
2. Bybee's analysis of zero expression (1985: 52–57) also deals with iconic structure. Her findings, showing that the inflectional categories of perfective, present, indicative, singular, and 3rd person (all *unmarked*) tend to be coded by zero, fit ideally into the natural framework, in particular the universal version. It also forms part of Bybee's conception of the 'basic' vs. 'derived' relation in paradigms.

---

7. This was called *syntagmatic iconicity* at the outset of this chapter.

3. Finally, let us consider suppletion. Bybee's theory, based on relevance, predicts that "suppletion and allomorphy tend to co-occur with the most highly relevant inflectional categories" (1985: 209). Suppletive structure would not be highly valued within universal naturalness, as it obviously violates uniform coding, transparency, and iconicity. However, it is a very common phenomenon in fusional, inflecting languages. It could certainly be part of the SDSPs, thus be 'system congruent', in languages like Latin. We have seen that what is 'natural' in morphological structure may depend on typological factors. As a consequence, in both Bybee's theory and in Natural Morphology, suppletion finds a 'natural' explanation.[8]

1.2.2 Paradigmatic structure

Carstairs (1987) concentrates his investigation on the logically possible ways in which inflection may deviate from an ideal one-to-one pattern of meaning-form realization, arriving at four types (14–17):

Deviation I: One property to many exponents syntagmatically. This has been labeled *extended exponence*, and it would be illustrated by Ancient Attic Greek *elelykete* "you (pl) had loosed", in which the perfect is marked twice, by the reduplicated prefix *-le-*and the suffix *-k-*.

Deviation II: One property to many exponents paradigmatically. Simple *allomorphy* is describable in this way and may be manifested by the two Latin allomorphs for the 2nd person singular, *-isti* in the perfect, *-s* elsewhere.

Deviation III: Many properties to one exponent syntagmatically. This describes *cumulative exponence*, shown in any person/number verbal suffix in Latin and the Romance languages.

Deviation IV: Many properties to one exponent paradigmatically. *Homonymy*, or *syncretism*, is at work here, seen in, among many other examples, Classical Latin 1st declension nouns in the singular genitive and dative in *-ae*.

The paradigmatic deviations form the center of interest in Carstairs's study, and they will be expressed in terms of three principles, the *Paradigm Economy Principle* (PEP) and the *Peripherality Constraint* (PC) filling in Deviation II, while the *Systematic Homonymy Claim* (SHC) represents Deviation IV.

The PEP receives the following formulation (Carstairs 1987: 51):

> When in a given language L more than one inflexional realization is available for some bundle or bundles of non-lexically determined morphosyntactic

---

8. See now Fertig (1998) for a thorough discussion of these issues.

properties associated with some part of speech N, the number of macroparadigms for N is no greater than the number of distinct rival macroinflexions available for that bundle which is most generously endowed with such rival realizations.

A very dramatic illustration of this principle is given by Carstairs by way of the Latin declensional system, which is said to possess the following inflectional desinences:

	Singular	**Plural**
Nominative	-s, -m, zero	-i:, -s, -a
Vocative	-e, -s, -m, zero	-i:, -s, -a
Accusative	-m, zero	-s, -a
Genitive	-i:, -is	-rum, -um
Dative	-o:, -i:	-i:s, -bus
Ablative	-o:, -e	-i:s, -bus

If we multiplied the number of suffixes available for each morphosyntactic property-bundle, the total of possible distribution patterns for Latin nouns would be 27, 648 (1987: 33)! The fact that only four different paradigms, traditionally assigned to two declensions (not all Latin nouns are included), are actually represented in the above, far reduced from the astronomical logical maximum, illustrates well the essence of Carstairs' PEP. It is a major contribution to our understanding of paradigmatic organization, how suffix allomorphy patterns 'economically', to make possible learnability.

Another aspect of allomorphic variation concerns the concept of *sensitivity*, essentially equivalent to (non-phonological) conditioning. It is fleshed out in detail by means of the PC (Carstairs 1987: 162):

> The realization of a property may be sensitive inwards, i.e. to a property realized more centrally in the word form (closer in linear sequence to the root, but not outwards, i.e. to a property realized more peripherally (further from the root).

This principle is based on the regularities discovered by Carstairs in a variety of languages: (1987: 161)

> In Latin the 2SG ending *-isti* triggered by the property Perfective is further from the root (or more peripheral) than the realization of Perfective; in Turkish and Hungarian the relevant Person-Number markers are more peripheral than the Tense-Aspect-Mood markers that determine the choice between them; and in Zulu the special set of possessive markers which occur with singular nouns of Class 1a are more peripheral than the Class 1a marker itself, *ka-*.

Constructing a constraint on Deviation IV must answer the question: What ambiguities become intolerable in a language, and when? A satisfactory solution in this matter could then also yield predictive power as to what homonymies are possible. Carstairs first establishes a dichotomy between *accidental* and *systematic* homonymies, the first type being caused by regular sound change. Of more interest to him is the second one, which is further subdivided into *syncretism* and *take-over* varieties. Parts of the German verb system illustrates syncretism (Carstairs 1987: 94):

		Singular		**Plural**	
a.	1st	*bin*	"am"	*sind*	"are"
	3rd	*ist*	"is"		
b.	1st	*habe*	"have"	*haben*	"have"
	3rd	*hat*	"has"		
c.	1st	*liebe*	"love"	*lieben*	"love"
	3rd	*liebt*	"loves"		
d.	1st	*esse*	"eat"	*essen*	"eat"
	3rd	*isst*	"eats"		
e.	1st	*wasche*	"wash"	*waschen*	"wash"
	3rd	*wäscht*	"washes"		

The properties Definite and Indefinite in the Hungarian past tense involve the other kind of systematic homonymy, a takeover (Carstairs 1987: 119):

Indicative "write"

		Indefinite	**Definite**
Present:	1SG	*ír-ok*	*ír-om*
	2	*ír-sz*	*ír-od*
	3	*ír*	*ír-ja*
	1PL	*ír-unk*	*ír-juk*
	2	*ír-tok*	*ír-átok*
	3	*ír-nak*	*ír-jak*
Past:	1SG	*ír-t-am*	*ír-t-am*
	2	*ír-t-ál*	*ír-t-ad*
	3	*ír-t*	*ír-t-a*
	1PL	*ír-t-unk*	*ír-t-uk*
	2	*ír-t-atok*	*ír-t-átok*
	3	*ír-t-ak*	*ír-t-ák*

The German example fulfills the definition of a syncretism: the same form in both persons in the plural has been stable over time. In the Hungarian paradigm, there is homonymy between the two 1st singular past forms, in *írtam*. The *-m* ending identifies the form as Definite. This is a takeover, because part of the context, i.e., past tense, is realized separately from the neutralized properties by means of the suffix *-t-* throughout (Carstairs 1987: 119).

The general claim about homonymy in inflection is given the following formulation by Carstairs (1987: 123) for the SHC:

> All systematic homonymies within inflexional paradigms are either (a) syncretisms or (b) takeovers, in which relevance conflicts with dominance (i.e., the morphosyntactic context contains properties belonging to categories that are lower on the relevance hierarchy than the category to which the neutralized properties belong).[9]

One of the interesting consequences of the analysis of homonymy concerns language change, since "there is a tug-of-war between memorability (to which syncretism contributes) and the avoidance of ambiguity (with which syncretism conflicts)" (1987: 124). If this constraint is valid, then fusional languages are specifically suited for homonymies, in particular syncretisms. If one assumes that large scale inflectional homonymy hastens the change to analyticity, then the SHC predicts that fusional languages become analytic faster than agglutinating ones. Such a prediction is, of course, borne out strongly in the evolution of the Romance languages from Latin (pp. 125–126).

What are specific traits of Carstairs's work which indicate some *rapprochement* with the theory of Natural Morphology? It has already been pointed out, above, that his PC is equivalent to what was referred to as *syntagmatic iconicity*, also being prominent in Bybee's view on inflectional organization. Carstairs's PEP could easily be seen as a parameter in Wurzel's system-dependent naturalness, or as part of the latter's PSCs. However, the PEP could also be conceived of as representative of *uniform coding* and *transparency*, explainable within universal naturalness. Finally, as has been stated in the preceding paragraph, the SHC uncovers aspects of the typological dimension of naturalness parameters, characterizing syncretism to be natural for fusional, or 'inflectional', languages like Latin and Romance.[10]

---

9. In this formulation, the concept of 'relevance' is introduced in the sense of Bybee (1985).

10. In the discussion of syncretism and the formulation of the SHC, it is puzzling that no mention of markedness is made. A quick inspection of the 43 homonymies outlined in the Appendix to Chapter 4 (Carstairs 1987: 141–143) reveals that at least half of them would profit from such a

1.3 Grammaticalization

1.3.1 *The metonymic-metaphorical model*

Heine et al. (1991) develop a theory of grammaticalization within "a conceptual framework", representable by means of the following flow chart:

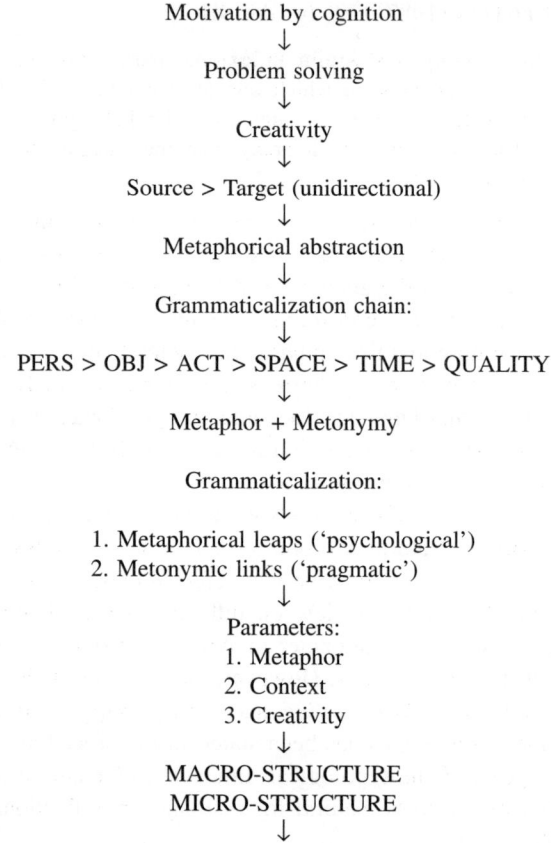

---

consideration. The absence of markedness in Carstairs' approach separates him from Natural Morphology, of course.

The authors stress from the beginning that the creation of metaphorical abstraction is to be conceived of as a problem-solving activity, motivated by cognitive structures. It proceeds from 'source' to 'target', *unidirectionally*, essentially from *concrete* to (more) *abstract*. Source concepts, codified in lexemes, are normally part of the "basic vocabulary" (1991: 33), and they include body parts, natural phenomena, human items, dynamic verbs, posture verbs, mental process verbs, etc. The unidirectionality[11] from a source to its target, which does not, however, equate to *biuniqueness*, is captured by way of a grammaticalization chain (p. 48). In addition to metaphor, metonymy plays an important role in the chain, resulting in a complete characterization of grammaticalization as consisting of (1) a 'discontinuous' phase, described in terms of *metaphoric* jumps; and (2) a 'continuous' phase, made up of *metonymic* connections, as, according to Heine et al. (1991: 70),

> metonymy and metaphor [...] are not mutually exclusive but rather complement each other, that is, that a development from a lexical item to a grammatical marker might not be possible unless there is an intermediate stage whereby distinct conceptual domains are bridged by means of metonymical understanding.

The model defended by Heine et al. (1991) fits into a dichotomy of *macro-* and *micro*-structure, "the overall network of conceptual ramifications" and "the transition from one sense to another" (98–99), respectively. As illustrations of the process outlined, Heine et al. (1991) use examples from African languages, showing, for instance, how the Ewe noun *ví* is conceptually expanded from the concrete word meaning "child", by way of the concepts of "young", "inexperienced", and "not yet having passed an exam", to "unsuccessful' (1991: 79–87). In addition, noun and adpositions are shown to grammaticalize out of body parts and landmarks (125).

In order to account for "more abstract grammaticalization", such as the evolution of case marking, an additional chain is proposed by Heine et al. (1991: 159):

Ablative >	Agent >	Purpose >	Time >	Condition >	Manner
Allative	Comitative	Instrument		Cause	
Locative	Benefactive	Dative			
Path		Possessive			

This second chain fits into the first one (above, in the flow chart) to the right of SPACE, underlining its higher degree of abstraction.

---

11. This issue, controversial for some, will be discussed in detail below, in 5.2.1.

The metonymic-metaphorical model of Heine et al. (1991) is also shown to be capable of dealing with the world of probabilities, text, and expectations, extensively illustrating the metaphorical nature of grammaticalization with examples like the development of the future, "textual" markings like relative pronouns from demonstratives (1991: 183), and "counter-expectation" markers (cf. *already, still*) (193). Finally, grammaticalization may also be integrated into a cyclical *cline* (1991: 245):

Discourse > syntax > morphology > morphophonemics > zero (> discourse)

Heine et al. (1991) is mainly concerned with the early stages of grammaticalization, but, as they correctly state, the process potentially may go to zero, that is, complete phonetic erosion of the affix may occur.[12] After this logical endpoint, but possibly also before, a new cycle of grammaticalization may be triggered, beginning with another discourse stage. The why and how of this cycle (or spiral?) have been discussed for a long time in historical linguistics, usually under the *synthesis/analysis* dichotomy.[13] This concern belongs to the pre-1970 period of the study of grammaticalization, according to Heine et al., when diachronic concerns were predominant. However, more recent studies consider grammaticalization as 'panchronic grammar', as for Heine et al., since metaphor is essentially based in panchrony, a combination of cognition and diachrony (1991: 258).[14]

---

12. See below, in Chapter 3, a complete analysis on why suffixation would atrophy, and not prefixation.

13. Cf. below in this chapter, 1.4.1., a review of the most recent study on this subject, Schwegler (1990).

14. Hopper & Traugott (1993: 1–2) succinctly summarize two meanings of grammaticalization, without the emphasis on metaphor and metonymy found in Heine et al. (1991): "As a term referring to a framework within which to account for language phenomena, it refers to that part of the study of language that focuses on how grammatical forms and constructions arise, how they are used, and how they shape the language. The framework of grammaticalization is concerned with the question of whether boundaries between categories are discrete, and with the interdependence of structure and use, of the fixed and less fixed in language. It therefore highlights the tension between relatively unconstrained lexical structure and more constrained, syntactic, morphosyntactic, and morphological structure. It provides the conceptual context for a principled account of the relative indeterminacy in language and of the basic non-discreteness of categories. The term "grammaticalization" also refers to the actual phenomena of language that the framework of grammaticalization seeks to address, most especially the processes whereby items become more grammatical through time."

1.3.2 *Paths of grammar*

Bybee et al. (1994) recognize, like Heine et al. (1991), that metaphor plays a role in the grammaticalization process. However, they suggest that (1994: 24–25)

> the actual formation of metaphors is not the major mechanism for semantic change in grammaticization. Rather, we see metaphor operating only on the more lexical end of grammaticization paths rather than propelling grams into the more and more abstract domains of grammatical meaning.

This 'more abstract' level of grammaticalization is developed and illustrated in this study in a thorough investigation and examination of tense, aspect, and modality in the languages of the world, of which 76 were carefully selected with criteria of genetic and typological classification and balance in mind (1994, Appendix A). The theoretical background for the analysis is laid by means of the following "set of hypotheses" (1994: 9–22):

1. Source determination.

Bybee et al. (1994) claim that the sources of grammaticalization must be 'irreducible' notions, basic to human experience, and culturally independent. The sources will determine the *path*, not the final result, of grammaticalization.

2. Unidirectionality

The existence of this feature in grammaticalization assures the 'orderliness' of semantic change and is obvious for the phonetic aspect of grammaticalization: reduced or deleted structure cannot be 'recreated', and therefore true 'reversibility' is inconceivable. It also allows for the 'predictability' of grammaticalization.

3. Universal paths

These are the consequences, if Hypotheses 1 and 2 turn out to be correct, since they reflect "common cognitive and communicative patterns underlying the use of language" (Bybee et al. 1994: 15).

4. Retention of earlier meaning

As instantiated by the English coexistence of *shall* and *will*, a source and the grammaticalized result may continue side by side for some time. This is also shown in the occurrence of inflectional suppletion and doublets.

5. Consequences of semantic retention.

These are crucial for (i) synchronic analyses in general, as grammatical meaning is seen to be a *continuum*, (ii) comparative studies, and (iii) internal reconstruction, where possible phonological change parallels possible grammatical change.

6. Semantic reduction and phonological reduction

Bybee et al. propose that such a 'parallel reduction' is causally linked, in that the phonetic and semantic continua overlap in a "dynamic coevolution of meaning and form"(1994: 20). Specifically, they make these two claims (ibid):

  a. "There is a link between frequency of use and phonetic bulk such that more frequently used material, whether grammatical or lexical, tends to be shorter (phonetically reduced) relative to less often used material".
  b. "Grams are phonetically reduced relative to generalized lexical items, which in turn are reduced relative to more specific lexemes".

One important consequence of these claims would seem to be that some grammatical categories are (universally?) signaled periphrastically (i.e., *habitual* and *progressive*), and belong to 'early' grammaticalization, and that others are signaled inflectionally (i.e. *imperfective* and *perfective*), belonging to 'later' or 'advanced' grammaticalization.

7. Layering

This hypothesis refers to the existence of more than one grammatical means of expressing some category, and to the fact that their "different ages" can be determined. For instance, the (modal) expression of obligation in English turns out to be three-fold in the spoken language of today:

  (i)   *You must respond to this IRS notice immediately.*
  (ii) *You have to respond to this IRS notice immediately.*
  (iii) *You(ve) gotta respond to this IRS notice immediately.*

Here we have multiple grammaticalizations along the same path and their 'ages' are clearly in the order given (Bybee et al. 1994: 22).

8. Relevance

The concepts of *relevance* and *generality* had been introduced in an earlier study of Bybee's (Bybee 1985, reviewed above, in 1.2.1). Grammaticalization may be said to determine "the way that generality is achieved in the development of grammatical morphemes" (Bybee et al. 1994: 22).

A good illustration of the theory encapsulated in the preceding eight hypotheses is found in Chapter 3 of Bybee et al. (1994: 51–105). Here, they examine tense and aspect interms of five 'evolutions', as sketched in the following, adapted from p. 105:

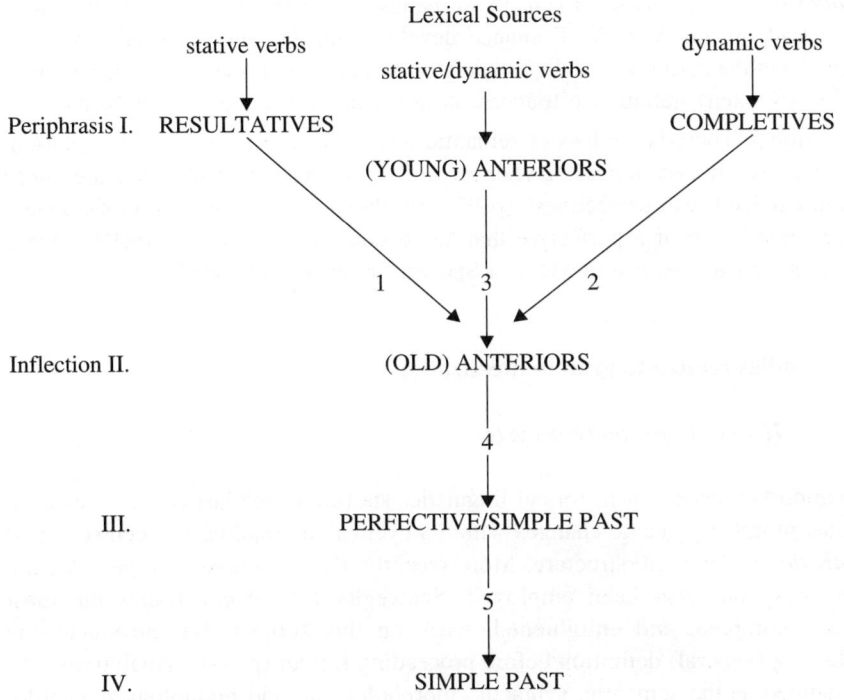

The numbers in this chart refer to the evolutions involved, briefly summarized as:

Evolution 1. Resultatives change to anteriors, which concerns the loss of the feature of 'state', or specificity, associated with the result stage. This development is the well-known history of Latin *habere* plus past participle: The resultative/possessive sense of the auxiliary was changed to "anterior" in most areas, but some minor Romance dialects retain the resultative meaning, while others, like Modern French, have 'progressed' to the perfective, or even simple past stage (Bybee et al. 1994: 69).

Evolution 2. There is a loss of 'completedness' or thoroughness in this changeover. It is a less well-known source for anteriors, essentially expressed by the verb 'to finish', occurring in the English Creole Tok Pisin *pinis* (1994: 71).

Evolution 3. In this development, we are witnessing a "finer" grammaticalization of the sense of *anterior*, accompanied by a structural shift from *periphrasis* to *inflection*. [Globally, the chart above shows the formal parallelism from periphrastic to inflectional structure juxtaposed to the semantic evolution].

Evolution 4. This consists principally of the loss of the sense of 'present relevance'. As already mentioned, the Romance developments fit here, especially Modern French, but the discussion of the meaning of the compound past in Castilian Spanish and in (Spoken) Italian also touches on this specific changeover (1994: 87).

Evolution 5. There is the loss of semantic relevance to the verb in this evolution, an increase in *remoteness*. Bybee et al. argue that "simple pasts are more grammaticized than perfectives" (p. 91), but they add that "we know of no clear documented case of a perfective that has become a simple past" (p. 93). Arguably, the *passé composé* in Modern Spoken French could qualify.

1.4 Studies related to grammaticalization

1.4.1 *The synthesis/analysis cycle*

An important aspect of historical linguistics starting in the last century has been to cast morpho-syntactic changes within a cyclical alternation between so-called *synthetic* and *analytic* structure. More recently, the *inflectional* vs. *periphrastic* dichotomy has also been employed. Schwegler (1990) constitutes the most recent, complete and enlightened, work on this subject. He introduces the following (general) definition before proceeding further (p. 48): "Analyticity will be defined as the semantic, syntactic, morphological, and phonological interdependency (or relatedness) of morphemes within a speech unit". The following criteria are used throughout to flesh out the details of the definition, to be applied to the specifics of the morpho-syntactic history of the Romance languages:

1. Relevance
2. Generality (semantic)
3. Displaceability
4. Isolatedness
5. Obligatoriness
6. Linearity
7. Transparency
8. Separability (morpho-syntactic)
9. Phonological bonding

One may claim that Schwegler's contribution revolves around the introduction of the concepts of *linearity* and *transparency*, in particular, as will be shown in the following.

In his Chapter 4 (pp. 75–116), Schwegler tackles the notorious and difficult issue of the history of person/number marking in French, touching on the questions of the rise of obligatory subject pronouns in Old French, the accompanying erosion of Latin personal endings, the status of the subject pronoun in Modern French, and the rise of a new set of personal pronouns in the colloquial language.[15] Two claims are to be substantiated in his analysis (1990: 77):

1. the French verb group has never passed through a distinctively analytic period; and
2. analytic and synthetic tendencies have existed simultaneously at all stages in the development of the French verb group.

The following is an overview of the evolution in question (cf. p. 112), incorporating the beginning and end points:

	Classical Latin (CL)		**Informal Spoken French (ISF)**	
1SG	(ego)	-o, -m	(moi)	[ʒ-]
2SG	(tu)	-s	(toi)	[t-]
3SG	(ille, -a)	-t	(lui, elle)	[i(l)-]
1PL	(nos)	-mus	(nous)	[õ(n)-]
2PL	(vos)	-tis	(vous)	[vu(z)-] [-e]
3PL	(illi, -ae)	-nt	(eux, elles)	[i(z)-]

Extant studies on this history have focused on the criteria of 'separability' and 'obligatoriness'. What is the effect of the two factors introduced by Schwegler for this analysis? *Linearity* differs from *separability* as it "focuses on the accumulation and fusion of meanings or functions in a single morpheme" (1990: 59). When such merging occurs, 'alinear' forms are created, to be equated to syntheticity, while entirely linear speech units imply a one-to-one relationship between meaning and form, and analyticity. This criterion plays an important role in the Latin to French verbal evolution, only two aspects of which will be pointed out. First, stem diphthongization, for instance, would characterize this stage (Old French) of the language as more synthetic than Latin, largely continuing into the modern period. Thus, ISF may be seen as more synthetic than CL, or at least as equivalent, because also *alinear*. Second, a consideration of the French periphrastic verb forms will have to deal with the status of the auxiliary. In both the *passé composé* and *futur proche* it may be seen as supplying an

---

15. See below, 3.2.1, for another view on this topic.

additional set of P/N suffixes, and, as a consequence, alinearity. The latter, of course, already applies to the regular future, since the discontinuous marking of P/N by both prefixed pronoun and verbal suffixes also adds up to alinear structure.

Transparency is divided by Schwegler (1990: 64–68) into 'structural' and 'semantic'. It also concerns allomorphy, its regularity and restrictiveness, affecting the "tightness" of the morphological system: "A high level of syntheticity is reached when a morpheme has an abundance of allomorphs whose alternations can be captured only by a multitude of rules" (p. 64). Structural transparency also depends on the formal interrelation of various morphemes constituting a paradigmatic set. By such a reasoning, both CL and ISF person/number marking must be considered as tending toward the synthetic pole of the analytic/synthetic continuum. Semantically, however, degrees of analyticity are contributed in the compound forms of French, in that the auxiliary in both the past and the future may occur as a free lexeme (p. 67).

Typically in the literature on the cycle, only syntactically contiguous units have been considered as candidates for possible synthesis. In Chapter 6 (pp. 151–74), Schwegler, however, treats in some detail the so-called 'embracing' negation *ne pas* of French, and similar structures in various Romance dialects, in terms of the degree of synthesis they have reached. The author claims that such bonding was very comparable to that between *habeo* and the past participle, with semantic synthesis being dominant (Schwegler 1990: 173).[16] Further steps in this synthesis are outlined as follows (1990: 155–156):

1. Syntactic restrictions: both elements occur only within the verb phrase
2. Obligatoriness: *pas* was the eventual winner among all the negative emphasizers of Old French (cf. *point, mie, goutte,* etc.)
3. Morphological freedom: no possibility of *ne* and *pas* as single negatives
4. Reduction to morphological variability: *pas* (and others) derive from nouns to sentence qualifiers, becoming invariable morphologically
5. Phonological units: both parts of the embracing negation must be incorporated in one phonological word

However, according to Schwegler, *ne* and *pas* never had the chance to develop into an inseparable unit because of (a) the prevailing verb-object word order in French, and (b) the rapid development of *pas* into the negator proper, "thereby eliminating the semantic attraction that might have united *ne* and *pas* at a later

---

16. See below, 3.1, for details.

stage in the history of French" (1990: 161). This may serve as a new hypothesis concerning the gradual loss of *ne* in Modern Spoken French: synthesis of the two elements had to be aborted due to (a) and (b), and *ne* lacked lexical meaning and became redundant.

Schwegler's view challenges, in a global sense, the traditional dichotomy of Latin as *synthetic* and Romance as *analytic*. Rather, degrees of analyticity may be contained in the former and degrees of syntheticity in the latter. The criterion of *linearity*, as seen in the lack of allomorphy, adds analyticity to the synthetic structure of Latin verbal suffixation, while semantic bonding makes analytic sequences candidates for syntheticity.

1.4.2 Perception and processing issues

Hall (1992) constitutes a revised and improved version of the processing explanation for the *suffixing preference*, or, better perhaps, the *prefixing dispreference* in morphology. One may trace the evolution of this approach by way of the following three proposals:

1. Lüdtke (1980: 279):

    ... due to the linear processing of the speech signal [inflections] are better perceived if the place where they are expected is indicated beforehand.

2. Cutler et al. (1985: 754):

    ... linguistic and psychological evidence together suggest that language structure reflects the preference of language users to process stems before affixes, in that the component preferred for prior processing receives the most salient position in the word, the component to be processed second a less salient position.

3. Hall (1992: 170):

    ... a comparison of the processes involved shows that entertaining a flirting prefix should require two cohorts, whereas entertaining a flirting suffix should require, in effect, only one.

The essence of Hall's explanation of the suffixing preference is contained in this statement, but it becomes comprehensible only through his presentation of various psycholinguistic models, including the Cohort Model (Chapter 5, pp.112–163). The goal is "to clarify matters by constructing an explicit model of access and representation from which specific predictions can be made and tested", but he agrees that "the result of such explicitness may be increased complexity in what is already a complex area" (1992: 162).

The major contribution of this work is found in Chapter 6, "A microanalysis of historical change" (164–194). In it, Hall supplements Cutler et al.'s (1985) processing account with 'linkage' to the evolution of affixation in order to find "the exact historical locus of the engagement of the dispreference" (1992: 164). The latter is assumed to come into existence during the "flirting stage", the end-point in a sequence sketched briefly as (1992: 166):

free morpheme > meaning generalization > redundancy > phonological reduction > flirting stage

'Flirting', in Hall's framework, captures the stage just before a formerly free form, now phonetically and semantically degraded, is bound to another (still) free form, on which it depends and to which it has been adjacent. Hall then also includes the results of a test involving novel combinations of prefix + stem from English derivational morphology, examples like *reambush, untile, non-vague, prepledge, exclown,* and *demoss* (1992: 197). The results establish that novel prefixed forms have recognition points significantly *after* those of bare stem forms. Hall assumes that the processing of these novel combinations closely resembles that of flirting prefixed forms and should thus provide at least indirect evidence for the prefixing dispreference (1992: 191). As a general characterization of the latter, the author suggests that "the putative processing dispreference for prefixes must have taken place in many languages all over the globe during long stretches of time, many now over, some still in progress and presumably yet to come" (1992: 164).[17]

Supporting evidence for Hall's thesis comes from typological studies, such as Greenberg (1966), who reveals a suffixation preference in his data: seventeen of the thirty languages are both prefixing and suffixing, but only one is exclusively suffixing. Hall, based on other studies involving up to 200 languages, extracts the following regularities(1992: 43):

a. i. Languages which are exclusively suffixing are considerably more frequent than those which are exclusively prefixing.
   ii. Across languages, suffixing morphology is more frequent than both prefixing and infixing, i.e., more functions are expressed by suffixes than by prefixes or infixes.
b. i. If a language is exclusively prefixing, it is prepositional (one exception) and verb-initial.

---

17. An application of this approach to the status of Modern French subject pronouns is found below, in section 3.2.1.

ii. Around sixty per cent of postpositional and verb-final languages are exclusively suffixing; the majority of prepositional and verb-initial languages are both prefixing and suffixing.

It can be said that Hall's concerns directly impact on the 'final stages' of grammaticalization and they have to be incorporated for a complete account of the latter.

1.4.3 *Syntactic branching*

Rejecting the conventional approach using the synthesis/analysis cycle, Bauer (1995) observes that

> ... the principal change in morphology was not the tendency toward analytic forms, but the reversal of the order of elements: archaic forms, in which the endings followed the stem, have been replaced by structures in which the grammatical element precedes the lexical element. In an inflected nominal form, for example, the lexeme precedes the grammatical marker, whereas in the prepositional — hence right-branching — phrase, the lexical element follows the head. The development parallels the change in syntax.

This left vs. right branching alternation, and evolution, is then illustrated by way of the following Latin and Modern French structural equivalents (Bauer 1995: 25–26):

A. PHRASES

	Classical Latin	**Modern French**
1.	object + verb	verb + object
	exercitum duxit	*il conduisit l'armée*
2.	prep phrase + verb	verb + prep phrase
	in partes discindere	*diviser en parties*
3.	adverb + verb	verb + adverb
	leniter ridere	*rire doucement*
4.	adjective + copula	copula + adjective
	avidus est	*il est avide*
5.	noun + adposition	preposition + noun
	mecum	*avec moi*
.	*temporis causa*	*à cause du temps*
6.	adjective + noun	noun + adjective
	longissimus truncus	*un tronc très allongé*
7.	genitive + noun	noun + genitive (prep phrase)
	deorum munus	*le présent des dieux*

8.	noun (gen.) + adjective	adject. + noun (prep phrase)
	pecuniae avidus	*avide d'argent*
9.	referent + comparative	comparative + referent
	Paulo grandior	*plus grand que Paul*

B. INFLECTED FORMS

10.	adjective + degree	degree + adjective
	grandior	*plus grand*
11.	noun + ending	prepos. + noun (prep phrase)
	legibus	*avec des lois*
12.	verb + ending	auxiliary/pronoun + verb
	amaverit	*il aura aimé*
13.	noun + conjunction	conjunction + noun
	populusque	*et le peuple*

For Bauer, each structure is binary, containing a *head* and a *complement*, with these equations in effect:

Left Branching = Complement + Head
Right Branching = Head + Complement

The identification of the *head* is accomplished by two characteristics, as "the head assigns a syntactic function to its complement and it indicates, hence expresses, the grammatical value of this element" (1995: 44). The data given above receive, therefore, the following branching analysis.

A. PHRASES

1. Latin: object = complement   verb = head (*left branching*)
   French: verb = head   object = complement (*right branching*)
2. Latin: prep phrase = complement   verb = head (*left branching*)
   French: verb = head   prep phrase = complement (*right branching*)
3. Latin: adverb = complement   verb = head (*left branching*)
   French: verb = head   adverb = complement (*right branching*)
4. Latin: adjective = complement   copula (verb) = head (*left branching*)
   French: copula (verb) = head   adjective = complement (*right branching*)

5.	Latin:	(pro)noun = <u>complement</u>	adposition = <u>head</u> (*left branching*)
	French:	preposition = <u>head</u>	(pro)noun = <u>complement</u> (*right branching*)
6.	Latin:	adjective = <u>complement</u>	noun = <u>head</u> (*left branching*)
	French:	noun = <u>head</u>	adjective = <u>complement</u> (*right branching*)
7	Latin:	genitive = <u>complement</u>	noun = <u>head</u> (*left branching*)
	French:	noun = <u>head</u>	genitive = <u>complement</u> (*right branching*)
8.	Latin:	noun = <u>complement</u>	adjective = <u>head</u> (*left branching*)
	French:	adjective = <u>head</u>	noun = <u>complement</u> (*right branching*)
9.	Latin:	referent = <u>complement</u>	comparative = <u>head</u> (*left branching*)
	French:	comparative = <u>head</u>	referent = <u>complement</u> (*right branching*)

B. INFLECTED FORMS

10.	Latin:	adjective (root) = <u>complement</u>	degree (suffix) = <u>head</u> (*left branching*)
	French:	degree (adverb) = <u>head</u>	adjective = <u>complement</u> (*right branching*)
11.	Latin:	noun (root) = <u>complement</u>	ending = <u>head</u> (*left branching*)
	French:	preposition = <u>head</u>	noun = <u>complement</u> (*right branching*)
12.	Latin:	verb (root) = <u>complement</u>	ending = <u>head</u> (*left branching*)
	French:	auxiliary/pronoun = <u>head</u>	verb (participle) = <u>complement</u> (*right branching*)
13.	Latin:	noun = <u>complement</u>	conjunction = <u>head</u> (*left branching*)
	French:	conjunction = <u>head</u>	noun = <u>complement</u> (*right branching*)

Bauer's analysis is characterized by "flexibility"[18], as various parts of speech may switch back and forth between 'head' and 'complement' status:

Verb: Functions consistently as the *head* (1, 2, 3, 4)

Noun: Functions as *complement* (to both the verb and the adjective) (1, 2, 5, 8, 9), but also to conjunctions (13), and to an ending (suffix), when in the shape of the root (11); functions as *head* to both the adjective and the genitive (6, 7)

Adjective: Functions as *complement* to both the verb and the noun (4, 6) and, as a root, to a comparative suffix; functions as *head* to the noun (8, 9)

It turns out that a syntactic branching proposal such as Bauer's has direct application to the process of grammaticalization, since the position of *head* will determine the eventual suffixation and (lack of) prefixation result, as detailed in Chapter 3, below.

Globally, Bauer assumes an evolutionary trend from left branching to right branching in the history of Indo-European languages. This could be captured in the following diagrammatic representation, adapted from Bauer, as applicable to grammaticalization:

---

18. This aspect has been criticized in Lightfoot (1996).

INTRODUCTION

LEFT BRANCHING > RIGHT BRANCHING

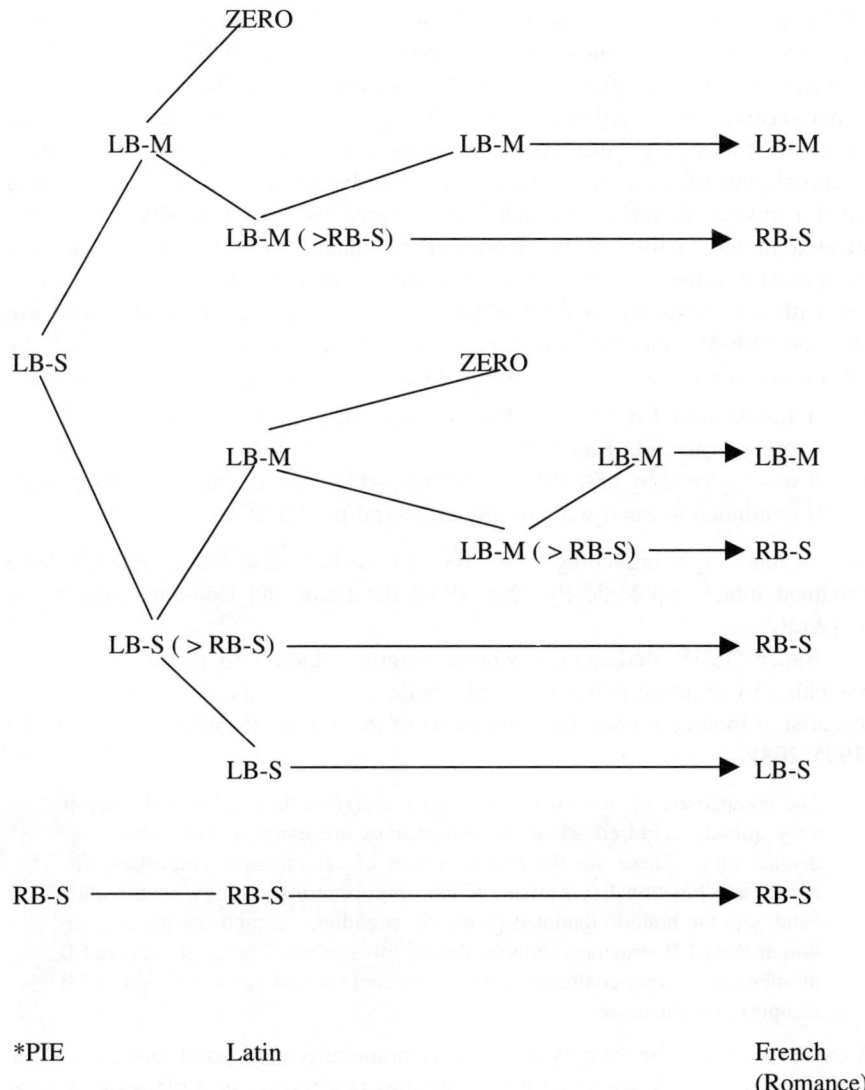

The following is an explanation of the above sketch.

Indo-European is assumed to have consisted of only 'syntactic' (periphrastic) structure, left branching syntactic (LB-S) and right branching syntactic (RB-S). In the normal course of grammaticalization, LB-S will develop into LB-M, left branching 'morphological' structure, better known as *inflectional suffixation*. Latin, of course, is principally characterized by such, but it is important to recognize that not all of LB-S became LB-M. The schema then tries to demonstrate what further changes can apply to the LB-M/LB-S dichotomy. First, LB-M may go to zero, that is, the 'logical' end point of grammaticalization — atrophying of suffixes — may occur. On the other hand, LB-M may also either continue as such, or it may be *replaced* by a (novel) RB-S, certainly attested in the history of the Romance languages from Latin (cf. both the 'periphrastic' future and past tense formations, analyzed in Chapter 3, below). In line with arguments advanced in Hall (1992), it is assumed that RB-S will not turn into *RB-M, since that would constitute *inflectional prefixation*. Second, the LB-S remaining in Latin from Indo-European is shown to have three possible fates:

1. it turned into LB-M, with later changes analogous to that of the LB-M coming from Indo-European;
2. it was replaced by new RB-S structures, which cannot change typologically;
3. it continued as such without any structural modifications.

All 'original' right branching structures of Indo-European are assumed to have remained intact, typologically, throughout the Latin and Romance periods, in perpetuity.

Bauer (1995) dedicates a whole, lengthy, chapter to the acquisition of branching by children (Chapter 6). She believes that the data available to her in this area of inquiry support her hypothesis of the diachronic shift from LB to RB (1995: 208):

> The comparison of these data has shown, therefore, that LB morphology is very quickly acquired when the morphemes are clear, unambiguous, and distinct units. These are the characteristics of agglutinative languages. The formal and functional syncretism of Indo-European morphology, on the other hand, and the nondifferentiated nature of its endings, complicate the acquisition of these LB structures. Finally, the easy mastering of the agglutinative LB morphology sharply contrasts with the slow and painstaking acquisition of LB complex constructions.

It can be said that the themes of syntactic branching/word order and acquisition hierarchy of Bauer's are to be tied to grammaticalization in a plausible way as follows:

WORD ORDER TYPOLOGY
1. (S)OV> (S)VO
2. LB > RB

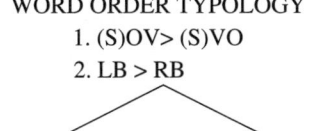

ACQUISITION HIERARCHY
1. RB <u>before</u>
2. LB

GRAMMATICALIZATION
1. LB > suffixation
2. RB > *prefixation

The studies reviewed in this introduction are referred to at various points in the body of the monograph, (Chapters 2 through 4). They will also enter into the theoretical summary on grammaticalization, (Chapter 5), and in the conclusion (Chapter 6). It is hoped that the synthesis of approaches labeled "natural morphology" and those falling under the heading of "grammaticalization" will emerge not only as a possible one, but rather one that is both plausible and productive, in particular for the subject matter of this study, Latin-Romance morphosyntax and inflectional morphology.

CHAPTER 2

Verbal Inflection

2.1 Overview

In the following, the Latin verb system will be represented by way of three first conjugation verbs, *cantare, amare,* and *laudare* ("sing", "love", "praise"), both synchronically and diachronically, in its evolution into two Romance languages, French and Italian. This corpus will serve as the basis for the detailed discussion of sections 2.2.-2.4., which examine the three verb morphologies globally and also investigate specific analogical developments (cf. Manczak 1980). In Chapter 3, additional data will be adduced in order to complete the Latin to Romance verb history, filling in the spaces left vacant for French and Italian. [The data for the analysis are found in the Appendix].

2.2 Latin system

The data of first conjugation verbs permit more than one segmentation into individual morphemes (for some discussion of problems involved in this analysis, cf. Touratier 1971 and Matthews 1972). If other conjugations and, in particular, irregular verbs are included, difficulties multiply rapidly. I believe that for the purpose of this examination within the theory of Natural Morphology the most 'regular' class of Latin verbs serves best and it will be supplemented by examples from other conjugations only infrequently.

Latin morphologists agree on the division of the verb system into the categories of aspect, tense, mood, person, number, and voice, each characterizable as binary, except for tense and person, which manifest a three-way split. A presentation of the morphemes of most regular verbs incorporating these grammatical categories is given in the following table:

		Imperfective ∅			**Perfective** -v-, PPP	
Aspect						
		IND	SUB		IND	SUB
	PRES	∅	-e	PERF	∅	-eri
Tense/Mood	IMP	-ba-	-re-	PLUP	-era	-isse
	FUT	-bi, bu, be-		FPERF	-er, eri	
		ACT	PASS		ACT	PASS
	1SG	-o,m	-(o)r	1SG	-o, -m, -i	AUX
	2SG	-s	-ris	2SG	-isti,s	AUX
Person/ Number/	3SG	-t	-tur	3SG	-t, it	AUX
Voice	1PL	-mus	-mur	1PL	-(i)mus	AUX
	2PL	-tis	-mini	2PL	-(i)tis	AUX
	3PL	-nt	-ntur	3PL	-(eru)nt	AUX

Globally, the entire system consists of 120 forms, one-fourth of which demonstrate periphrastic, or analytic, structure, in the perfective passive forms. For these, the preceding table merely indicates AUX, referring to the auxiliary *esse* "to be", employed in various tense-mood combinations to be discussed below, in 3.1.1. Actually, this subsystem is signaled by both the auxiliary and the perfect passive participle (PPP), included as a marker of perfective aspect.

The difficulties of segmentation alluded to above concern the bulk of the verbal forms, the seventy-five percent remaining 'synthetic' structure. As can be seen, uncertainties remain in my overview, shown by segments in parenthesis. However, it can be argued that most of such hesitations do not crucially handicap an appreciation of the system in terms of parameters of naturalness.

Let us begin by proposing the following (uncontroversial) markedness dichotomies (UM = unmarked, M = marked):

	UM	**M**
Aspect	IMP	PERF
Tense	PRES	-PRES
Mood	IND	SUB
Person	3rd	-3rd
Number	SING	PL
Voice	ACT	PASS

Considered individually, not fusionally for the moment, four of the morphological categories in the Latin verb, aspect, tense, mood, and voice, manifest correspondence of markedness values with overt marking, resulting in a highly iconic system. The zero morpheme is very clear for tense (pres) and aspect (imp), less so for mood (ind), and not at all obvious for voice: here only 3rd person differentiates the passive form from its active counterpart by the added suffix -*ur*.[1]

As is well known, Latin belongs to the fusional type of languages (Skalička 1979), in which inflections are combined in *portmanteau* formations. Person and number are the classic examples of such inseparable categories, but I have found it necessary to add voice to this complex, as can be seen. Tense and mood are quite easily combinable, of course. The segmentation hesitations involve the assignment of vowels in the future and in the perfect. They will create allomorphy either in the tense-mood or the person-number-voice morpheme. Carstairs' peripherality constraint (PC) will argue for allomorphy in the P/N/V marker, probably, since that would constitute 'inward sensitivity'. However, it is possible that incorporating the vowels in the future morpheme would qualify as "legal" outward sensitivity in his theory (Carstairs 1987, Chapter 5).

A different set of allomorphic alternatives may be seen in the realization of the first person singular (1SG). The table shows its limitations in not being able to cross-reference the variants with respect to tense-mood: within active allomorphs of the 1SG, variation is sensitive to tense-mood, as *-m* is found in the PS, II, IS, PeS, PPI, and PPS, *-o* in the PI, F, and FP, and *-i* only in the PeI. This constitutes inward sensitivity in Carstairs' sense, to be considered as an additional parameter of naturalness.

Does the Latin verbal system, as represented by the 1st conjugation, display any weak points, areas which (predictably) will lead to changes in order to eliminate marked features (cf. Wurzel 1988)? For us to uncover such markedness requires first a determination of the *system defining structural properties* of the Latin verb. Wurzel (1984: 82) distinguishes these properties to be applied to specific language (sub)systems:

1. an inventory of category sets and the categories attributed to these;
2. the occurrence of either base form or stem inflection;
3. separate vs. combined symbolization of categories;
4. the number and manner of formal distinctions in the inflectional forms of a paradigm;
5. the types of marker existing in relation to the sets of categories involved; and
6. the presence vs. absence of inflectional classes.

The first criterion has been uncovered in the presentation of our table and the

---

1. See the analyses in Touratier (1971: 339) and Matthews (1991: 238).

review of the segmentation. These categories are valid, or course, for all Latin verbs, not only the 1st conjugation. With regard to (2), Latin was typified by stem inflection, again applicable throughout.[2]

Property (3) has been exhaustively discussed in terms of *portmanteau* structure. Syncretism, suggested in point (4), occurs remarkably rarely in the Latin verbs shown. It is limited to the zero morph for *imp*, *pres*, and *ind*. However, for this property, the difference between 1st and other conjugations does become crucial, as the formation of the future and present subjunctive constitutes a well-known syncretism for some non-1st conj verbs, the future 1sG in *-am*. Property (5) seems to be easily determinable for Latin, the important feature of inflectional suffixation for all extant categories. Yet, as has been mentioned, one-fourth of the system departs from this norm, the perfective passives. The inclusion of non-1st conj verbs would, of course, also uncover other inflectional means, such as the formation of the perfect by vowel lengthening and reduplication. Criterion (6), by definition, must involve all conjugation classes of Latin. Summarized succinctly, a Latin verb form may thus be said to obey *system congruity* (SC), if (1) it contains the feature constellation of aspect, tense, mood, person, number, and voice, (2) it shows inflection of the stem, (3) it manifests fusional formatives, (4) it is not syncretic, it exhibits suffixation, and (6) it belongs to one of the recognized conjugations.

It can be demonstrated that the 1st conjugation of verbs constituted the default *paradigm structure condition* (PSC), as it replicated itself in the following three developments of Late Latin, taken from the *Glossary of Reichenau*:

(1) *cecinit : cantavit*
(2) *dem : donem*
(3) *minatur : manatiat*

Regarding (1), the reduplication in the perfect clearly amounted to a marked feature in the verb system, since the unmarked type of formation consisted of the perfective marker *-v-* plus the suffixation of person-number. This marked point was eliminated by substituting a "regular" 1st conj form. Item (2) makes use of the 1sGPS of a 1st conj verb *donare*, either coexisting in Latin with the irregular *dare* or newly created. It has the advantage of belonging to the dominant PSC. Finally, *minatur* represents perhaps the most anomalous, and therefore most highly marked, feature of the Latin verb system, so-called deponent verbs. These

---

2. One minor adjustment of the stem involves the deletion of stem-final *-a* before both 1sGPI *-o* and the subjunctive *-e* in the PS, both phonologically conditioned.

were characterized by "passive form but active meaning". It is easily predictable that such formations will be very unstable and the replacement with *manatiat* (with some minor phonetic changes) integrates this verb within the default PSC.[3]

Two areas of inflectional markedness can, globally, be detected in the Latin verb:

    a.   the analytic perfect passive formations
    b.   the deponents.

With respect to (a), Pulgram (1977: 98) suggests that synthetic structures like **laudavir*, **laudavitur*, or **laudaveruntur*, in place of the occurring 1SG *laudatus sum*, 3SG *laudatus est*, and 3PL *laudati sunt*, had "nothing un-Latin about them." As a matter of fact, he lists attested passives like *iussitur, faxitur,* and *turbassitur*. However, such forms did not "catch on." This is surprising from the stand-point of system congruity, as such analogical changes would be exactly the ones expected. As will be seen below, in 3.1.1., the analytic passive expressions were, in fact, expanded in the evolution of Latin into Romance — a development strongly at odds with predictions according to the parameter of system congruity. In this instance, the latter came in conflict with an even stronger tendency, the analyticity trend, or morphosyntactic transparency (cf. Wurzel 1988: 492).

As the brief discussion of the 3rd item from the *Glosses of Reichenau* has shown, the other marked area of the Latin verb did get eliminated, and completely so, in its history into Romance. No language or dialect retains even a remnant of such medio-passive voice. Clearly, this type of verbal structure violated system congruity in multiple ways, in reference to properties (1) (no active expressed), and (5), since half of its paradigms were periphrastic. The example *minari* is cited in the 3SG below:

PI	*minatur*
PS	*minetur*
II	*minabatur*
IS	*minaretur*
PeI	*minatus est*
PeS	*minatus sit*
PPI	*minatus erat*
PPS	*minatus esset*
F	*minabitur*
FP	*minatus erit*

---

3. For details on how PSC's may change, see Wurzel (1987).

2.3 French and Italian results

2.3.1 *Data and segmentation*

Modern French and Italian include the future and conditional (= C), two synthetic structures not directly traceable to the Latin forms given. They are added now in order to complete a segmentation analysis for these languages. Their evolution will be discussed below, in section 3.1.2.

	French	**Italian**
F	*(je) chanterai*	*canterò*
	chanteras	*canterai*
	chantera	*canterà*
	chanterons	*canteremo*
	chanterez	*canterete*
	chanteront	*canteranno*
C	*(je) chanterais*	*canterei*
	chanterais	*canteresti*
	chanterait	*canterebbe*
	chanterions	*canteremmo*
	chanteriez	*cantereste*
	chanteraient	*canterebbero*

The six active inflectional paradigms of the two modern languages may now be segmented as follows:

French

		IND	SUB
	PRES	$\emptyset$	$\emptyset$
Tense/Mood	IMP	$-\varepsilon$ [4]	-a(s)
	F/C	$-R-$ [5]	
	PERF	$\emptyset$	

---

4. Requires glide formation rule in the 1PL and 2PL. The phonetic symbol ε is used to represent a mid lax front unrounded vowel throughout this study.

5. Requires a schwa insertion rule in the 1PL and 2PL

VERBAL INFLECTION

		PRES	IMP	F	C	SUB	PERF
	1SG	Ø	Ø	-e	-ε	Ø	-e
	2SG	Ø	Ø	-a	-ε	Ø	-a
Person/Number	3SG	Ø	Ø	-a	-ε	Ø	-a
	1PL	-õ	-õ	-õ	-jõ	-jõ	-am
	2PL	-e	-e	-e	-je	-je	-at
	3PL	Ø	Ø	-õ	-ε	Ø	-εR

Italian

		IND	SUB
	PRES	Ø	Ø
Tense/Mood	IMP	-av-	-as(s)
	F/C	-er-	
	PERF	Ø	

		PRES	IMP	F	C	SUB	PERF
	1SG	-o	-o	-ò	-ei	-i	-ai
	2SG	-i	-i	-ai	-esti	-i	-asti
Person/Number	3SG	-a[6]	-a	-à	-ebbe	-i	-ò
	1PL	-iamo	-amo	-emo	-emmo	-i(a)mo	-ammo
	2PL	-ate	-ate	-ete	-este	-(i)a(s)te	-aste
	3PL	-ano	-ano	-anno	-ebbero	-ino,ero	-arono

The preceding analysis dealt with the verb system of French and Italian only incompletely, of course, as it involved the synthetic forms exclusively. A generally accepted view would posit, probably, thirteen paradigms for each of the modern languages, illustrated for the active with the 3SG of the verb "to praise" as follows:

	French	**Italian**
PI	*(il) loue*	*loda*
PS	*(il) loue*	*lodi*
II	*(il) louait*	*lodava*
IS	*(il) louât*	*lodasse*
PeI	*(il) loua*	*lodò*
PeI-2	*(il) a loué*	*ha lodato*
PeS	*(il) ait loué*	*abbia lodato*
PPI	*(il) avait loué*	*aveva lodato*

---

6. Matthews (1991: 241) proposes a zero morpheme for 3SG, which establishes an iconic relationship between the 3SG and 1SG He would assign 'phonological markedness' to the low vowel /a/.

PPS	*(il) eût loué*	*avesse lodato*
F	*(il) louera*	*loderà*
FP	*(il) aura loué*	*avrà lodato*
C	*(il) louerait*	*loderebbe*
CP	*(il) aurait loué*	*avrebbe lodato*

As is evident, seven of the active paradigms, or forty-two verbal forms, constitute synthetic structure, while the remaining six, or thirty-six forms, plus all the passives, or seventy-eight forms, manifest themselves analytically. Thus, of the total of 156 forms for each verb having both active and passive structure, the ratio of analytic over synthetic is today 3:1, an exact reversal of the Latin situation.[7]

2.3.2 Comparison of differences

In comparing and contrasting the segmentations given for the synthetic forms of Latin, French, and Italian, three impressions stand out globally.

a. Canonical restructuring

The template for the Latin verb changed in its evolution into the Romance languages as follows:

Latin	STEM	+ A	+ T/M	+ P/N/V
Romance	STEM	+ T/M	+ P/N	

The linear order of Latin verbal morphemes made for clear-cut inward sensitivity of both T/M, conditioned by A, and P/N/V, conditioned by T/M, as expressed in the table of Latin segmentation given in 2.2, above. The loss of morphological aspect in Romance results in but one kind of inward sensitivity, that of P/N with respect to T/M, as illustrated in the preceding section. Let us compare directly the 3SG of the seven Romance synthetic paradigms with Latin.

Latin	**French**	**Italian**
lauda + Ø + Ø + *t*	[*lu* + Ø + Ø]	*lod* + Ø + *a*
laud + Ø + *e* + *t*	[*lu* + Ø + Ø]	*lod* + Ø + *i*
lauda + Ø + *ba* + *t*	[*lu* + ε + Ø]	*lod* + *av* + *a*
lauda + Ø + *re* + *t*		
lauda + *v* + *isse* + *t*	[*lu* + *a* + Ø]	*lod* + *ass* + *e*

---

7. The historical development of the analytic forms of these systems will be shown below, in 3.1.

lauda + *v* + Ø + *it*   [*lu* + Ø + *a*]   *lod* + Ø + *ò*
lauda + Ø + *bi* + *t*
 [*lu* + R + *a*]   *lod* + *er* + *à*
 [*lu* + R + *ε*]   *lod* + *er* + *ebbe*

This overview combines synchronic equivalence and diachronic correspondences: Latin *laudaret* can be considered the synchronic equivalent of the Romance imperfect subjunctive, although the latter derives from the Latin pluperfect subjunctive *laudavisset* etymologically. Likewise, the Romance future is not traceable to Latin *laudabit*, but it certainly must be considered its equivalent. The Romance conditional, however, has neither an etymological source (synthetically) nor a functional equivalent in Latin.

b. The complexity of P/N marking in Italian

This suffix, showing inward sensitivity with respect to T/M, seems to have gained in bulk compared to Latin, as it incorporated material from both the stem and the T/M morpheme. In addition, the near-uniform symbolization of Latin has been given up, the T/M conditioning producing quite a variety of allomorphs.

c. Zero marking in French

The P/N table on French, given in the previous section, exhibits fully one-third, or 12/36 of zero suffixes, for the PRES, IMP, and SUB columns. These are the results of the extensive sound changes, affecting both vocalic and consonantal signals, for which the history of French is notorious. The relationship of such atrophying of morphological markers with the rise of obligatory subject pronouns will be discussed below, in section 3.2.1.

Let us now consider the effect of the changes from Latin to Romance with respect to the parameter of SC, or the SDSPs to be isolated for French and Italian verbs.

Cf. SDSP 1:   there have been important changes, since the Romance verb, at least synthetically, no longer signals the categories of aspect and voice
Cf. SDSP 2:   no change[8]
Cf. SDSP 3:   no change in the forms considered
Cf. SDSP 4:   one could claim that there has been an increase in syncretism, in particular in French, clearly proven by the high percentage of the zero morpheme

---

8. Kilani-Schoch (1988: 197) suggests that French may be turning to base inflection.

Cf. SDSP 5: the most essential changes have occurred here, as the synthetic/analytic ratio has been reversed, thus making analyticity system-defining: the remaining synthetic verb forms now constitute the marked portion of the verb system
Cf. SDSP 6: there has been a restructuring of some verb conjugations, but this issue has not been investigated

2.4 Individual analogies

2.4.1 *Outline*

It was shown in section 2.1., above, that of the 120 possible forms of a Latin verb only 48, or eight paradigms, survive in both French and Italian. An even more drastic reduction of continuing Latin forms becomes apparent if the forms followed by +, indicating an analogical development, are excluded. In that case, French and Italian retain but ten and eleven verbal items, respectively:

French
PI *cantas > chantes*
cantat > chante
cantatis > chantez
cantant > chantent
PS *cantent > chantent*
PeI (A) *cantavi > chantai*
cantavit > chanta
PeI (P) *laudatus es > es loué*
laudatus est > est loué
laudati sunt > sont loués

Italian
PI *canto > canto*
cantat > canta
cantatis > cantate
II *cantabat > cantava*
cantabamus > cantavamo
cantabatis > cantavate
PeI (A) *cantavi > cantai*
cantavit > cantò
cantavimus > cantammo

PeI (P)   *laudatus est > è lodato*
PPI (P)   *laudatus erat > era lodato*

In French, thirty-eight of continuing forms may be considered analogical, in Italian thirty-seven, as a consequence. In both languages, these may be grouped into thirteen analogical processes, with these (informal) labels:

French
1. Schwa generalization in 1SGPI
2. 1PL *-ons*
3. Schwa in PS
4. Yod in 1PL and 2PL of PS
5. II suffix
6. *passé simple*
7. Haplology in Late Latin PPS
8. Stem leveling in some verbs
9. 1SG *suis*
10. 1PL *sommes*
11. 2PL *êtes*
12. PS of *être*
13. II of *être*

Italian
1. 2SG *-i*
2. 1PL *-iamo*
3. 3PL *-o*
4. Subjunctive *-i*
5. 1PL, 2PL of PS
6. 1SG II
7. *passato remoto*
8. Haplology in Late Latin PPS
9. 1SG *sono*
10. 2SG *sei*
11. 1PL, 1PL of PI of *essere*
12. PS of *essere*
13. 1PL, 2PL of II of *essere*

In the following, I will select what I consider from the perspective of naturalness parameters the most significant of the listed processes, combined into these groups:

French: A. (1), (3)
B. (2), (4)
C. (5)

[This will involve a total of 13 of the 38 analogical forms]

Italian: A. (1), (4)
B. (2), (5)
C. (3), (6), (9)

[This will involve a total of 17 of the 37 analogical forms]

2.4.2   *French*

2.4.2.1 *Schwa*

Analogical process A concerns the generalization of schwa in both the PI and PS of Old French. Let us first summarize the historical background.

From the segmentation of the Latin verb presented above, in 2.2, the following are the details relevant for our analysis:

a.   1SG = -*o, m* vs. 3SG = -*t*
b.   PI = Ø vs. PS = -*e*

Phonological changes from Latin to Old French (apocope of all vowels except /a/, deletion of final consonants) delivered the OF present tense paradigms of *cantare* as given:

PI			PS	
	1SG	*chant*		*chant*
	2SG	*chantes*		*chanz*
	3SG	*chante*		*chant*
	1PL	*chantons*		*chantons*
	2PL	*chantez*		*chantez*
	3PL	*chantent*		*chantent*

The morphological oppositions involved have now been changed to:

a.   1SG = Ø vs. 3SG = -*e* (schwa)
b.   PI = -*e* (schwa) vs. PS = Ø

Sound change has altered a non-iconic relationship in Latin to a counter-iconic one in Old French in (a), an iconic connection to counter-iconicity in (b). The effect of schwa generalization into the 1SGPI and into the PS resulted in this uniform paradigm (except for 1PL and 2PL) in Late Old French and Modern French:

PI, PS   *chante*
         chantes
         chante
         chantons ~ chantions
         chantez ~ chantiez
         chantent

As a consequence, non-iconicity is established for both oppositions (a) and (b). In accordance with the naturalness parameter of *constructional iconicity* the marked structure of counter-iconicity has been "improved" to non-iconicity.

There were two factors, however, that probably paved the way for iconicity, one phonetic/phonotactic, one morphological. It has been traditionally asserted that the extension of schwa to the 1SG PI was done in analogy to verbs like *entrer* or *doter* in Old French, derived from Latin *intrare* and *dubitare*. In the 1SG of such verbs, a schwa was inserted or triggered phonotactically, due to the presence of a final consonant cluster, either in both Latin and Old French, as in *entre*, or in Late Latin, after the operation of syncope, as in **dub'te*, later simplified to a single C: *dote*. In addition, one may refer to a possible pressure exerted by non-1st conj. verbs, which, in agreement with regular sound change, ended up with schwa in the subjunctive, since the vowel /a/ marked this mood in Latin in non-1st conj. verbs, as far as the generalization of schwa into the PS is concerned (Walker 1987a: 121). Thus, PS forms which develop etymologically from Latin, like *vienne, parte,* or *fenisse,* served as models for the new PS of *chante*. Walker (1987a: 122) also mentions the property of some Old French dialects to try to differentiate the PS from the PI iconically, by the addition of a special subjunctive suffix like *-ge* or *-che*. That these soon became extinct may be attributed to system congruity, as French acquired the characteristic of non-iconicity throughout its morphological system (cf. Klausenburger 1992a, b).

There is more involved in schwa generalization than the parameter of iconicity. If verbs other than *chanter* are taken into consideration, *paradigmatic transparency* for the stem appears clearly, as illustrated in what follows.

	Latin	**Old French**	**Mod. French**
PI	*lavo*	*lef*	*lave*
	lavas	*leves*	*laves*
	lavat	*leve*	*lave*
	lavamus	*lavons*	*lavons*

PS	lavem	lef	lave
	laves	les	laves
	lavet	let	lave
	lavemus	lavons	lavions
PI	gardo	gart	garde
	gardas	gardes	gardes
	gardat	garde	garde
	gardamus	gardons	gardons
PS	gardem	gart	garde
	gardes	garz	gardes
	gardet	gart	garde
	gardemus	gardons	gardions
PI	parabolo	parol	parle
	parabolas	paroles	parles
	parabolat	parole	parle
	parabolamus	parlons	parlons
PS	parabolem	parol	parle
	paraboles	parous	parles
	parabolet	parout	parle
	parabolemus	parlons	parlions

In Old French, final devoicing and l-vocalization were morphophonological rules which created allomorphy in the stem, which, however, is restored to uniformity after the operation of schwa generalization: [lav], [gaʀd], [paʀl]. (For *laver*, a vowel alternation unrelated to the final schwa is also involved; for *parler*, the extension of the syncopated stem [paʀl] complicated matters slightly).

Stem leveling as a trigger for schwa generalization seems to be confirmed by the fact that "-*e* appears much earlier and with greater regularity in consonant-final stems than it does in those ending in a vowel" (Walker 1987a: 119). (Cf. Dees et al. 1980). The parameter of paradigmatic transparency would be invoked within the theory of natural morphology, of course. The only question to be answered is whether this property could also qualify as one of the SDSPs of Old French (Latin) verb morphology. In that case, schwa generalization would be considered in compliance with system congruity.

Finally, Carstairs' *systematic homonymy claim* (SHC) must be touched on in this connection. Due to schwa generalization, syncretism between the PI and PS is obtained in Old French, fitting his definition of a systematic homonymy, not an accidental one, which is caused by sound change (Carstairs 1987: 123). Such a type is claimed to be stable over time — a seemingly correct prediction for the French inflectional system for both number and mood.

2.4.2.2 -ons

One of the most puzzling questions of Romance historical linguistics concerns the origin of the French 1PL suffix -*ons,* occurring in all tenses and moods except the *passé simple,* the continuation of the Latin perfect indicative (PeI). Over 100 years of research on this problem has not yielded a generally accepted (and acceptable) answer (Manczak 1980: 62). Mayerthaler (1972: 332) divides the approaches to this issue into seven groups of explanations as follows:

1. Analogy to *sons*
2. Analogy to *habere*
3. Analogy to the 1st conjugation
4. Stratum explanation
5. Labialization
6. Velarization
7. Homonymy conflict

Leaving aside the (least plausible) stratum view, these analyses may be divided, roughly, into phonetic/phonological and morphological sections. Let us briefly summarize the essence of the above suggestions.

The most widely accepted hypothesis is (1), first proposed by Diez. It claims that the Latin 1PL of the copula *essere, sumus,* developed into Old French *sons,* the *-ons* suffix of which was subsequently generalized to all PIs and, in a second phase, to other tenses and moods. Two major objections have been advanced against this theory:

a. the 1PL derived from Lat. *sumus* is actually *sommes,* and was in Old French already, at least most frequently, *sons* occurring rarely; and
b. it is implausible to attribute such "generalization power" to the 1PL of *essere.*

The other two analogy proposals must be combined with the phonetic factors of labialization or velarization. In order for *habere* to serve as analogical model, the 1PL *habemus* must first turn into *avons,* /e/ having been transformed to /o/ by both preceding and following labials. Similarly, the 1st conj 1PL *-amus* became *-*omus* due to the rounding effect of /m/. Mayerthaler (1972: 304) makes use of velarization, a general rule that is supposed to have applied to all verb endings in front of a (bilabial) nasal consonant in Gallo-Romance.

Corbett (1968) actually reinforces (1), suggesting that the analogical spread of *sons* is made more plausible if one sees it as a way of avoiding homonymy between the reflexes of the Latin PI *cantamus* and PeI *cantavimus*, the latter, after the loss of *-vi-*, compensated by gemination, but later degeminated in Old French, having coincided with the former (Corbett 1968: 424), or potentially so, if the PI had not diverged to *chantons*.

Manczak (1980: 63) rejects as well the analogical explanation for *sons* and proposes that *-ons* was due to an "irregular sound change conditioned by frequency." Frequency led to a reduced suffix, in that the vowel opening of /o/ is smaller than for /a/. Similar frequency-induced changes may be found in other Romance developments, as well as outside this language group. Manczak relates the evolution of French *-ons* from Latin *-amus* to that of Latin 3SGPeI *-avit* to Italian *-ò* (Spanish *-ó*) (p. 65).

Before integrating the history and status of this suffix into an account within natural morphology, let us sketch the etymological evolution to be expected for the first conjugation:

PI   *cantamus* > **chantains*
PS   *cantemus* > **chanteins*
II   *cantabamus* > **chantevains*
F   *cantare habemus* > **chantereins*
C   *cantare habebamus* > **chanterevains*

It is interesting that *none* of these "expected" reflexes actually occur in Old French. Instead, the extant forms were the following, preceded by reconstructed Late Latin sources (cf. Rheinfelder 1967: 193–200):

PI   **cantu/omos* > *chantons*
PS   **cantu/omos* ~**cantiamos* > *chantons* ~*chantiens*
II   **cante(b)amos* > *chantiiens*
F   **cantare omos* > *chanterons*
C   **cantare eamos* > *chanteriiens*

A natural morphological solution would predict that the 1PLPI suffix *-amus* must have been the source of French *-ons*, for two reasons:

a.   PI is unmarked for both tense and mood; and
b.   the 1st conjugation was the default PSC

A phonetic explanation, probably one of labialization (cf. de Poerck 1963: 23–6), must be added to deliver the *-ons*. Thereafter, principles (a) and (b) describe this path of evolution:

1. *-ons* is extended to F, since the auxiliary *habere* is involved in the PI, thus a generalization to another conjugation in the PI (cf. St. Léger *cantumps, cantomps*, but: *devemps*);
2. further generalization to the PS;
3. final extension to the II and C (the reflex of the PeI, of course, was never reached, making the modern *passé simple* so anomalous, or *system incongruent*).

The shift of distribution of the 1PL and 2PL P/N suffixes from Old French to Modern French is schematized clearly by Walker (1987a: 125–6) in this manner:

	Old French	**Modern French**
PI	*-ons, -ez*	*-ons, -ez*
PS	*-ons/-iens, -ez/-iez*	*-ions, -iez*
II	*-(i)iens, -(i)iez*	*-ions, -iez*
F	*-ons, -ez*	*-ons, -ez*
C	*-(i)iens, -(i)iez*	*-ions, -iez*

According to Walker, "the correlation of formal differences with meaning differences is re-established in a manner strikingly more functional than the complexity of the Old French situation" (p. 126). In accordance with markedness considerations, the UM tense and mood categories of PI and F are grouped together with the suffixes *-ons* and *-ez*, while the M tense/mood paradigms of PS, II, and C are grouped separately, by means of the suffixes *-ions* and *-iez*. In addition, iconicity is attained due to the extra marker of the yod in the latter group.

2.4.2.3 *Imperfect indicative*

By regular sound change, the Latin 1st conjugation paradigm would have delivered the following Old French forms:

1SG	*cantabam > chanteve*
2SG	*cantabas > chanteves*
3SG	*cantabat > chantevet*
1PL	*cantabamus > chantiiens*
2PL	*cantabatis > chantiiez*
3PL	*cantabant > chantevent*

Such imperfect verbs are in fact attested, in some eastern dialects of Old French

(Rheinfelder 1967: 197). However, it is generally agreed that the Francien dialect, and, as a consequence, the standard French of today, must be derived from a spoken Latin paradigm apparently modeled after the 2nd conjugation:

1SG	*cantebam > chanteie > chantais
2SG	*cantebas > chanteies > chantais
3SG	*cantebat > chanteit > chantait
1PL	*cantebamus > chantiiens > chantions
2PL	*cantebatis > chantiiez > chantiez
3PL	*cantebant > chanteient > chantaient

The remodeling of the unquestionably default PSC of Latin verbs by a (more) marked 2nd conjugation seems to counter parameters of naturalness. How do we explain this morphological shift?

Let us present a complete segmentation analysis of Latin imperfects and compare the evolution into French with that of Italian.[9]

	Latin	**Italian**
1st conjugation	cant + a + ba + t	cant + a + v + a
2nd conjugation	vid + e + ba + t	ved + e + v + a
3rd conjugation	scrib + e + ba + t	scriv + e + v + a
4th conjugation	part + ie + ba + t	part + i + v + a

	Old French	**Modern French**
	chant + ei + t	chant + ait
	ve(d) + ei + t	voy + ait
	escriv + ei + t	écriv + ait
	part + ei + t	part + ait

It becomes apparent from this comparison that the Italian imperfect kept intact the Latin structure, in two ways:

a. the canonical sequence of three morphemes, TV (theme vowel) + T (tense) + P/N (person/number), survives;
b. all three TV's are maintained (in the 4th conjugation, the -ie- turns into a "clearer" -i-, the distinctive vowel of this conjugation, seen in the infinitive *partire*, remodeled probably in late Latin already).

---

9. I am now giving examples of all the conjugations, but only in the 3SG

There has been a restructuring, as the vowel /a/ has been "cut" from the T marker /ba/ to signal P/N in Italian — but that does not change the typology.

In Old French, on the other hand, three morphemes have been reduced to two, with the loss of the TV, and from Old French to Modern French, P/N has atrophied (with the exception of 1PL and 2PL), schematically:

Latin (Italian)	Old French	Modern French
3	2	1
TV + T + P/N	TV + P/N	T + (P/N)

The complete paradigm of *cantare* is now given, with the segmentation of Latin and Modern French suggested above, and the Old French analysis taken from Walker (1981: 87–97).

Latin	**Old French**	**Modern French**
e + ba + m	*ej +* Ø	ɛ
e + ba + s	*ej + s*	ɛ
e + ba + t	*ej + t*	ɛ
e + ba + mus	*i + jens*	*j +* õ
e + ba + tis	*i + jets*	*j + e*
e + ba + nt	*ej + nt*	ɛ

I would claim that the evolution of the imperfect indicative in Old French does not violate the SC of Latin verbs, in particular the default PSC of the 1st conjugation, simply because the theme vowel, which characterized the various conjugations of Latin, no longer plays a major role in Old French. Expressed differently: sound changes from Latin to Old French have transformed the SDSPs of Latin. As a consequence, we may assume that *cantebat* was no longer to be considered "marked" over *cantabat*. This vowel exchange, as a matter of fact, can now be attributed to another parameter of naturalness, *uniform symbolization*: within late Latin that developed into French, /e/ became, in combination with the remaining ending(s), a unique marker of the imperfect indicative. Modern French pronunciation, of course, has obliterated the Latin segmentation even further.

The tense allomorphs of the imperfect proposed for Old French in Walker's analysis, /ej*e*, i, ej/, undergo conditioning 'outwards', sensitive to P/N (p. 91). It seems to be of the "legal" kind of outward sensitivity, however, as it affects "all the properties within a given category" (Carstairs 1987: 168). If we take /ej/ as basic, (i.e. the suffix of the 3rd person), it may be claimed that [i] and [ej*e*] are sensitive to the *marked* categories of 1st and 2nd person. Thus, a modification of Carstairs' PC is obtained by including markedness considerations.

2.4.3 *Italian*

2.4.3.1 *Final -i*

The Italian verbal ending *-i* occurs as a 2SG and subjunctive morpheme. Its evolution from Latin has received various interpretations and explanations, three of which will be outlined below and then evaluated in terms of parameters of naturalness.

For each of the presentations concerning the origin of *-i* I shall give the Latin suffixes (singular only), their etymological results according to the approach, and the actual Italian reflexes.

A. Meyer-Lübke (1967: 180–183) proposes a (special) sound change of the 2SG *-as* and *-es* to *-i*, to be placed into the following overall context:

	Latin	**Etym. Italian**	**Act. Italian**
PI	*-o*	*-o*	*-o*
	-as	*-i*	*-i*
	-at	*-a*	*-a*
PS	*-em*	*-e*	*-i*
	-es	*-i*	*-i*
	-et	*-e*	*-i*
II	*-abam*	*-ava*	*-avo*
	-abas	*-avi*	*-avi*
	-abat	*-ava*	*-ava*
IS	*-assem*	*-asse*	*-assi*
	-asses	*-assi*	*-assi*
	-asset	*-asse*	*-asse*

On this view, all the 2SG suffixes are obtained phonologically in the first conjugation given. The PI2SG of the 2nd conjugation is also predicted, as is the 4th conjugation, but not the 2SG of the 3rd, which has to be considered an extension of the others:

PI2SG *-as*
-es > *i*
-is
-is > *e* > *i*

For the PS paradigm, 2SG *-i* appears to have served as the base for the reformations of 1SG and 3SG to *-i,* creating a 'subjunctive' marker *-i,* for the 1st conjugation. For all the other conjugations, etymological *-a* continues, including the 2SG *-as* to *-a,* not *-i,* underlining the "special" sound change nature of *-as* to *-i* posited for the PI2SG, above. In the IS, etymological 2SG *-i* is generalized to the 1SG, but not to the 3SG

B.   Rohlfs (1968: 248) (and the majority of traditional opinion) sees the source of 2SG *-i* in the PI2SG of the 4th conjugation, thus delivering the following overview:

	Latin	Etym. Italian	Act. Italian
PI	*-o*	*-o*	*-o*
	-as	*-a*	*-i*
	-at	*-a*	*-a*
PS	*-em*	*-e*	*-i*
	-es	*-e*	*-i*
	-et	*-e*	*-i*
II	*-abam*	*-ava*	*-avo*
	-abas	*-ava*	*-avi*
	-abat	*-ava*	*-ava*
IS	*-assem*	*-asse*	*-assi*
	-asses	*-asse*	*-assi*
	-asset	*-asse*	*-asse*

This hypothesis not only has to motivate how a (marked) 4th conjugation can spread to all the others, including the default first, but also the extension of the *-i* into the subjunctive, both present and imperfect. On the other hand, the generalization of 2sGPI *-i* to 2sGII seems plausible. The inclusion of the 1SG and 3SG in the subjunctive by the *-i* repeats Theory A, above.[10]

C.   A third alternative, which may be considered "between" the two already given, has been proposed in Seklaoui (1989: 150):

---

10. The *-i* of the IS may be due to analogy to the PeI, cf. Jensen (1971: 56).

	Latin	Etym. Italian	Act. Italian
PI	-o	-o	-o
	-as	-e	-i
	-at	-a	-a
PS	-em	-e	-i
	-es	-i	-i
	-et	-e	-i
II	-abam	-ava	-avo
	-abas	-ave	-avi
	-abat	-ava	-ava
IS	-assem	-asse	-assi
	-asses	-assi	-assi
	-asset	-asse	-asse

Two phonological changes are proposed in this analysis, (1) final /s/ > yod, and (2) a raising of /a/ to /e/ and /e/ to /i/, caused by this yod. However, just like Meyer-Lübke's sound change, it is morphologically conditioned, as these two changes do not apply in non-1st conjugation verbs.

Which hypothesis of the origin of Italian *-i* fits best into parameters of naturalness? I would choose Meyer-Lübke's approach, despite the problematical sound change necessary. What remains to be explained is how the 2SG can serve as the base for reforming the 1SG and, especially, the (unmarked) 3SG of the PS. It seems that in the IS, the unmarked nature of the 3SG was "strong" enough to resist replacement. But in the PS, the parameter of *uniform symbolization*, in the direction of *-i* as a subjunctive marker, was victorious over 3SG It is striking to compare and contrast the indicative and subjunctive endings of Modern Italian outlined in this analysis:

PI, II	PS, IS
-o	-i
-i	-i
-a	-i, -e

The neutralization of the morphological category P/N is manifested in the *marked* subjunctive mood, while distinctive suffixes for all three persons are obtained in the *unmarked* indicative. The latter vocalic markers have replaced the loss of the Latin *-s* and *-t* in the 2SG and 3SG, restoring the Latin SDSP of differentiation between 2SG and 3SG, which had become syncretic, if "regular" sound change only is assumed.

2.4.3.2 *-iamo*

The evolution of the Italian 1PL suffix *-iamo* can best be traced within the context of (a) the four Latin conjugations and (b) together with the 2PL, limited to the PI and PS paradigms (cf. Wanner 1975: 154–6).

			Latin	**Etym. Italian**	**Old Florentine**	**Mod. Italian**
1 c.	PI	1PL	portamus	portamo	portiamo	portiamo
		2PL	portatis	portate	portate	portate
	PS	1PL	portemus	portemo	portiamo	portiamo
		2PL	portetis	portete	portiate	portiate
2 c.	PI	1PL	videmus	vedemo	vedemo	vediamo
		2PL	videtis	vedete	vedete	vedete
	PS	1PL	videamus	vediamo	vediamo	vediamo
		2PL	videatis	vediate	vediate	vediate
3 c.	PI	1PL	facimus	facemo	facemo	facciamo
		2PL	facitis	facete	facete	fate
	PS	1PL	faciamus	facciamo	facciamo	facciamo
		2PL	faciatis	facciate	facciate	facciate
4 c.	PI	1PL	dormimus	dormimo	dormimo	dormiamo
		2PL	dormitis	dormite	dormite	dormite
	PS	1PL	dormiamus	dormiamo	dormiamo	dormiamo
		2PL	dormiatis	dormiate	dormiate	dormiate

This overview incorporates three morphological shifts:

```
PS           — (1) →   PS           — (2) →   PI           — (3) →   PI
[−1 conj]              [+1 conj]              [+1 conj]              [−1 conj]
1PL, 2PL               1PL, 2PL               1PL                    1PL
```

1. Old Florentine texts attest the spread of [−1 conj] PS 1PL and 2PL suffixes to the [+1 conj] (*portiamo, portiate*);
2. in the Old Italian period, the 1PL *-iamo* also reaches the PI of the 1st conjugation (*portiamo*); non-first conjugations manifest *-iamo* in the PI in the modern language only. This last change involves both the transfer of the

suffix, as in *vediamo* and *dormiamo*, and the transfer of the entire 1PLPS verb form, as in *facciamo*, which cannot be interpreted as the addition of the suffix to the previous stem *fac-* (Vincent 1980: 389).

At first glance, two of the three shifts outlined seem to counter markedness and naturalness parameters. Only step (3) is immediately motivatable: it constitutes the extension of the default [1 conj] to the other conjugations, an application of the PSC parameter. Shift (2) has been given a plausible explanation by Nyman (1982). What is unexpected here is the move from the *marked* subjunctive to the *unmarked* indicative. From a pragmatic point of view, Nyman claims, this change-over is explainable, if we realize that the Latin subjunctive functioned as both a subjunctive and as a 'hortative' in the 1PL. He sets up the following interpretation of 1PL "we" (ms., p.7):

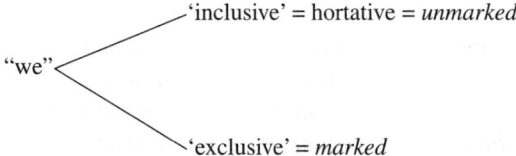

The complete transfer may be diagrammed thus:

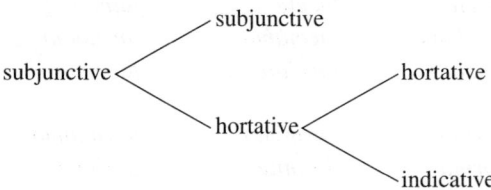

Seen as an extension of an unmarked hortative, the shift from PS *-iamo* becomes natural; it also explains the non-shift into the 2PL PI, erroneously predicted in Wanner's transderivational account.

Morphological shift (1), however, remains difficult to motivate. It involves the generalization of the marked [−1 conj] forms to the default PSC. It is agreed, of course, that only one of the non-first conjugation 1PL can be the etymological source of *-iamo*. One could be tempted to see a tie-in with the generalization of final *-i* as a subjunctive marker. However, the latter is not finalized until after the Old Italian phase, while step (1) in the *-iamo* spread must be posited for much earlier.

2.4.3.3 *Final -o*
Modern Italian P/N suffixes exhibit a final *-o* non-etymologically in the three contexts listed above, in 2.4.1, under Italian C:

(3)   3PL *-o*
(6)   1SG II
(9)   1SG *sono*

There cannot be any controversy concerning the explanation of the last two cases of analogy, both due to an extension of the default [1 conj] PI 1SG *canto*. Latin 1SG *sum* was the only 1SG PI not ending in *-o*, thus would have yielded etymologically It. *son*, sometimes attested in early texts. The Latin singular II paradigm delivered an example of (accidental) homonymy, as by regular sound change all three persons resulted in identical forms:

cantabam > *cantava*
cantabas > *cantava*
cantabat > *cantava*

Such homonymy, however, had no "synchronic underpinning" (Carstairs 1987: 13) and quite naturally was removed by having the II acquire the system-congruous three-way distinctiveness of:

cantavo
cantavi
cantava

In the 3PL, the final *-o* does not appear to have an etymological source, the expected result being *cantan* or *canta*, the latter then identical to 3SG, attested in medieval Italian dialects (Rohlfs 1968: 256). Three hypotheses as to the origin of the standard 3PL's *cantano*, *vedono*, and *dormono* have been proposed in the literature.

Probably the most frequently expressed view follows this rather tortuous analogical path: Latin *sum* acquired a final *-o* from 1SG regular *-o* and this epenthesis is duplicated in the evolution of 3PL *sunt* > Ital. *sono*. From the latter, all 3PL endings obtained a final *-o* (Jensen 1971: 39–40). Another analogical source proposed, considered as a "reinforcement" of the development just outlined, is the 3PL of the PeI, as, for instance, Lat. *fecerunt* to Ital. *fecero* (d'Ovidio 1899: 320, Grandgent 1927: 160).

These two proposals must be considered implausible for a theory of morphological naturalness. Why the 3PL of "to be" should add a 1SG morpheme *-o* makes no sense at all. In addition, the generalization of the irregular 3PL *sono* to all other verbs, including the dominant PSC of the first conjugation, must remain doubtful. Similarly, the marked PeI cannot be assumed reasonably to have been the model for all other tenses and moods.

There exists a lesser known hypothesis about It. 3PL -*o*, which, however, possesses a certain degree of attractiveness in terms of parameters of naturalness. It is the *danunt* theory, proposed by Foerster (1898). He claims that already in Old Latin, and continuing in the spoken dialects right into the history of Romance, there occurred 3PL doublets such as *dant* and *danunt*. The latter is seen as a secondary 3PL morpheme, necessary if the final -*t* of the first form gets weakened or deleted in fast speech. It can be compared to a "double" infinitive like spoken Latin *essere*, where the infinitival suffix -*se* in Classical Latin *esse* is no longer recognized, or the second plural marker being added in the history of English *children*, to be analyzed as *child-r-en* (cf. German *Kinder*, with only "one" plural). If we believe, with Foerster, that other double forms existed in spoken Latin, including 3PL's of first conjugation verbs, then Italian -*o* can now be explained etymologically (Foerster 1898:523):

amanunt > *amano*
danunt > *danno*
vidununt > *vedono*
dormununt > *dormono*

Paroxytonic stress in *danunt* triggered, presumably, gemination, while proparoxytonic stress, due to the regularization of stem accentuation, yielded the single /n/ in the suffix. The resulting vocalic ending fits Italian phonotactically, as consonant-final words are extremely rare.

In his response to Foerster's hypothesis, d'Ovidio doubts the soundness of attributing so much importance to some archaic Latin occurrences and also shows that some problems remain with the phonetic evolutions to be assumed (1899:320). Nevertheless, this proposal seems to be the most motivatable of those extant, being based on constructional iconicity, as a secondary 3PL marker would clearly reflect the markedness of plural over singular for the third person. Such a distinction between the two third persons can also be seen as a typological feature of the SDSPs of Latin, which have been retained rather intact in Modern Italian, already seen in previous sections.[11]

---

11. See Klausenburger (1992c).

2.5 "Minimal" inflections in Modern French

In the preceding sections, details of Latin, French, and Italian inflectional morphology have been examined within a framework of naturalness parameters.[12] Romance inflection has been due to two sources, (a) (original) Latin suffixation and (b) the evolution of Latin analysis to synthesis, in the case of the future and conditional. The continuation of Latin inflection has supplied the bulk of the Romance material analyzed (PI, PS, II). Modern French manifests globally non-iconic inflectional structure, characterized by (mainly) zero marking,[13] as may be gleaned from the following table (Klausenburger 1992a: 411):

Modern French Inflectional Morphology

		Orthography	Pronunciation
ADJECTIVE	a.	*mauvais, -e*	[movɛ + z]
gender (M/F)		*petit, -e*	[pəti + t]
	b.	*large*	[larʒ]
		nu,-e	[nü]
VERB:	a.	*lit, lisent*	[li + z]
number (3SG/p)	b.	*arrive, -nt*	[ariv]
		joue, nt	[ʒu]
		parle, nt	[parl]
VERB:	a.	*lit, lise*	[li +z]
mood (PI/PS)	b.	*arrive*	[ariv]
		joue	[ʒu]
		parle	[parl]
NOUN:	a.	*ami, -s*	[ami]
number (SG/PL)		*femme, -s*	[fam]
	b.	*oeuf, -s*	[oef], [ö]
		cheval, -aux	[ʃəval], [ʃəvo]

---

12. On a possible hierarchy of such parameters, see Wheeler (1993).

13. Herschensohn (1993: 104) asserts that "the most significant morphological alternation in spoken French is that of *final consonant* vs. *zero* in adjective and verb paradigms." It is illustrated by an adjective like *petit*, with the final consonant /t/ in the feminine, and by a verb like *attendre*, which manifests a stem-final /d/ in its paradigm in all forms except the (unmarked) present indicative singular. It is clear that this "FCA" of Modern French ranks as a PSC of the language, second only to that of "invariance" of the stem, and it must be considered the trigger for the well-known Canadian French insertion of a final consonant (either /s/ or /z/) to a vowel-final verb stem in the marked contexts of 3rd plural of the PI and in the 1,2,3,6 forms of the PS (cf. Walker 1995), creating an iconic relationship between 3rd person singular and plural in the PI, and between the singular forms of the PI and the PS.

The non-iconic structure, characterized by zero-marking, is manifested in ADJECTIVE by the example *large*, in VERB by *arriver*, and in NOUN by *ami*. It is the predominant pattern, while iconicity is demonstrated by an adjective like *petit*, a verb like *lire*, and a noun like *cheval* (partial), and counter-iconicity in SG *oeuf*, PL *oeufs* [ö]. One may detect, in fact, a *minimal* level of inflections (Klausenburger 1989: 232) in this system of forms, one in which more "burden" is put on the syntactic side, in order to compensate for the loss of inflectional suffixes from Latin and Old French to Modern French. Such an erosion can be nicely shown by the following verbal endings, comparing stage (a) (= a more conservative standard version of Modern French) and stage (b) (= trends in the spoken language) (Klausenburger 1992b: 230–231):

Modern French Spoken Verbal Endings

		PI	PS	II	F	C
a.						
	1SG	-Ø–Ø	Ø–Ø	-ε-Ø	-r-e	-rɛ-Ø
	2SG	-Ø–Ø	-Ø–Ø	-ε-Ø	-r-a	-rɛ-Ø
	3SG	-Ø–Ø	-Ø–Ø	-ε-Ø	-r-a	-rɛ-Ø
	1PL	-Ø-õ	-Ø-jõ	-j-õ	-r-õ	-rj-õ
	2PL	-Ø-e	-Ø-je	-j-e	-r-e	-rj-e
	3PL	-Ø–Ø	-Ø–Ø	-ε-Ø	-r-õ	-rɛ-Ø
b.		PI	PS	II	F	C
	1SG	x	x	x	-Ø–Ø	(x)
	2SG	x	x	x	-Ø–Ø	(x)
	3SG	x	x	x	-Ø–Ø	(x)
	1PL	-Ø–Ø	-Ø–Ø	-ε-Ø	-Ø–Ø	(-rɛ-Ø)
	2PL	x	x	x	-Ø–Ø	(x)
	3PL	x	x	x	-Ø–Ø	(x)

In (b), the x's indicate duplication of the table in (a). Three changes are recognizable from (a) to (b):

1. The elimination of the 1PL *nous* form in favor of *on*, which has the consequence of requiring 3SG verbal endings;
2. the replacement of the synthetic future by the *futur proche*, or the *go-future*. As a result, no suffixes exist any longer, since the analytic sequence of the auxiliary *aller* plus the infinitive of the verb is employed;
3. the conditional endings are shown in parentheses, as the possibility exists to equate the conditional to a syntactic sequence of *aller* in the imperfect indicative plus the infinitive of the verb (cf. *allait chanter*), at least in certain contexts of indirect speech (cf. Harris 1978).

It may be seen that these trends in progress fit perfectly into the *system congruity* of Modern French, as it features (a) a lack of suffixes and (b) analytic structure with anteposition (Kilani-Schoch 1988: 194ff). The latter is actually re-enforced by the obligatory use of the subject pronouns in Modern French, to be considered either proclitics or prefixes (cf. below, Chapter 3). Modern Spoken French may be considered as 'pro-drop', with the stipulation, however, that while 'classical' null subject languages like Spanish and Italian have a suffix on the verb, French makes use of a "prefix" as a result of the grammaticalization of the former clitic pronoun subject with the following finite verb. Such a proposal would supply ingredients for both points (a) and (b), above: the "old" clitics have become prefixes, supporting the feature "lack of suffixation", but the anteposition also occurs analytically by way of the "new" subject pronouns, traditionally considered 'tonic': *Moi, je chante...*

Although the existence of a minimal inflectional system is clearly a fact of Modern French, the relationship with syntax hinted at above has to be clarified further. In particular, the teleological and cause-and-effect scenario suggested must be rejected. It is not tenable to consider the rise of periphrastic (i.e. analytic, syntactic) structures as a *consequence* of the loss of inflectional endings. Such a claim misunderstands the *dynamics* of inflectional morphology (cf. also Vincent 1987), the final output of a process of grammaticalization, traditionally summarized in the analysis to synthesis change-over. Focusing entirely on the evolution of Latin and Old French inflections into Modern French leads us to believe that almost "catastrophic" reductions in signaling have produced minimal and useless morphology today. In addition, some of these changes have gone from iconic to non-iconic, apparently in contradiction of expectations of "maintenance and enhancement of ... iconicity" (Matthews 1991: 244) in language change.

The theoretical framework of grammaticalization supplies the crucial link and the explanatory context needed. It makes clear that grammatical structure is found at some point on the continuum of grammaticalization. As will be developed in particular in Chapter 3, 3.2.1, Latin suffixation constituted a (quasi) endpoint of the evolution of earlier periphrasis. Romance inflections continue this structure, but do also develop further, culminating in Modern French in the real *Endstation* of grammaticalization, i.e., the atrophying of suffixes. Grammaticalization chains or continua coexist and manifest various degrees of finality, and it is not necessary for one to be completed before another one starts anew (with the same functional role in the language). Therefore, morphology and syntax always show a certain reciprocity to one another, subtly being shifted along the way.

Although the bulk of Romance inflectional material analyzed above apparently had completed grammaticalization already in Latin, and only a smaller part of it, the paradigms of the future and conditional, still are transparently understood as due to the synthesis of erstwhile periphrasis, it is those structures which supply the key to an understanding of all of inflectional morphology. In a sense, then, we began in this chapter in *medias res*, or even at the "end of the story". The next chapter will add the "beginning".

Chapter 3

Grammaticalization Processes Involving the Verb

3.1 Synthesis and analysis in Romance verbs

3.1.1 *The rise of analyticity*

As determined in section 2.2, above, the Latin verb system was aspectual, manifesting a dichotomy between *imperfective* and *perfective*, illustrated with the 3SG form in the indicative active as follows: (Harris and Vincent 1988: 56)

	Past	**Present**	**Future**
Imperfective	CANTABAT	CANTAT	CANTABIT
Perfective	CANTAVERAT	CANTAVIT	CANTAVERIT

It is generally agreed that the Romance system must be considered temporal, the equivalences in French to be most accurately diagrammed as: (Harris and Vincent 1988: 229, Harris 1978: 152)

			aura chanté	
			p/a	
Present axis	a chanté	chante		chantera
	a	s		p
Past axis	avait chanté	chantait		chanterait
	a	chanta		p
		s		
			aurait chanté	
			p/a	

Abbreviations: *a* = anterior, *s* = simultaneous, *p* = posterior

There appears to be no objection to presenting the Italian verb analogously:

		avrà cantato	
ha cantato	*canta*		*canterà*
aveva cantato	*cantava*		*canterebbe*
	cantò		
		avrebbe cantato	

There has occurred a fairly radical restructuring of the Latin system, as there are only three etymological survivors, all in the simultaneous column, and there have been six additions, augmenting the overall Romance system to nine paradigms, compared to six in Latin. For the six additions, one uncontroversially posits these late Latin sources:

PRESENT PERFECT	*habet cantatum*
PLUPERFECT	*habebat cantatum*
FUTURE	*cantare habet*
CONDITIONAL	*cantare habebat (habuit)*
FUTURE PERFECT	*habere habet cantatum*
CONDITIONAL PERFECT	*habere habebat (habuit) cantatum*

The abandonment of the Latin system and the rise of these new analytic structures seem to pose serious difficulties for the two principal parameters of natural morphology, since (a) the Classical Latin verb architecture presented no counter-iconic, thus highly marked, instances, appearing, instead, to be neatly transparent; and (b) retention of synthetic forms would have been perfectly system-congruous, as it made up three-fourths of the system globally. As a matter of fact, the rise of the new analyticity can be seen as the imposition of the marked type, being manifested in only one-fourth of the total occurrences. The motivation for the verbal restructuring must principally be sought on a deeper level than overt morphological architecture. The surface Latin system obscured three crucial morpho-syntactic instabilities, involving (1) the future, (2) the perfect, and (3) the passives, each of which will now be analyzed in detail.

A. The future and conditional

Fleischman (1982: 31) attributes an inherent instability of the future due to "the continual fluctuation of the balance of modality and temporality". She presents the following diachronic overview from PIE to Romance (p. 109) [I am substituting French for the Spanish examples given by Fleischman]:

		A.		B.			C.
I. PIE	MODAL	*ama-bhu		MODAL			
II. Latin	TEMPORAL	amabo			cantare habeo		
III. Romance	MODAL	Ø	ASPECTUAL TEMPORAL		chanterai	ASPECT.	vais dormir
IV. Contemporary Romance			MODAL		chanterai	TEMP.	vais dormir
						MODAL	vais dormir

Fleischman also correlates the assumption of temporal function in these developments with synthetic structure (pp. 153–154). As a consequence, one can reason that such a synthetic-temporal state will trigger (the next) modal/aspectual period, exactly to be posited for late Latin (and contemporary spoken Romance, although *not* Italian).[1] This morphosemantic explanation of the rise of the analytic future in spoken Latin appears much more convincing than two traditional hypotheses, one referring to the phonetic merger of the Latin future and perfect (in the intervocalic confusion of the bilabial fricative), and the other pointing to the non-uniformity of future formation in Classical Latin, consisting of the -*b*- constellation for the first two conjugations, and forms equivalent to subjunctives in the other conjugations.

The new future served as the catalyst for two other compound formations, the future perfect and the conditional. The first can easily be motivated on the model of the simple future, as part of the replacement of the abandoned perfective/imperfective aspectual system by a new temporal constellation, relating also, of course, to the rise of new compound pasts. It is interesting to note that the structure of the new tense constellation, outlined above, seems to "require" a "future in the past", or the *posterior* category on the past axis. It is the Romance conditional, its source having an architecture analogical to the future, also being paired with a *p/a* correspondence. As to the interaction between these two new structures, four possibilities present themselves:

a. The future and conditional arose independently, one due to the long-standing instability mentioned above, the other necessitated in the new tense system;
b. The future served as a model for the conditional;

---

1. For a very specific plotting of the development of the semantics of future, cf. Bybee (1988).

c. The conditional served as a model for the future (although this sequence may appear less convincing, it has been proposed by some analysts);
d. There existed both independent and combined motivation, the most plausible approach.

B. The Latin perfect

It is well known that the Latin perfect was bivalent, incorporating the functions of the inherited Indo-European aorist and perfect.[2] This double meaning is largely hidden within the aspectual system of Classical Latin as portrayed traditionally (cf. above) and becomes overt only in the diagramming of the developing tense constellations: *cantavit* would have to fill both the *a* slot on the present axis and the *s* slot on the past axis. The first function is selected for the new analytic formation in spoken Latin by means of the *habet cantatum* periphrasis, since the present tense of the auxiliary is able to express what is needed, direct relevance and connection to the present moment. Actually, such a compound also introduced aspectual perfectivity once again, leading Fleischman (1983: 203) to propose a parallelism between this evolution and that of the future, both shifting "predictably" from pragmatic device > aspect > tense.[3]

The immediate consequence of the rise of *habet cantatum* would seem to have been the filling of the parallel *a* slot on the past axis, the pluperfect. The latter had been appointed modally in some Romance languages (cf. the imperfect subjunctive in Spanish) in its synthetic Latin guise. The indicative pluperfect ties in clearly with the imperfect of the *s* slot in the morphological architecture of the auxiliary *habebat*.

C. The passives

As has already been mentioned, the Classical Latin passive paradigms were characterized by an analytic pattern, at least in the perfective, later to become the dominant structure, but considered marked at the outset. The loss of the aspectual dichotomy may be seen as the principal reason for the transformation of the perfect passive to the present passive (Harris and Vincent 1988: 58). The PPP is no longer interpreted as 'perfective' and the dominant member of the sequence *est laudatus* becomes the auxiliary. Furthermore, the tense of the auxiliary determines now the tense of the whole passive structure, integrated as it is within

---

2. For some recent studies on this matter, cf. McCray (1979), Vincent and Harris (1982), Fleischman (1983), and Pulgram (1987).

3. The only clear-cut aspectual distinction of Modern Romance concerns the dichotomy of the **s** on the past axis, the *durative* of the imperfect vs. the *punctual* of the preterit.

the new temporal constellation. Let us now outline Latin and Romance equivalents of the passive in the following way, limiting ourselves to the indicative 3SG:

Latin	**French**	**Italian**
laudatur	*(il) est loué*	*è lodato*
laudabatur	*(il) était loué*	*era lodato*
laudabitur	*(il) sera loué*	*sarà lodato*
est laudatus	*(il) a été loué*	*è stato lodato*
erat laudatus	*(il) avait été loué*	*era stato lodato*
erit laudatus	*(il) aura été loué*	*sarà stato lodato*

The reanalysis of the passive in terms of the tense of the auxiliary makes plausible the takeover and replacement of the synthetic Latin forms.

We find, thus, the recurrent factor in the rise of all three areas of periphrastic innovations to be the radical restructuring of the Classical Latin aspectual dichotomy, an underlying cause which cannot easily be determined from the surface architecture of the morphology. However, we should not conclude that the Romance languages make natural parameters useless, but rather that they have to be supplemented by morpho-semantic considerations like the ones discussed in the preceding analysis.[4]

3.1.2 *The motivation for synthesis*

In the most recent and complete treatment of the classic issue of the synthetic/analytic cycle,[5] Schwegler (1990: 132–3) outlines the trajectory of the synthesis of the Romance future (and conditional) in these four steps:

1. The semantic reanalysis of *habeo*, from full verb to marker of futurity;
2. the loss of morphosyntactic freedom, manifesting increasing lack of transportability and separability of the auxiliary;
3. the phonological binding of infinitive + *habeo*, the whole sequence gaining one primary stress, with various phonetic reductions as consequences;
4. the decrease in morphological variation of the auxiliary *habeo*, as it is no longer inflected for mood and the tense/aspect possibilities become limited to the present and imperfect/perfect.

---

4. For further discussion, see Klausenburger (1993a). For the attribution of the rise of analyticity to a shift from left-branching to right-branching, see Bauer (1995: 166).

5. A well-documented study of synthesis out of analysis outside the Romance domain may be found in Steever (1993). See also Stolz (1987).

Schwegler (1990: 133) succinctly summarizes and elaborates thus:

> While semantic reanalysis must have occurred prior to any other type of synthesis, it is clear that diachronically these processes overlapped and interacted. Though the morphological and phonological conditions were decisive in SHAPING the morphemes of modern Romance future forms, without continued semantic relevance between *cantare* and *habeo* the construction would never have conflated into a single, inflectional lexeme.

According to Schwegler, the morphosyntactic history of *habeo cantatum* repeats that of *cantare habeo*, except for the "relative analyticity" of the former. He demonstrates that in this evolution morphological freedom has also been restricted, as has transportability and separability (pp. 133–135). Schwegler (1990: 136) even claims a certain phonological unity between these two elements, clearly apparent when they are contiguous, as

> ... the phonological behavior of juxtaposed *avoir* + PP suggests, then, that French aspires to replicate on the level of phonology as well the strong semantic relationship inherent in the construction, but that this phonological unity is often overridden by stronger syntactic considerations.

It remains to be explained why *cantare habeo* synthesized "completely" while *habeo cantatum* did not, one of the long-standing mysteries in Romance linguistics. Schwegler argues that syntactic conditions alone were responsible as (a) a high degree of separability must have existed for *habeo cantatum* prior to and during its grammaticalization, and word order was more rigid during the (partial) merging of the compound past. He agrees with Fleischman's (1982: 120) claim that OV word order still dominated at the time of the formation of the future, while the consolidation of *habeo cantatum* occurred AFTER the basic syntax of Latin had switched form OV to VO. During the older period greater syntactic flexibility was allowed by Latin inflections such that potentially intervening items could readily be placed OUTSIDE the ever more "relevant" *cantare habeo* complex." The more rigid syntax of late Latin and Romance, however, according to Fleischman (1982: 138),

> ... made alternative positions for intervening items ... less readily available. Consequently, elements separating *habeo cantatum* could not be squeezed out easily, and the kind of morphosyntactic synthesis which had earlier brought together *cantare* and *habeo* so effectively was either delayed or, in some instances, halted altogether.

[For a similar analysis, see Kefer (1985)].

Focusing on the morphological features of the auxiliary, the infinitive, and the past participle, Joseph (1988: 200) assigns I (= inflection) to two of the elements involved, depicting their combinations in four sets:

a.   *habe*-I *cantat*-I   b.   *habe*-I *cantare*
c.   *cantat*-I *habe*-I   d.   *cantare habe*-I

According to this hypothesis, sequences (a) and (c) are not available for synthesis because both constituents are inflectionally marked. The non-inflectional nature of the infinitive would qualify both (b) and (d) for fusion. However, (b) will be eliminated, as "colloquial Latin word order ... was fixed pragmatically, following a THEME RHEME order" (1988: 197).

Neither of the two preceding hypotheses considers the suffixation result in the future opposed to the (potential) prefixation end-point of the synthesis of the compound past as a crucial factor. Yet, one could certainly make a case for its relevance in this context, on two levels. First, the rise of inflectional prefixation in a (completely synthesized) *passé composé* would constitute typological markedness in terms of the history of Latin and Romance. Second, from the psycholinguistic perspective, recent work has shown a general tendency of languages to prefer suffixes over prefixes, since stems are more easily processed before affixes "in that the component preferred for prior processing receives the most salient position in the word, the component to be processed second a less salient position" (Cutler et al. 1985: 754).[6]

What parameters of natural morphology impact on the analyticity vs. syntheticity issue? Plausible candidates appear immediately to be Dressler's (1985b) *morphotactic* and *semantic transparency*. These criteria, along with Mayerthaler's (1981) *constructional iconicity* (*diagrammaticity*), can be said to argue for the analytic phase of the cycle to be "more natural" (Mayerthaler 1981: 146–147). The *peripherality constraint* proposed in Carstairs (1987) supplies an interesting perspective. He hypothesizes (1987: 256) that

> ... for an inflexional affix to be sensitive to some lexically or syntactically determined property of its 'host' (or stem) is commonplace; on the other hand, it seems at least unusual for clitics to be sensitive to their hosts as such, other than phonologically.

The tense auxiliaries in the compound pasts in French (along with the *aller* paradigm which signals the periphrastic future) qualify as *affixes* according to this reasoning, thus constituting morphological synthesis.

I believe that naturalness considerations must be widened to include reference to *encoding* and *decoding* strategies (Geisler 1982). Synthesis of syntax

---

6. For a detailed analysis of the processing hypothesis, see section 3.2.1, below.

becomes "natural" for the speaker when viewed as encoding, amounting to most efficient for production. This has been expressed clearly by Lüdtke (1980: 279):

> The advantage of morphology lies in the fact that grammatically (not lexically) processed information (i.e. cognitive items) is communicated with comparatively little physical exertion (small size of units, easy articulation) and little expense of time.

The listener, on the other hand, employs a decoding strategy, which becomes natural for perception: analyticity may qualify as preferred from this vantage point.

A typological classification of the French (and Italian) indicative active systems outlined above, in 3.1.1, logically permits three possibilities:
1. A mixture of synthetic and analytic
2. (Mainly) analytic
3. (Mainly) synthetic

It may appear to be uncontroversial to choose the first option, determined by the "obvious" surface morphological architecture. Many, if not most, descriptions of the Romance verb structure continue to select possibility (2), buttressed as it seems to be, by the analytic passive formations. Our foregoing discussion of synthesis, however, actually may force choice (3). This holds in particular if the "semantic relevance" aspect of fusion, as stressed convincingly by Schwegler (1990), is maintained as decisive. Five of the nine paradigms of modern Romance are uncontroversially synthetic, of course, having achieved phonological synthesis in the future and conditional and also displaying three etymological successors of Latin synthetic structure. The remaining four compound tenses exhibit semantic synthesis, the most crucial link for (eventual) morphological formation. The latter would also be applicable if the periphrastic future of French, and possibly even a new periphrastic conditional (cf. Harris 1978), were to be substituted in the overall constellation.

3.1.3 *The grammaticalization of auxiliaries*

Schwegler (1990) attempts to delimit the syntheticity/analyticity dichotomy by means of the criteria of *relevance, generality, displaceability, isolatedness, obligatoriness, linearity, transparency, separability*, and *phonological bonding*. Original to Schwegler are the two factors of *linearity* and *transparency*, which, interestingly, tend to make the analytic/synthetic dichotomy rather fuzzy, requiring reference to "relative" syntheticity and "relative" analyticity (Klausenburger 1994: 222). The "phasing-out" of the traditional concepts of analytic and synthetic, especially prominent in the history of the Romance languages, is definitively accomplished within a theory of grammaticalization (Heine 1993; Bybee et al. 1994), rendering the A/S dichotomy linguistically undefinable. Let us briefly sketch the evolution of the Romance verbal system with respect to periphrastic structures within the grammatic(al)ization framework.

Heine (1993:58) summarizes four parameters of grammaticalization in combination with seven possible stages they may reach in the "verb-to-TAM chain" (that is, in the evolution of a full verb to tense/aspect/mood markers):

	Stage						
Overall stage	A	B	C	D	E	F	G
Desemanticization	I	II	III				
Decategorialization	I		II	III	IV	V	
Cliticization	I				II		III
Erosion	I				II		III

Succinctly, the parameter of *desemanticization* refers to the semantic change occurring during grammaticalization, usually referred to as 'bleaching'. *Decategorialization,* referring to the neutralization of morphological and syntactic markings, applies on the morpho-syntactic level, *cliticization* in the morpho-phonology, and *erosion* concerns phonetic detail (Heine 1993:54–58). For the study of auxiliaries, Heine (roughly) establishes these correspondences in terms of stages: at stages A and B, verbs are considered lexemes or full verbs, at stage C quasi-auxiliaries, or semi-auxiliaries, stages D and E representing the "real" auxiliary phase, and F and G affixal development (1993:65). In the global schema presented, each parameter is also considered in terms of individual stages (or degrees), indicated by Roman numerals, necessitating five for decategorialization, only three for the other parameters, to "run the complete course". A conclusion to be gleaned immediately from the above table "suggests in particular ... that conceptual shift from lexical to grammatical content ... precedes all other shifts ... and that cliticization and erosion normally start later than the other shifts" (1993:58).

A different view of this evolution may be given as follows (Heine 1993:87):

Domain	Starting point	Endpoint
Semantics:	Full verbal meaning	Grammatical function
Syntax:	High degree of variability	Fixed position
Morphology:	Inflected for TAM, person, number, negation, etc.	Invariable element
	Free word	Affix
Phonology:	Full form	Reduced (typically monosyllabic) form

The whole process of *auxiliation* begins, however, with up to twelve "event schemas" as sources, reduceable to three basic ones, location, motion, and action (1993: 31). For the history of the Latin *habere* in Romance, Heine employs the source meaning of possession (originally derivable from location?) and makes the important point that the double grammaticalization of this verb into both a perfective marker and a future indicator in Romance can only be understood if entire periphrases are taken into consideration (1993: 30):

1. *habere* + perfect passive participle = Romance perfect
2. *habere* + infinitive = Romance future

What seems to have played a crucial role in this dual evolution, according to Heine, is the 'static' nature of the Latin PPP vs. the 'dynamic' character of the infinitive (pp. 46–47). This idea is corroberated by Pinkster's detailed analysis in terms of the "*praedicativum* as the channel of auxiliarization" (1987: 210). According to this hypothesis, both developments began with the combination of *habere* + object + *praedicativum*, the latter being represented by (a) the PPP, resulting in the object having a property from anterior action, delivering the perfect formation, and by (b) the *gerundivum*, later to be replaced by the infinitive, indicating a posterior property of the object. The (active present) infinitive as the substitute for the (passive future) *gerundivum* seems to produce the "dynamic" character mentioned by Heine.[7]

Let us now show how the model of grammaticalization outlined by Heine offers a more explanatory and linguistically significant means of deriving the Romance verbal developments than the traditional S/A cycle.

The goal will be to determine, as exactly as possible, where in Heine's overall scheme of the grammaticalization of verb to TAM the Romance future

---

7. For further details, cf. Green (1987) and Vincent (1987). For a thorough discussion, cf. Bybee et al. (1994). See also Smith (1995) for past participle agreement.

and perfect markers could be placed. The end-points for each parameter are described by Heine as follows:

Desemanticization: (completion at step III, overall at C)
"The subject is no longer associated with willful/human referents and the verb acquires a grammatical function" (p. 54)

Decategorialization: (completion at step V, overall at F)
"The verb loses virtually all remaining verbal properties, and the complement acquires the morphosyntax of a main verb, although it may retain some relics of a nominalizing and/or adverbial morphology" (p. 55)

Cliticization: (completion at step III, overall at G)
"The verb develops into an affix. The verb and its complement merge into a single word unit, where the erstwhile verb constitutes an affix and the erstwhile complement the main verb stem" (p. 56)

Erosion: (completion at step III, overall at G)
"The verb loses its ability to carry distinctive tone and stress" (p. 56)

One can conclude with confidence that the history of the Romance future has "run the course" on all four parameters and that, therefore, it qualifies as a case of complete grammaticalization. What about the perfect formation? Here, for the parameter of *cliticization*, Heine's description of step II seems to fit best: "The verb loses its status as a separate verb and develops into a clitic. The verb and its complement are now likely to form a 'simple phrase', which permits only one expression of tense, negation, passivization, etc." (p. 56). As a consequence, our conclusion will be that one of the parameters has not run its course in this change, thus not having reached complete grammaticalization yet.

What is the difference between the description of these histories in terms of the A/S cycle (given above, in 3.1.2) and within grammaticalization theory? Clearly, the traditional dichotomy of concepts reveals itself as superfluous, as degrees of grammaticalization can be (fairly) clearly established, but the additional binary labeling turns out to be arbitrary and linguistically not defensible. Schwegler had to resort to "relative" analyticity and syntheticity in his detailed examination, thus opening the door, in fact, to the abandonment of this dichotomy. The question as to the synthetic or analytic nature of a given structure will no longer have to be asked, since it will be considered irrelevant. The essence in all these histories, the change-over into grammatical marking, has always been the point of interest for scholars. It can now be focused on even better, since the "distraction" of the determination of analyticity or syntheticity has been removed.

In Bybee et al. (1994), degrees of grammatic(al)ization are correlated "quantitatively" with the parameters of (phonetic) shortness, dependence, and fusion. A score is calculated for each of these, contrasting the English past tense *-ed* with the future marker *will*. For *shortness*, they assign the past tense a score of 9, the future a score of 8, thus reflecting almost the same degree of grammaticalization (1994: 109).[8] Regarding *dependence*, the authors give *-ed* a score of 7, *will* a score of 6, again very close in the stage of grammatic(al)ization reached (p. 112). Finally, the third parameter, *fusion*, does reflect a radical difference between the two structures, as the past is assigned a score of 8 while the *will* future draws a blank (p. 114). Five criteria are made use of in this last tabulation:

1. "written bound" (no = 0, yes = 2)
2. "open class intervening" (no = 1, yes = 0)
3. "phonological process conditioned by stem" (no = 0, yes = 1)
4. "lexical conditioning" (no = 0, yes = 2)
5. "stem change" (no = 0, yes = 2)

In total, then, the English *-ed* past may be given a grammaticalization score of 26, the English *will* future a score of only 14. The crucial gap between the two tenses in the analysis of Bybee et al. centers around *fusion*, which sounds suspiciously like the traditional "synthesis". One could conclude that all that is being discovered here is that the English past is a "synthetic" structure, while the English future may best be characterized as "analytic", a well known fact, of course. However, the authors are careful to relate all three parameters to degrees of grammaticalization, arriving at an overall index of the latter, similar to Heine's presentation. What scores would be obtained for the two Romance tenses?

One would expect the Romance future to be similar to the English past in this matter, but not quite the same. Taking *fusion* first, criterion (1) is answered by yes, yielding 2 points. Criterion (2) yields 1 point. However, no apparent phonological process conditioned by the stem is involved in the Romance future, thus adding 0. Lexical conditioning does apply, adding 2 points. Unlike the English past, however, there is no Romance stem change conditioned by the future suffix, equating criterion (5) to 0. Thus, the Romance future *fusion* score is 5, not 8. The calculation of scores on the other two parameters turns out to be quite complicated, if attempted in detail. It is reasonable to assume, however,

---

8. Details of the criteria used and the analysis cannot be reproduced here.

that the parameters of *shortness* and *dependence* will be fairly even for the two Romance tenses, just like for English. But let us get back to *fusion*. If the Romance future ends up with a score of 5, what about the Romance perfect? Unlike the English *will* future, the Romance perfect will obtain 2 points for lexical conditioning, criterion 4. Therefore, the gap between the two for this parameter in terms of grammaticization is only 3, possibly the same in total. This quantification of grammatic(al)ization, thus, really erases the syntheticity/analyticity split completely. What remains crucial in this scheme, just like in the one offered by Heine, is not the S/A dichotomy, nor the exact scores assigned, but the linguistic factors or parameters introduced in order to measure degrees of grammaticalization. These may vary from author to author, and they have to be motivated in each analysis.

In response to a skeptical evaluation of the concept of grammaticalization such as that of Steele (1994), who wonders "why and how do lexical items make that first step away from their end or the gradient?" (p. 820), Heine (1994) essentially equates the process to an *explanans* itself, constituting (p. 259) a "complex explanatory parameter, in its cognitive and pragmatic manipulation of more concrete concepts ... into expressions of grammatical concepts" (p. 277). It is, in fact, *predictive*, because unidirectional (p. 281).[9] Nevertheless, grammaticalization can only be considered probabilistic, in line with other aspects of Natural Morphology, which have been labeled "claims of explainability", or *Erklärbarkeitsbehauptungen*. The cognitive-conceptual side in grammaticalization has also been stressed in the metonymic-metaphorical model of Heine, Claudi, and Hünnemeyer (1991), with metaphor as the creative force. Finally, the important role played by the parameter of (diagrammatic) iconicity, especially obvious in the parallelism between reduced (eroded) form and "bleached" meaning in grammaticalization, has been described in great detail in Giacalone-Ramat (1994). She proposes, in addition, that one must assume "level specific iconicity", separately in the lexicon, in the syntax, and in the morphology, each component being characterized by "re-iconization" (p. 134).

A much more sober assessment as to the explanatory power of grammatic(al)ization, on the other hand, is offered in Bybee et al. (1994). They see no motivation, or functional teleology, in this process, since language really has no need for grammatical morphemes. They take a purely mechanistic view (p. 298): "The processes that lead to grammaticization occur in language use for their own

---

9. See, however, Joseph and Janda (1988) and Ramat (1992). The issue of unidirectionality or irreversibility in grammaticalization will be discussed more thoroughly in Chapter 5.

sakes; it just happens that their cumulative effect is the development of grammar".[10] In this, they join Labov, who has maintained that the evolution of grammar has the same "automatic" character that we recognize in sound change.

Grammaticalization has also been dealt with within the Principles and Parameters syntactic theory, in Roberts (1993), with an application to the Romance future. As a first step of a formal characterization, Roberts (1993: 221) calls grammaticalization "a change from a lexical to a functional category (with associated semantic bleaching)". He considers this change, in addition, as involving "the loss of thematic structure and a related shift in category from V to I" (1993: 227). However, the *why* of grammaticalization is part of a general mechanism of syntactic change, *Diachronic Reanalysis (DR),* during which the "category change V to I takes place when a structure where V has moved to I is reanalysed as one where the verbal element is base-generated in I'. *DR* is "a relationship between the grammars of successive generations" (p. 228). More to the point, finally, grammaticalization is to be analyzed as the "elimination of syntactic movement by a *DR*" (p. 228). Roberts then asks the further question as to why there should be a preference for the elimination of movement in this way. He concludes that this desire for simplicity is due to a strategy of languages acquisition, labeled by him the *Least Effort Strategy (LES)*: "Representations assigned to sentences of the input to acquisition should be such that they contain the set of the shortest possible chains consistent with (a) principles of grammar and (b) other aspects of the trigger experience" (p. 228–229). Grammaticalization is a frequently encountered change because it "is a *DR* driven by the *LES*". The grammaticalization of Latin *habere*, then, is seen as an instance of a *DR*, as the movement of *habere* to I has been eliminated in favor of base generation of the verb in I. *Habere* has metamorphosed from a lexical to a functional auxiliary. The *DR* was triggered by the *LES*, the innovated structure having one less step of movement than the old structure (p. 236). In its global evolution, the history of *habere* in the Romance future, according to Roberts, takes on a familiar account, in these four stages: (pp. 249–250):

a. lexical auxiliary (3rd century Latin)
b. functional auxiliary (late Latin)
c. clitic auxiliary (old Romance)
d. affix (modern Romance)

In the last section of his paper, Roberts integrates his analysis of grammaticalization into a wider frame of syntactic change involved in parameter (re)setting.

---

10. See Chapter 5 for an extension of this view into an 'invisible hand' explanation of grammaticalization.

The major contention is that "there is no logical relation between the notions of *DR* and parametric change, but that there is a causal relation" (p. 253). Thus, "*DR* deriving from *LES* may affect the trigger experience for acquisition in such a way that parameters are set to values different from those of the adult grammar underlying the trigger experience" (p. 253). However, we have already seen that grammaticalization also is caused by *DR*, or, simply, *is* a *DR*. In addition, Roberts considers the possibility of parameter resetting leading to more diachronic reanalysis. This is so, because "parametric changes are usually observable as clusters of diachronic re-analyses" (1993: 253).

Hopper and Traugott (1993: 206) list six properties of new parameter settings, taken from Lightfoot (1991):

a. they are manifested in a cluster of changes;
b. they can set off chain reactions;
c. they tend to take place rapidly;
d. they may appear as obsolescence of earlier rules or forms;
e. they produce significant change in meaning;
f. they occur in response to shifts in embedded clauses.

According to Hopper and Traugott (1993: 207)

> ... the perspective of grammaticalization challenges virtually all of these claims. Fundamentally, the approach from grammaticalization argues that the grammaticalization of lexical items or constructions is enabled by pragmatic factors ...

Such a point of view seems to agree with Roberts' contention about the absence of a logical relation between *DR* (and thus grammaticalization) and parametric change. However, does it allow the causal relation envisaged by Roberts? One may conclude in the affirmative, if that relation is essentially conceived of along the lines outlined for the evolution of the Latin verb into Romance in 3.1.1, above.[11]

3.2 The grammaticalization of Romance personal pronouns

3.2.1 *Subject proclitics or prefixes in French?*

In Chapter 2, above, the Latin, French, and Italian verb systems were presented entirely in terms of suffixation. In the present section, some of that analysis will

---

11. The metaphor of 'switching off' of parameters may have to be replaced by one of 'dimming', given the nature of grammaticalization.

be repeated, but, most importantly, I will add the subject pronouns for Modern French and will entertain various possible hypotheses concerning these structures.

In order to illustrate the similarities and (crucial) differences between Classical Latin and Modern (Spoken) French, I will juxtapose three paradigms, those of the PI, II, and F, transcribed phonetically and having undergone the morphemic divisions generally accepted for these forms. (T/M = Tense/Mood, P/N = Person/Number)

	Classical Latin			Modern Spoken French			
	ROOT +	T/M +	P/N	P/N +	ROOT +	T/M +	P/N
PI	am	Ø	o	ʒ	ɛm	Ø	Ø
	ama	Ø	s	t(y)	ɛm	Ø	Ø
	ama	Ø	t	il	ɛm	Ø	Ø
				ɛl	ɛm	Ø	Ø
	ama	Ø	mus	õn	ɛm	Ø	Ø
	ama	Ø	tis	v(u)z	ɛm	Ø	e
	ama	Ø	nt	i(l)z	ɛm	Ø	Ø
				ɛ(l)z	ɛm	Ø	Ø
II	ama	ba	m	ʒ	ɛm	ɛ	Ø
	ama	ba	s	t(y)	ɛm	ɛ	Ø
	ama	ba	t	il	ɛm	ɛ	Ø
				ɛl	ɛm	ɛ	Ø
	ama	ba	mus	õn	ɛm	ɛ	Ø
	ama	ba	tis	v(u)z	ɛm	j	e
	ama	ba	nt	i(l)z	ɛm	ɛ	Ø
				ɛ(l)z	ɛm	ɛ	Ø
F	ama	b	o	ʒ	ɛm	R	e
	ama	bi	s	t(y)	ɛm	R	a
	ama	bi	t	il	ɛm	R	a
				ɛl	ɛm	R	a
	ama	bi	mus	õn	ɛm	R	a
	ama	bi	tis	v(u)z	ɛm	R	e
	ama	bu	nt	i(l)z	ɛm	R	õ
				ɛ(l)z	ɛm	R	õ

Some, but not all, of the morphophonemic variation of the French subject pronouns in the spoken language is indicated in the data by way of parentheses:

(cf. Lambrecht 1981: 34)

a. 2nd person singular: [ty] or elided [t]
b. 2nd person plural: [vuz] or [vz]
c. 3rd person plural: [ilz] or [iz], [ɛlz] or [ɛz]

In addition, since the sample verb is vowel initial, allomorphs occurring before a consonant initial verb are not illustrated:

1st person singular: [ʒə] appears before consonants, but the elided allomorph will also undergo devoicing to [ʃ], as in [ʃpaʀl] (= *je parle*), for instance

3rd person singular: most frequently, the vowels [i] and [ɛ], along with [il] and [ɛl], represent this person, for the masculine and feminine, respectively

1st person plural: [õ] occurs before consonants

2nd person plural: [vu], but also [v], are found preconsonantally

3rd person plural: before consonants, both [i] and [ɛ], along with [il] and [ɛl], may be heard

The following is an overview of these subject markers:

	Pre-vocalic	**Pre-consonantal**
1SG	ʒ	ʒə, ʒ, ʃ
2SG	t, ty	ty, t
3SG	il, ɛl	i, ɛ, il, ɛl
1PL	õn	õ
2PL	vuz, vz	vu, v
3PL	iz, ilz, ɛz, ɛlz	i, il, ɛ, ɛl

Let us now introduce two more paradigms of spoken French, the *passé composé* and the *go*-future.

	P/N +	T/M/P/N +	ROOT +	T/M
passé composé	ʒ	e	ɛm	e
	t(y)	a	ɛm	e
	il	a	ɛm	e
	ɛl	a	ɛm	e
	õn	a	ɛm	e
	v(u)z	ave	ɛm	e
	i(l)z	õ	ɛm	e
	ɛ(l)z	õ	ɛm	e

go-future	ʒ(ə)	ve	ɛm	e
	t(y)	va	ɛm	e
	i(l)	va	ɛm	e
	ɛ(l	va	ɛm	e
	õ	va	ɛm	e
	v(u)z	ale	ɛm	e
	i(l)	võ	ɛm	e
	ɛ(l)	võ	ɛm	e

The canonical structure of the Latin verb is well known, as illustrated by the three paradigms given: the root precedes the two suffixes, T/M always preceding the 'peripheral' P/N.[12] The Modern French inflectional values of T/M and P/N, as displayed in the five paradigms above, are signaled heterogeneously, by way of suffixes and preposed markers, the status of which, proclitics or prefixes, remains to be determined. Thus, for the PI, it is legitimate to speak of a zero suffix for T/M, and almost exclusively zero for P/N suffixation also, with the exception of the 2PL [e]. One has to add, of course, the "real" markers of P/N, the preposed paradigm of the "personal pronoun", with its extensive morphophonemic variation. The same canonical structure holds for the II and F, although in these two groups the zero suffix is in the minority. In a direct comparison between the Latin and French forms of the PI, II, and F, what is striking is the way that P/N marking envelops the verb in the shape of a discontinuous marker in French, partly preposed and partly postposed. On the other hand, the remaining two paradigms of Modern French are best analyzed with the additional complexity of a *portmanteau* signaling of T/M/P/N in the occurrence of the suppletive auxiliaries of *avoir* and *aller*, T/M also being discontinuous.[13]

Perhaps the most immediate issue to develop with respect to the heterogeneous markers of inflection in Modern French is their obligatoriness. Here, an interesting split develops concerning the third person. While the other two persons incorporate all the markers outlined, always, the third person presents the additional allomorph of zero in the preposed P/N slot, if a noun phrase functions as subject of a sentence: [ilɛmɛ] becomes [ɛmɛ] if appearing in the sentence *mon*

---

12. In some verbs, in particular "irregular" ones, a neat morphemic cut like this is not always possible, and T/M and P/N may merge in a *portmanteau* formation.

13. This sample verb does not show any stem allomorphy. If the latter were taken into account, one could point to P/N marking in that alternation also.

ami aimait ses parents, and [*i(l)zɛmɛ*] in similar manner turns into [*ɛmɛ*] in *mes amis aimaient leurs parents*. The following distribution rule seems to be at work: (cf. Baldinger 1968: 89–90)

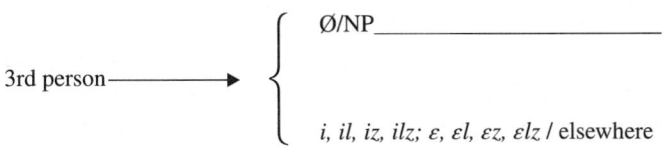

3rd person ⟶ { Ø/NP_____

i, il, iz, ilz; ɛ, ɛl, ɛz, ɛlz / elsewhere

Two facts must be added to this rule. First, in a typical (spoken) corpus of Modern French, the NP as a subject in a sentence is rare, less than 8% of occurrences, as "im (empirisch-quantitativen) 'Normalfall' ist das Subjekt nicht als Substantiv realisiert, und das Substantiv steht im 'Normalfall' nicht als Subjekt" (Jacob 1990: 125). Second, it has been remarked for a long time that a tendency toward leveling exists in this matter, the zero allomorph being eliminated in favor of the 'elsewhere' case: *Mon ami il aimait ses parents* may be heard quite frequently, being no longer socially stigmatized. One may conclude confidently, then, that the zero allomorph following the NP subject has marked status, the 'elsewhere' variant, on the other hand, unmarked. Trends in the spoken language represent but the natural evolution in the direction of the unmarked realization. Jacob (1990: 135) lists several syntactic contexts in which Modern French structure appears to exclude the 3rd person personal pronoun "in principle", among which these three:

a. Relatives: *Le chien qui il mange ...
b. Indefinite articles: *Un chien il mange ...
c. Interrogatives: *Qui il parle?

Jacob himself discusses a possible system of relatives of some speakers which would permit the presence of the preposed pronoun, one in which the only "relative pronoun" is *qu(e): Le chien qu'il mange...* will occur in such a dialect. Most surprising is Jacob's example (b), since it is generally assumed that such a sentence is possible (Schwegler 1993: 97). The only systematic obstacle to the occurrence of the subject pronoun, remains the interrogative in (c).

In the century-old controversy dealing with the prefix nature of the French personal pronoun, the most prominent factor mentioned has been the difference between the Latin suffix of the 3rd person, *-t*, which (surely) is totally categorical, and the French 3rd person personal pronoun, which is not. Ashby (1977: 58) implies that if the coexistence of this pronoun with a noun is no longer interpreted as a *reprise* construction of emphasis, evidence may exist for the prefix nature of this marker. Jacob (1990: 126) objects, saying that even if the occurrence of the 3rd person pronoun in this structure became categorical this would not yield proof of (a) its non-emphatic function, nor, most importantly, of (b) its prefix status. In general, he concludes that the presence of the *pronom conjoint* does not prove its prefix nature, but its absence might argue against it.

Jacob (1990) is the most complete recent empirical study of the status of the French personal pronouns, placing them in the larger context of the morphosyntax of the modern language. However, the author does not take a firm position on the "prefix, yes or no" controversy, responding, rather, with a resounding *Jein*. His goal is an objective assessment of Modern French synchrony.[14] The almost emotional attachment to a position for or against a *Konjugationsthese* evident among certain researchers comes to light quite forcefully in Hunnius (1977). Jacob's rigorous work constitutes a salutary counter point to such an attitude, and it makes us realize that the constant reference to Latin in the long-standing analysis of the status of French (subject) personal pronouns may have done a disservice, since it unquestionably has distracted from a really concise description of the Modern French system on its own terms. The whole idea of a *Konjugationsthese*, which implies a total equating of the function of the French personal pronoun with P/N marking to the Latin P/N suffix, should henceforth be abandoned. What remains, however, is the crucial issue of how to characterize as exactly as possible such P/N marking, elaborating its historical evolution.

In the following, a new interpretation of the history and status of the preposed structures in question will be attempted with the help of three recent studies, which, in my opinion, complement each other nicely in this effort: Bauer (1995), who supplies the beginning of the story, Heine (1993), who fills in the middle, and Hall (1992), who explains the end-point reached today and suggests why further developments may or may not be forthcoming. The essential concepts for my hypothesis are condensed in the form of a flow-chart entitled *Scenarios for grammaticalization*, as follows:

---

14. See also the studies by Hunnius (1977, 1991); Ashby (1977, 1980); Pignatelli (1988); Baldinger (1968).

SCENARIOS FOR GRAMMATICALIZATION

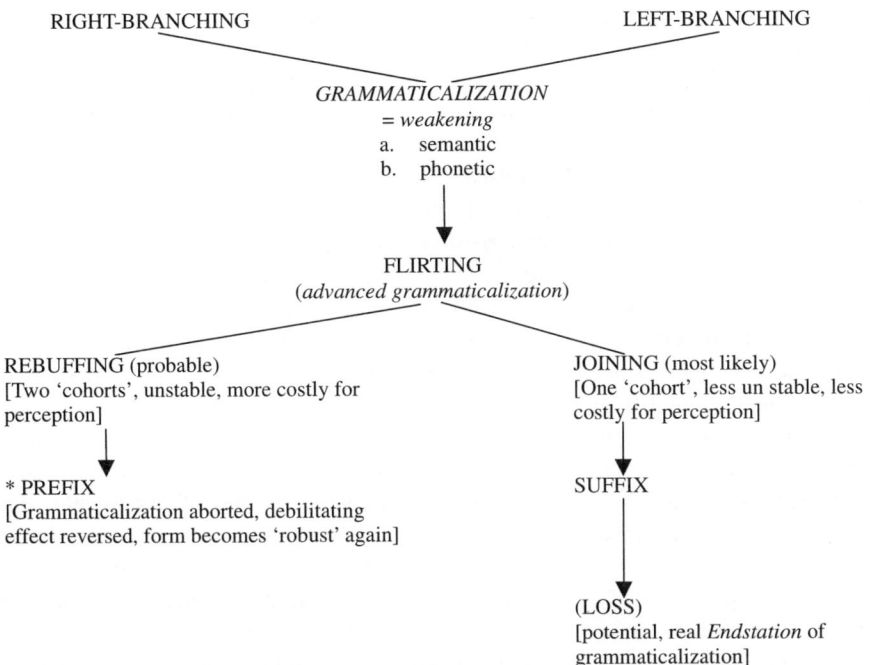

In the context of the global evolution of right-branching structures from left-branching ones, characteristic of the emerging SVO patterning in the history of French, Bauer (1995: 118) alludes to the personal pronoun as follows:

> The preposed pronoun ... had a distinctive feature: it was right-branching. Its rise therefore was integrated in the creation of RB structures: as the preposed auxiliary, which replaced the ending, the personal pronoun became increasingly important. The creation of the subject personal pronoun, therefore, marks one the last stages in the reorganization of the verb phrase.

As we will show, this right-branching nature of the personal pronoun has determined its evolution in an important way. Furthermore, it will be claimed that the determination of its branching type constitutes one of only two "certainties" about its nature, the other being its grammaticalized character.

It is, of course, well known that the Romance 3PL personal pronouns descend from the Latin demonstrative *ille*.[15] The first phase of grammaticalization, from demonstrative to personal pronoun, will not be re-examined here. We begin with the stage at which these forms function as "personal pronouns", considering it the starting point for a second phase of grammaticalization, one which, potentially, could reach inflectional prefix status. Making use of Heine's (1993) four parameters of grammaticalization, discussed above, in 3.1.3, we can conclude that the French personal *pronoms conjoints* unquestionably have run the course in *desemanticization* and *decategorialization*. One may say that these two lead to a 'semantic weakening' of the forms. As we saw above, in Heine (1993: 58), both *cliticization* and *erosion* start early also, at stage A, along with the semantic parameters. However, their advanced degree, at III, is set for later. A curious detail must now be added, one which seems to derail, typically or probably, the orderly progression of grammaticalization, usually aborting it, *if the original form to be grammaticalized stood in RB position*, no such obstacle being put in the way of LB grammaticalization. Such a hypothesis is based on Hall (1992: 96), who states that "a ... tenable claim is that the processor influences the diachronic process of fusion ... according to whether the erstwhile lexical item stands before or after the element with which it fuses." As to why this would happen, Hall responds: "The answer ... lies in the demand of the hearer for clarity of expression, at least at the beginning of words" (p. 101). Furthermore, "the principle of economy directs the reduction of semantically general free forms to affix status ... [It] will not favor prefixes as highly as suffixes, since the former entail greater representational complexity than the latter" (p. 108). In Hall's analysis, two key concepts appear, (a) *flirting*, "in which a semantically decayed free form attempts to become bound to (i.e. 'flirts' with) a full free form on which it depends and with which it is habitually ... contiguous" (p. 166), and (b) *cohort*, "a list of all the words in the mental lexicon which match the acoustic onset properties of the input signal" (p. 119). The reason, then, that potential prefixes are (usually) 'rebuffed' during the flirting process can be pinpointed exactly: two cohorts, one for the prefix and one for the stem, are released, while a flirting suffix does not generate a second cohort (after that of the stem). Therefore, according to Hall (1992: 176),

> ... prefix representation entails more storage complexity than suffix representation ... since prefixing disturbs the uniformity of the 'address' of the lexical entry, as represented by the initial acoustic specification of the stem.

---

15. For a recent review of this evolution, see Carrasquel (1995).

Actually, all flirting forms, which I would label 'highly grammaticalized', are characterized by an "instability of the morpheme combination and the tentative nature of the bound analysis" (1992: 167). The prefix dispreference is engaged, however, because it entails the greater cost, as detailed in terms of the cohort model.[16]

Grammaticalization inexorably weakens a free lexical item, both semantically (Heine's first two parameters) and phonologically (the second two parameters). One may add that grammaticalization uncovers the 'fragility' of LB structures, since it leads (almost invariably) to suffixation, which might lead to complete disappearance. On the other hand, grammaticalization reveals a certain amount of 'robustness' in RB structures, since it is (usually) arrested/aborted at an advanced stage, not delivering prefixes. As a consequence, the debilitating effect of grammaticalization is reversed for RB structures and they regain some robustness, albeit still possessing a certain degree of grammaticalization.

Is there, then, a common explanation for the prefixation dispreference and the unidirectionality of the replacement of LB by RB structures in the history of the Indo-European languages? Bauer (1995: 171) claims that "a thorough analysis of the acquisition of branching patterns in a number of languages will show the advantage of right branching over left branching". Although not addressed as such by Bauer, Hall's processing hypothesis may be an appropriate means of defining this "advantage" children are said to have in mastering RB languages at a quicker rate than the (archaic) LB structures. A possible reasoning could be the following.

Two evident forces may be seen in conflict with each other, grammaticalization and the principle of economy in processing and clarity of expression. Grammaticalization may be said to 'threaten' the latter, being destructive to RB structures in its advanced stages, rendering them opaque, when clarity of expression is reduced too greatly by phonological attrition, blocking the formation of prefixes. At the end of words, on the other hand, grammaticalization is free to proceed to advanced levels, since processing is not hindered by the formation of suffixes. It is interesting to add, however, that the logical *Endstation* of grammaticalization is zero, or the loss of the erstwhile postposed lexical item. If that happens, the ultimate effect of grammaticalization has clearly been destructive here also, even more so, since it has not been stopped in its inexorable drive to zero. In some sense, then, LB structures seem to exist

---

16. See Bybee et al. (1994: 163) for a discussion of the difference between inflectional and derivational affixation developments.

simply to disappear, potentially, programmed by grammaticalization. The most common replacements for lost LB structures are ungrammaticalized RB formations. They will then undergo (inevitable) grammaticalization, but only to a certain degree, remaining generally robust, after the flirting and rebuffing scenarios, as outlined by Hall. With this reasoning, one may conclude that since RB is a locus non-conducive to advanced grammaticalization, unlike LB, which is conducive to even the end-point of the latter, an *explanans* for the rise of RB structures has been found. In addition, the "advantage" for acquisition of right branching lies in its ability "to protect itself against the destructive effects of grammaticalization" as outlined above.

Bauer (1995: 217), although having stressed the importance of the preference of RB over LB in terms of acquisition in Chapter 6, concludes her study with a brief explanation of the preponderance of LB in earlier periods of the Indo-European languages in terms of syntactic typology, as

> ... originally left branching corresponded to a specific syntactic system that conveyed nontransitive, more concise structures with a subordinate value. With the change of the conception of action, transitivity developed and the 'relative' clause changed its syntax and consequently its place in the sentence. Hence the importance of the early emergence of RB subordinate clauses ...

This hypothesis, provisional as yet, according to Bauer, requiring an evaluation and understanding of the underlying principles of ancient Indo-European syntax, may complement the processing/grammaticalization account given above. However, the more universal aspects of the latter would seem to offer a more explanatory reward.[17]

Let us now flesh out more concretely the evolutionary stage of the Modern French subject pronoun, placing it in the context of (a) other changes within the grammaticalization scenario, and (b) the co-existence of LB and RB structures today.

The logic of the arguments presented in Bauer (1995) and Hall (1992) would lead us to predict an (eventual) dominance, if not monopoly, of (partially grammaticalized) right branching structures in the modern Indo-European languages, in particular in Modern French. What is the actual situation in the language today?

It is clear that the four possible structure types coexist, even in spoken French:

---

17. There seems to be a relationship between RB, or periphrastic, structures and the signaling of grammatical categories which are found in the 'early' stages of the semantic evolution (cf. Bybee et al. 1994). Thus, can RB formations ever express the most 'advanced', i.e., the most abstract, functional categories?

1. *Right branching*
   Examples: Determiner + noun, Pronoun + verb, SVO word order, Noun + adjective
2. *Left branching*
   Examples: Adjective + noun, Interrogative verb inversion
3. *Prefixation*
   Examples: Limited to derivational morphology
4. *Suffixation*
   Examples: Verbal endings, as shown in the data, above

Why do all four formations occur, even though only (1) is predicted?

Every synchronic slice of the language incorporates, it is well known, diachronic remnants, the survival time of which cannot generally be established. Every example of inflectional suffixation in Modern French constitutes such a continuation, either from Latin directly, as with the imperfect tense suffix, or from a complete LB grammaticalization, such as the future. The following is a (partial) context for the historical evolution of some Modern French structures from Latin.

RIGHT BRANCHING
a. Perfect → *passé composé*
b. Demonstrative → 3rd person personal pronoun, definite article
c. *go*-future

LEFT BRANCHING
a. *habeo*-future
b. *mente*-adverb
c. Latin verbal suffixes

In terms of the grammaticalization scenario given above, all three right branching structures underwent grammaticalization to a certain point, but no prefix formation occurred, due to the flirting/rebuffing stage posited. I am therefore placing the evolutionary point of the French subject personal pronoun on a par with the *habeo* plus PPP development, analyzed in 3.1.3, and with that of the periphrastic future, becoming dominant in the spoken language. Left branching has fully grammaticalized in the future and in the *ment*-adverb, having reached the suffix stage, as expected. Finally, under (c) I refer to the fate of the Latin verbal endings, some of which survived phonetically (i.e. the imperfect), but some of which illustrate the logical end-point of grammaticalization, loss of the erstwhile lexical item, as in the case of the atrophied P/N suffixes of modern spoken French. The (partial) replacement of these lost suffixes by new right branching structures, the *pronoms conjoints*, illustrates well how left branching has been phased out in the history of French. However, a "balance" appears to be maintained among the two types of branching, due to the historical survivals. An important question arises: Does a source exist for new LB formations? It is difficult to conceive of such a source, in any modern language, especially French, although Hall (1992: 109) vaguely refers to the possibility of word order changes which would yield new LB's.[18]

Within the theoretical framework of (language specific) naturalness, the co-occurrence of these four structure types is unstable, and it would predict the disappearance of two of the marked formations, left branching and inflectional suffixation. Of course, prefixation must also be seen as marked, but its exclusive locus is derivation. Clearly, the *system defining structural properties (SDSPs)* of Modern French will include right branching, characterized by an appreciable, yet not advanced, degree of grammaticalization, as typified by the status of the *pronom conjoint*.

3.2.2   Pro-drop in Old French and Modern (Spoken) French

It is of special interest to examine the status of the subject pronoun in Old French. There has always been agreement among scholars about the essential difference between the Old and Modern French phase, summarized in the optionality and stressability of the pronoun in the medieval period, opposed to its obligatoriness and clitic nature today. Within the theoretical framework offered in this study, such a difference will be seen as reflected in the varying degree of grammaticalization reached at each stage.

The status of the subject pronoun in Old French is intimately tied to word order configurations of the language. In a well-documented study, Marchello-Nizia (1995: 52) outlines 19 hypothetically possible declarative orders, consisting of the constituents of *S* (ubject), both nominal and pronominal, *V* (erb), (noun) *O* (bject), and *C* (omplement) (a cover term for a variety of constituents, especially adverbials). Only two of these orders are unattested. The following are the nine sequences involving pronominal (*Sp*) subjects, divided into "visible" and "invisible" categories, listed in the order of frequency:

A.   *Visible* subject pronouns: *Sp V O*
　　　　　　　　　　　　　　　　　　O V Sp
　　　　　　　　　　　　　　　　　　C V Sp O
　　　　　　　　　　　　　　　　　　Sp O V
　　　　　　　　　　　　　　　　　　O Sp V
　　　　　　　　　　　　　　　　　　V Sp O

---

18. See the discussion of right dislocations in spoken French, below in 3.2.2.

B. *Invisible* subject pronouns: C V O
                                    V O
                                    O V

Five of the nine sequences illustrate the well-known V-2, or 'verb in second position in the sentence', structure of Old French. But the dominance of this configuration becomes even clearer in Marchello-Nizia's detailed accounting (pp. 71–90) of two texts, one of poetry, the *Chanson de Roland* (11th/12th century), and one of prose, the 13th century *Queste del saint Graal*. Four orders, CVO, OV, SVO, and VO, describe 90% of the occurrences in the *Roland*, while only two others, CVO and SVO, cover 86% of the existing declarative sentences in the *Graal*. A crucial additional statistic for our purposes is the fact that, according to Marchello-Nizia (1995: 82),

> ... il y a [in the *Graal*] ... 51% d'énoncés déclaratifs transitifs à sujet nul. L'expression du sujet n'est pas encore une contrainte très forte, mais elle a nettement progressé: dans le *Roland*, elle n'était que de 28% dans les énoncés déclaratifs; sa fréquence a presque doublé.

As can be seen above, CVO may be said to be the unmarked order *par excellence* for Old French, since it satisfied both the V-2 constraint and the Pro-drop characteristic assumed for this period. Thus, Adams (1987b: 44) introduces this typical sentence: (cf. also Adams 1987a)

> *Si firent ___ grant joie la nuit.* "They celebrated greatly that night"

In her analysis (1987b: 56), such a surface structure was due to verb fronting, producing an inversion of subject and verb, and subject pronoun deletion, resulting in the blank following the verb, corroborating her earlier claim that "in Old French null subjects only show up in the context of verb second" (1987b: 5). Bauer (1995: 117) objects, however, stating that

> ... this hypothesis is somewhat doubtful since it is based on data in absentia: subject inversion is claimed to be 'hidden', because it is assumed that the pronoun subject is deleted in inversion. Yet this interpretation is difficult to verify.

Her objection is principally due to the introduction of a left-branching subject-verb inversion in the course of Adams' derivation, above, which contradicts Bauer's assumption of the steady evolution into right-branching in the history of French. There is no denying that the subject pronoun is usually absent in the CV constellation, and even Einhorn (1974: 64), representing a rather traditional approach to Old French grammar, mentions that the pronoun subject "is ... usually omitted in inversions". Marchello Nizia (1995: 53) seems to say that CVO (her 14') can be

derived from an 'underlying' subject pronoun in three different positions:
a. pre-verbal
b. post-verbal
c. post-object

However, she does not present a theoretical framework of derivations. Bauer's alternative explanation of the absence of the subject pronoun in CVO is simply to say that it was "optionally" being introduced in the language at the time, having no distinctive function as yet, since verbal suffixes were still operative (1995: 118). It fits with Harris (1978: 112), who claims that

> ... the use of the subject pronoun is one device used by the language as part of a conspiracy to achieve its current syntactic target, namely the observance of the verb-second constraint.

This was a decisive stage in the global evolution of word order from Latin SOV to French SVO, by way of the intermediate TVX, when the T slot became gradually filled by the subject, whose "topicalization ... may be regarded as normal and unmarked" (1978: 20). Similar views are found in Geisler (1982: 195) and Schwegler (1990: 82).

According to Marchello-Nizia (1995: 61),

> ... deux traits fondamentalement différents semblent en effet en oeuvre dans ces différents changements: d'une part l'obligation d'exprimer le sujet, et d'autre part l'obligation de placer l'objet nominal juste après le verbe.

She concentrates on the latter point, which she considers more important, "la vraie caractéristique de la prose française naissante" (1995: 83), but she recognizes that it is dependent on the first, both leading to the fixing of the SVO order, which became dominant (in the declarative main clause) during the 12th century, in her opinion. Adams (1987b) claims that "V2 effects ... are entirely *epiphenomenal*, the accidental consequence of two distinct and independent properties of grammar." These may be listed as (1) verb movement, and (2) a prosodic structure containing clause-initial secondary stress, stress *eurythmy* (cf. also Horne 1990). Old French had both, but the prosodic structure began to change, culminating in the development of fixed oxytonic stress (cf. also Klausenburger 1970) around 1500. This leads to (a) the break-down of V-2 effects and (b) the rise of obligatory cliticized subject pronouns. The cliticization stage emerges at the point when a dichotomy between disjunctive and conjunctive personal pronouns arises, the new tonic forms being derived from the (stressed) accusative of Latin (i.e. *moi* from *me*) (cf. also Dufresne and Dupuis 1994: 113, and Vance 1995). We may enter these details into a grammaticalization continuum, deciding that the syntactic rigidification into SVO essentially equates to the second parameter proposed in Heine's scheme, decategorialization (cf. above, 3.1.3), for the subject pronouns. They also show a low degree of grammaticalization in Old French by being non-obligatory, displaceable, separable, and morphologically unbound (Schwegler 1990: 84–85). They have not yet reached parameter three, cliticization, by the Middle French period. By the end of this phase, however, it appears that " ... Modern French usage with respect to the syntax of subject pronouns was virtually attained" (Adams 1987b: 187). When (pro)cliticization was achieved, "die Voraussetzungen für den Aufbau einer prädeterminierenden Morphologie" (Geisler 1982: 246) existed. However, the latter will be prevented from turning into prefixation, in all likelihood, due to the factors in our grammaticalization scenarios concerning the *flirting* phase, as outlined and shown above.

While it is universally accepted to consider Old French a pro-drop language, it would be highly controversial to propose this characterization for Modern Spoken French. Thus, Brandi and Cordin (1989: 116) conclude that

> ... subject clitics of Trentino and Fiorentino differ from French subject clitics both in categorical status and in syntactic position. French subject clitics are phonological clitics which fill the subject position, a position where *pro* could not be licensed, given the typological nature of the language. In Trentino and Fiorentino subject clitics are syntactic clitics which spell out AGR specifications ...

However, Roberge (1990: 154) finds a closer *rapprochement* between (an uncontroversial pro-drop language like) Italian and French, saying that

> the difference lies in the way each language licenses *pro* in subject position. French has recourse to clitic pronouns whereas rich agreement is sufficient for the licensing of *pro* in Standard Italian.

The concept of "rich agreement" is replaced in Jaeggli and Safir (1989: 30), who claim that the requirement for null subjects to be permitted is a "morphologically uniform inflectional paradigm", which is defined as follows:

> An inflectional paradigm is morphologically uniform iff it has either only underived inflectional forms or only derived inflectional forms.

In the following, I would like to make a case for considering spoken French a pro-drop language. The prerequisite of inflectional uniformity seems to be in the process of being met in the decisive tendency of the spoken language to become base inflected, one of its system defining structural properties, according to Kilani-Schoch (1988, Chapt. 6). Data to illustrate pro-drop effects come from erstwhile left and right dislocated structures, termed *topic* and *anti-topic* in Lambrecht (1981). Let us begin with these simple examples (Lambrecht 1981: 1):

1. *Ces Romains sont fous.*
2. *Ces Romains i-sont fous.*
3. *I-sont fous ces Romains.*

Due to the presence of the subject clitic in (2) and (3), the noun phrase *ces Romains* has been "desyntacticized" (Lambrecht 1981: 7), appearing in a subject verb inversion in (3). Desyntacticization may also apply if the NP slot is filled by a disjunctive pronoun, converting the second and third sentence into:

2′. *Eux i-sont fous.*
3′. *I-sont fous eux.*

Now, it is not far-fetched to qualify *eux* in these examples as the real subject pronoun, which, quite evidently, may then undergo pro-drop, since *I-sont fous* is a perfectly well formed sentence in French. Two slightly more complex sets of examples will corroborate this analysis:

A. 1. *J'adore Marie.*
   2. *Moi j-l-adore Marie*
   3. *J-l-adore Marie moi*
   4. *J-l-adore moi Marie.*
B. 1. *On va à la plage.*
   2. *Nous on-y-va à la plage.*
   3. *On-y-va à la plage nous.*
   4. *On-y-va nous à la plage.*

Moi and *nous* are the subject pronouns in these sets, clearly deletable, as shown in the 'canonical' sentences A.1. and B.1. However, these examples become more complex by the presence of the direct object in A and the prepositional phrase in B, represented by the clitics *l* and *y*. For (2) to (4), the 'verb' is best analyzed as *j-l-adore* and *on-y-va*, respectively. Again, desyntacticization occurs, allowing an apparently 'free' word order, only some of the possibilities of which are exploited in the data cited. This corpus manifests a fairly rich agreement system, delivering, in a sense, a 'case' structure on the verb (cf. Auger 1993).[19]

It is important to make clear what such data prove and do not prove. I have proposed that pro-drop may be plausibly claimed, if dislocation structures are considered unmarked within the spoken language, given its typology of uniform inflection. Actually, the prerequisite of 'rich inflection' certainly seems to hold also, as illustrated. However, it is crucial to add that even if all the preceding is

---

19. For a discussion of non-subject clitics in Romance, cf. below, 3.2.3. Cf. now also Blasco (1997).

accepted, these facts do not constitute sufficient evidence for the prefix status of the unstressed pre-verbal elements: they can just as easily be seen as proclitics, co-extensive with the (stressed) subject pronoun (and nonsubject noun phrases) (cf. Jacob 1990). In this way, Modern Spoken French shows a return to Old French, not only if pro-drop is accepted as part of it, but also by the apparent 'free' word order evident at both periods. The tonic subject pronoun today, thus, is beginning a new cycle of grammaticalization, on a par in its low degree with that of Old French, it would seem. One interesting difference, however, concerns the option there exists between right branching and left branching, indicated in the left and right dislocation possibilities. If the left branching (= right dislocation) should eventually dominate, which is predicted in Harris (1978), but which is not born out in the most recent studies by Ashby (1982, 1988), and Barnes (1985), an eventual advanced grammaticalization could lead to a new set of suffixes. However, such a future evolution can in no way be evaluated by the current state of affairs.[20]

3.2.3 Object clitics

In the preceding section, object clitics in French were introduced in connection with the possible status of the spoken language as pro-drop and the apparently free word order in existence. The latter, as a matter of fact, would be permitted only if non-subject clitics are analyzed as verbal case markers in the context of (erstwhile) left and right dislocated structures. In the present section, some object clitics of various Romance languages will be analyzed with the goal of evaluating the evolution of an "object conjugation".

Roberge (1990: 152) considers subject and object clitics as "two different realizations of the same syntactic element", the latter being base-generated on the verbal head, the former in AGR of INFL. The fact that the "internal argument position [is] associated with the object clitic, which is affixed to the inflected verb" implies, within the theoretical framework offered in this study, a higher degree of grammaticalization reached for object pronouns (in all of Romance) than in subject pronouns (for French exclusively). In fact, as long ago as in Rothe (1966), a Romance "object conjugation" was proposed, although based on factors quite different from those of Roberge. Rothe found that Portuguese, in particular, compares favorably in terms of the criteria needed in an object

---

20. Kaiser (1992) characterizes Modern Spoken French as *both* a null subject and null object language, and Modern Portuguese as a null object language. Cf. Petruck (1996). For an excellent bibliography of clitic studies, see Nevis et al. (1994).

conjugation language, a classical and 'ideal' example of which has always been Hungarian. He juxtaposes the two languages as follows (1966: 537):

	Hungarian		**Portuguese**	
	Subj. conjugation	Obj. conjugation	Subj. conjugation	Obj. conjugation
	/-ok/	/-om/	/-u/	/-uu/
	/-s/	/-od/	/-ʃ/	/-lu/
	Ø	/-jo /	Ø	/-u/
	/-unk/	/-juk/	/-muʃ/	/-mulu/
	/-tok/	/-ja:tok/	/-d(ə)ʃ/	/-d(ə)lu/
	/-nok/	/-ja:k/	/-ẽi/	/-ẽinu/

The three distinguishing characteristics examined are: (1966: 533–4)
1. the object markers are 'bound' forms
2. the subject markers change form as soon as an object marker is present
3. the object markers are obligatory

Portuguese fulfills criterion (1), in that the direct object appears as an enclitic/suffix, as in the second paradigm of "to see" (1966: 535):

Paradigm 1		Paradigm 2	
vejo	/vɛʒ-u/	vejo-o	/vɛʒ-u -u/
vês	/ve-ʃ/	vê-lo	/ve -lu/
vê	/ve/	vê-o	/ve -u/
vemos	/ve-muʃ/	vemo-lo	/ve-mu -lu/
vedes	/ve-d(ə)ʃ/	vede-lo	/ve-d(ə)-lu/
vêem	/ve-ẽi/	vêem-no	/ve-ẽi -nu/

In the presentation of Paradigm 2, the object 'suffix' (3rd person singular masculine) exhibits three allomorphs, /u/, /lu/, and /nu/, phonetically conditioned in contact with the preceding subject suffix. However, Rothe proposes a "restructured" subject marker in his comparison of Portuguese with Hungarian, as seen above, merging the two suffixes into:

    1SG /-uu/
    2SG /-lu/
    3SG /-u/
    1PL /-mulu/
    2PL /-d(ə)lu/
    3PL /-ẽinu/

Thus, condition (2) for an object conjugation is fulfilled. In the remaining feature (3), finally, Portuguese joins the other Romance languages, in that it is met exclusively in anaphoric contexts, similar to French dislocations. But in such an environment 'object doubling' is required, not just optional (Stolz 1992: 453). Here, Portuguese corresponds most closely to Spanish, for which "categorical pronoun duplication", in addition to "no interpolation and fixed position of the clitic pronoun" are established by Rini (1990: 367–368) as the three crucial indications of "a grammaticalized, morphologically bound verbal flexion" (1990: 354), in effect since the early 17th century. One of these factors, fixed position of the (object) clitics, is considered by Wanner (1981) as the principal factor in the grammaticalization/morphologization of clitic placement in the history of Italian, manifesting a transition from syntactic change into "localized morphosyntactic governance" (Wanner 1981: 331).

Condition (3) may be said to be fulfilled in varying degrees in the following four Romance equivalents (Rothe 1966: 544):

Portuguese:	*Vejo-o o meu amigo*
Spanish:	*Le veo a mi amigo*
French:	*Je le vois mon ami*
Italian:	*Lo vedo il mio amico*

A possible ranking of the likelihood of such occurrences would probably put Portuguese and Spanish first, French second, and Italian in a third category. The most interesting detail of Rothe's proposal concerning a Romance object conjugation, for present purposes, however, concerns condition (2), to which we will now return.

Rothe makes a fairly good case for his restructuring analysis of a new 'subject' marker in Portuguese, when the object is also present, thus duplicating the situation in Hungarian. This completely obscures the historical evolution, of course, exhibiting such radical changes for subject marking as 2SG */-ʃ/* to */-lu/* and 1PL */-muʃ/* to */-mulu/*. Such a merged option, however, focuses on a crucial difference between Portuguese and the other Romance languages, in which it would not be possible since (1966: 539)

> ... die Objektsmorpheme in diesen Sprachen nicht wie im Portugiesischen postdeterminierend verwendet werden, sondern ... prädeterminierenden Status haben, die Subjektspersonen hingegen weiterhin wie im Lateinischen postdeterminierend angegeben werden.

Actually, a complete accounting of the Romance languages has to include not only proclisis and enclisis, but also mesoclisis (cf. Stolz 1992). In the following overview, probable markedness values are included:

	French (Sub/Ob)	Spanish/Italian (Ob)	Portuguese (Ob)
PROCLISIS	*um*	*um*	*m*
ENCLISIS	*(m)*	*m*	*um*
MESOCLISIS			*m*

In this table, French 'enclisis', limited to positive imperatives, like *faites-le*, obviously a marked structure, is also put in parenthesis, since, for some, there is really no clitic here, as, given French oxytonic stress, *le* would be a 'stressed enclitic'. The existence of enclisis is more widespread in Spanish and Italian, involving infinitives and participles, for instance. Still, no one would disagree that proclisis is the unmarked pattern. Finally, Portuguese differs from the others in two ways: (1) It has mesoclisis, although confined to the future and conditional, as in *verme á* 'he/she will see me' (Stolz 1992: 446); (2) enclisis can be considered unmarked, as it is found in finite declaratives, as in the examples above.

Stolz (1992) investigates the degree to which Portuguese qualifies as an object conjugation language, attempting to discover, beyond the goal of Rothe (1966) (who, surprisingly, is not mentioned by Stolz!), how well it would fit eight criteria gleaned from Natural Morphology (1992: 440):

a. separate coding of the object marker
b. uniformity of marking
c. paradigmatic transparency of object marking
d. morphotactic stability of the marker
e. iconic signaling of object marker
f. marker is semantically additive
g. marker is bound
h. object marking occurs as suffixation

It turns out that no language known fulfills all 'natural' characteristics, even an object conjugation language *par excellence* like Classical Aztec, since it crucially violates the above in having prefixes, not suffixes (p. 441). For Portuguese, several violations are found by Stolz: Re (a), the issues of Rothe's third criterion, discussed above, resurface, having to do with the categorical nature of the object clitic. Re (e), iconicity is partially disturbed, if both accusative and dative objects are considered, since these are formally distinguished only in the 3rd person: *o, a* vs. *lhe* in the singular, and *os, as* vs. *lhes* in the plural (p. 444). Re (d) and (h), the tripartite proclisis, enclisis, and mesoclisis configuration constitutes a problem, although the unmarked nature of enclisis goes in the direction of fulfilling both. Re (c), the morphophonological alternations obtained due to contact between P/N suffix and object, mentioned above, obscure transparency, of course. However, these fusions amount to new "subject" suffixes for Rothe, as we saw, and they are of greatest interest to the concerns of this study. We may claim that Portuguese in this way demonstrates a high degree of grammaticalization of object clitics, having reached the suffix stage. These contractions, once again, point to the way that left branching structures are powerless in the face of on-rushing grammaticalization. As a matter of fact, Stolz (1992:455) hints that even the *Endstation* of grammaticalization, that is, loss, may have been reached for object markers, at least in Brazilian Portuguese, where "... das System der Objektklitika — wenn nicht ohnehin schon obsolet — so doch wenigstens in der Auflösung begriffen [ist]".

With respect to the phonetic erosion parameter of grammaticalization, it is significant to compare the left branching/suffixation Portuguese situation with that of right branching of the other Romance languages, in particular French. At first glance, the allomorphy of the subject pronouns of the spoken language, outlined in 3.2.1, above, along with the object clitics reduced to case markers, both functionally and phonetically, proposed by Lambrecht (1981:34), seem to point in the same direction of (eventually) complete erosion. However, I would claim that this similarity is misleading: Right branching/proclisis manifests erosion only *to a certain degree*, never to the point of contraction/fusion/inseparability. French clitic combinations undergo adjustments such as the well-known processes of liaison, elision, and *e-caduc*, which are *applicable throughout the language*, not limited to proclitic combinations. The restructuring into a new subject prefix containing the object marker, as proposed for the Portuguese suffix by Rothe, seems implausible for French. The underlying reason for (relatively) robust object proclitics, preventing their degrading into prefixes, must again be sought in processing/perception factors, as detailed in the analysis of French subject markers in 3.2.1.

3.3 The (un)likelihood of Romance inflectional prefixation

In the preceding two sections, aspects of Romance verb morphology have been examined within the framework of grammaticalization, demonstrating how both tense/aspect/mood (TAM) and person/number (P/N) marking evolved from Latin. Materially, these analyses dealt with the history of (1) Latin verbs into auxiliaries in Romance and (2) Latin personal pronouns, both subject and object, into clitics/affixes in the Romance languages, especially French. Degrees of grammaticalization were determined for each case, succinctly summarized in the flowchart on "scenarios of grammaticalization", above. I will now attempt to tie the preceding discussions together by focusing on the advanced stages of grammaticalization reached in all of them, verifying, in particular, whether affix status may be assumed anywhere.

Let us first illustrate various canonical sequences that have been looked at in the preceding sections:

Portuguese: Root +   P/N +   DO
              vej +   o +   o
              "I see him"

Spanish: DO +   Root +   P/N
              lo +   hag +   o
              "I do it"

Italian: IO +   Root +   P/N
              mi +   parl +   a
              "He/she speaks to me"

French: P/N +   IO +   DO +   T/P/N +   Root +   T
              tu +   me +   l' +   as +   donn +   é
              "You (SG) gave it to me"

The French example incorporates all details relevant to our summary, allowing us to comment on degrees of grammaticalization evident in the sequence. "Traditionally" it would be considered as containing three pronouns/proclitics, one auxiliary verb, the root of the main verb, and an inflectional suffix. However, such discrete labeling no longer obtains once specifics of grammaticalization are pointed out. Schwegler (1990) introduced the criteria of *linearity* and *transparency* for the purpose of establishing analytic vs. synthetic structure. We have decided to abandon such a dichotomy, as discussed in 3.1.3, above. These two criteria, however, may now be employed with profit in measuring degrees of grammaticalization in the French sample given.

Clear aspects of *alinearity* are visible in the duplicate signaling of tense in both the auxiliary and the suffix of the past participle, as well as in the co-occurrence of P/N marking in the subject pronoun and in the auxiliary, as linearity "focuses on the accumulation and fusion of meanings of functions in a single morpheme" (Schwegler 1990: 59).[21] (Structural) transparency may be

---

21. Similar mergers can be detected in the P/N signaling of both futures. Cf. the samples in 3.2.1.

somewhat lacking, within Schwegler's definition of this criterion, in that various markers, such as the subject and object pronouns, are tightly interwoven within Modern French morphosyntax, by case, number, and gender. Such a state contributes to a higher degree of grammaticalization (points to the synthetic pole in Schwegler's terms). On the other hand, the fact that the auxiliaries used in the *passé composé* and the *futur proche, **avoir, être, aller***, also occur as full verbs, may indicate a lesser degree of grammaticalization (Schwegler 1990: 67). This underlines a very important characteristic of this process, the fact that advanced grammaticalization permits earlier (more concrete) stages to "shine through" later in the evolution (Bybee et al. 1994, Chapter 1). There is, therefore, a conflict and tension always in existence, between a (unidirectional) evolutionary process and the extant continuum. It will make the determination of the "completion" of grammaticalization especially difficult, as it may not really exist, and a new cycle of grammaticalization may certainly commence without a completion. In this connection, there remains also the crucial question as to how deeply the morphosyntax of a language must be penetrated in order to uncover connections pertinent to grammaticalization. No obvious answer seems to be forthcoming in this matter.

If such tighter criteria for determining grammaticalization are applied, even "obviously completed" cases must now be questioned. The Portuguese enclitic object pronoun was considered as qualified for suffixation, due to its original left branching nature, on a par with the Romance future formation from Latin infinitive + *habere*. The factor of *transparency* would be relevant for this marker, probably re-enforcing its grammaticalized status, although other, perhaps not yet apparent, features may be uncovered in a thorough investigation of its interaction with the rest of the morphosyntax. These may, finally, offer evidence of less grammaticalization, as is clearly the case with the Romance future, since transparency actually exists in the fact that the verb *habere* is used as a full verb, at least in French and Italian. The point is that the introduction of Schwegler's two parameters of *linearity* and *transparency* seems to be opening a Pandora's box, not easily closed. Nevertheless, a ranking in terms of degrees of grammaticalization could still be made of the Romance verb constellations which include personal pronouns:

1. Portuguese object pronouns
2. Spanish object pronouns
3. Italian object pronouns
4. French object pronouns
5. French subject pronouns

In some (crucial) ways, this constitutes merely an intuitive evaluation, in particular the order (2) through (5). Since left vs. right branching does remain the one clear criterion in contributing to the level of grammaticalization, the top ranking of Portuguese will be understood. Among the others, however, uncertainty reigns, depending not only on the variety of factors that could be unearthed in a thorough examination of each language's morphosyntax, but also on the weight one decides to place on each. How should one assess, for instance, the allomorphy of *mi, ti, si, gli, ci, vi* vs. *me, te, se, glie, ce, ve* in Italian or the 'spurious' *se* of Spanish, which in *selo* may have five meanings (Rothe 1966: 543)? In French, the separation of object and subject markers is due to their distribution: the 'peripheral' location of the subject pronoun, as opposed to the more central placement of the object pronouns, may be considered a factor in the degree of grammaticalization reached.

Halpern (1995), a most recent work on the morphology of clitics, proposes a theory of "extended inflection", in which he distinguishes "... true clitics, which are syntactically independent prosodically bound words, and those which, like inflectional affixes, are lexically attached" (p. 32). He speaks of "... the intriguing minimal pair of Old and Modern French" (p. 236), considering the former to have possessed the 'true' kind, while suggesting that clitics in Modern French are best equated to inflectional affixes (p. 186). For Halpern (1995: 186) the clitic/affix distinction seems to undergo total effacement, as "it seems reasonable ... to claim that lexical clitics and canonical inflections are added by the same morphological level or stratum (1995: 186)".[22]

Halpern provides ample argumentation in his study for his claims, within the theoretical apparatus he has chosen. The latter is unrelated to the one offered in this study. However, this framework may be forced to a similar conclusion as to the clitic/affix distinction, for the following reasons.

If the difference between clitic and affix is meant to be one of *degree of grammaticalization*, which is a reasonable criterion, it forms but part of the grammaticalization continuum. However, no discrete point can be found along this slope at which the transition from clitic to affix must be located. Quite similarly, in the continuum from "Latin" to "French", it is impossible to date the moment when people began "speaking French". Yet, Latin and French are distinguished, usually. But the reason/motivation for this dichotomy must be sought *outside* the linguistic evolution.

---

22. Anderson (1992) makes a distinction between clitic and affix in terms of a "domain difference." For an alternative view on pronominal clitics, cf. Everett (1996). See now also Watson (1997: 86), who considers the grammaticalization of clitic clusters in French as a kind of "parallel syntax".

What does it mean, then, so say that prefixation is less likely than suffixation? All that we can be certain of seems to be that a higher degree of grammaticalization can be reached in the evolution of left branching than in the evolution of right branching. This higher degree is principally obtained in the phonological aspect of grammaticalization, involving erosion/fusion, due to perception/processing (perhaps *decoding/encoding*, cf. Geisler 1982), as outlined above.[23] However, an absolute determination on the transition from enclisis to suffixation cannot be made any more definitively than on the one necessary to proceed from proclisis to prefixation. It may, then, be *theoretically* possible to establish such a dichotomy based on more or less grammaticalization, 'more' referring to affix, 'less' to clitic. But the cut-off point will be elusive and no evident factor external to the grammaticalization continuum could be invoked to aid in the matter. Thus, the theory of grammaticalization is incapable of selecting one concept over the other for a particular synchronic slice of a language, and a question like "Inflectional prefixation in Romance"? remains, quite simply, unanswerable.

It is more useful to focus on what insights our grammaticalization framework *has* brought to an understanding of the history of Latin > Romance morphosyntax. It has underlined the importance of the rise of right branching structures, traditionally equated to analysis or periphrasis. Their 'robustness', and thus preferred nature, can best be understood by their ability to resist advanced grammaticalization, arguably for the reasons given above, in section 3.2.1. The facts concerning the replacement of grammaticalized left branching by new right branching in the history of Romance are incontrovertible, illustrated, among others, by the rise of proclitic P/N marking in French, the *go*-future in French and Spanish, and the tendency to abandon object-enclisis in Brazilian Portuguese. These details have always formed the bulk of historical Romance morphosyntax, usually framed within the synthetic/analytic cycle. As was shown in this chapter, this dichotomy can and should be abandoned, as it is made linguistically superfluous within grammaticalization theory. The logic of the latter, however, also forces the loss of the clitic/affix distinction, although such does not seem to be the conclusion in previous studies of the subject. Although the factors to be retained as *for sure* from our analysis seem to be reduced to two, (1) that

---

23. An RB structure from Latin to Romance which did go all the way to inflection may be found in the demonstratives: the 'deictic' *ecce* preceded the Latin demonstrative *ille* to deliver the French demonstrative *celui/celle*. However, no synchronic "prefix" *c- would be (normally) isolated. (The same deictic is assumed to be a "suffix" in the Latin demonstrative *hic*, deriving from a left branching combination.)

structures are (universally) "more or less grammaticalized", and that right branching is preferred with a "limited level" of grammaticalization, they amount to important conclusions. They permit us to investigate further the myriad of details involved in the history of Latin to the Romance languages, providing a context free of terminological baggage, reduced to the necessary minimum of concepts.[24]

---

24. The "unlikelihood" of Romance prefixation may be explained within Heath's approach to grammaticalization, in which "... the prior system, in its formal patterning as well as its unique categorial system, is seen as providing the models for would-be grammaticalizations ... (1998: 754)".

CHAPTER 4

Nominal Inflection and Grammaticalization

4.1 Rumanian noun inflection

4.1.1 Data and synchronic analysis

The inflection of the Rumanian noun, including the well-known case distinction between a nominative/accusative (N/A) case and a genitive/dative (G/D) case, may be illustrated as in the following tabular presentation (Mallinson 1986: 206, 251):

MASCULINE

		Type A	
		Singular	Plural
[−def]	N/A	*un lup*	*un-i-i lup-i* 'wolf'
	G/D	*un-ui lup*	*un-or lup-i*
[+def]	N/A	*lup-u-l*	*lup-i-i*
	G/D	*lup-u-lui*	*lup-i-lor*

		Type B	
		Singular	Plural
[−def]	N/A	*un arbor-e*	*un-i-i arbor-i* 'tree'
	G/D	*un-ui arbor-e*	*un-or arbor-i*
[+def]	N/A	*arbor-e-le*	*arbor-i-i*
	G/D	*arbor-e-lui*	*arbor-i-lor*

FEMININE

		Singular	Plural
[−def]	N/A	*o cas-ă*	*un-e-le cas- e* 'house'
	G/D	*un-e-i cas-e*	*un-or cas-e*
[+def]	N/A	*cas-a*	*cas-e-le*
	G/D	*cas-e-i*	*cas-e-lor*

NEUTER

		Singular	Plural
[−def]	N/A	un num-e	un-e-le num-e 'name'
	G/D	un-ui num-e	un-or num-e
[+def]	N/A	num-e-le	num-e-le
	G/D	num-e-lui	num-e-lor

As presented, the examples have already undergone the appropriate morphemic cuts, demonstrating two sets of suffixes, noun suffixes and definite articles:

NOUN SUFFIXES

Masculine	*Type A singular*: Ø, u	*plural*: i
	Type B singular: e	*plural*: i
Feminine	*N/A singular*: a [ə]	*plural*: e
	G/D singular: e	*plural*: e
Neuter	*singular*: e	*plural*: e

DEFINITE ARTICES

			Singular	Plural
Masculine	*Type A*	N/A	l	i
		G/D	lui	lor
	Type B	N/A	le	i
		G/D	lui	lor
Feminine		N/A	a	le
		G/D	i	lor
Neuter		N/A	le	le
		G/D	lui	lor

It is clear that no case distinction exists in the noun suffixes, the continuations of the Latin declensional desinences, with the exception of the feminine singular: the vocalic segment [ə], which elides before the article [a] in the [+def] N/A, is opposed to [e] in the G/D. These noun suffixes serve to mark both number and gender, a situation parallel to that of Italian (cf. below, in 4.3).

The real innovation in the Rumanian noun inflection may be found in the enclitic definite article, the actual locus of its case system. The two cases are unambiguously distinguished in this second suffix in all the paradigms given, both in the singular and the plural. Case inflection is also present in the indefinite article, appearing proclitically in Rumanian, just like in the other Romance languages. This inflection is sometimes transparent for case, i.e. *un-e-i*, which looks like a [+def] feminine noun, or *un-i-i*, like a [+def] masculine plural, or *un-e-le*. Yet it also contains shortened forms, like G/D *un-ui* and *un-or*, instead of the "expected" **un-u-lui* and **un-i-lor* or **un-e-lor*, and the totally suppletive/opaque FEM SG *o* (for **un-a*?). Case inflection by way of the definite article suffix can also be part of the (attributive) adjective, when it precedes the noun: *Bunul om* occurs alongside (more common) *Omul bun* "the good man" (Mallinson 1986: 296–298).

The Rumanian case dichotomy fits well into Greenberg's (1966: 37–38) markedness split: his 'direct' cases (Nominative, Accusative, Vocative) are considered unmarked, while his 'oblique' cases (Genitive, Dative, Locative, Instrumental) are marked. Following this scheme, we have in Rumanian an unambiguously unmarked case in the N/A and a marked case in the G/D. This taxonomy would characterize the Rumanian case inflection as very stable, opposing it to the instability of the Old French (and Old Provençal) system (cf. Klausenburger 1990).[1]

Using these markedness values, the following connections may be established for the Rumanian case system in terms of iconicity (for the masculine, Type A is shown only):

1.	N/A/sg/m	vs.	G/D/sg/m	(*l* vs. *lui*)	ICONIC
2.	N/A/pl/m	vs.	G/D/pl/m	(*i* vs. *lor*)	ICONIC
3.	N/A/sg/f	vs.	G/D/sg/f	(*a* vs. *i*)	NON-ICONIC
4.	N/A/pl/f	vs.	G/D/pl/f	(*le* vs. *lor*)	ICONIC
5.	N/A/sg/m	vs.	G/D/sg/m	(*le* vs. *lui*)	ICONIC
6.	N/A/sg/m	vs.	G/D/pl/m	(*le* vs. *lor*)	ICONIC

The almost total iconic manifestation of case in this sketch strongly corroborates what was said above about the stability of the system. In addition, no disappearance, or even weakening, of this structure in colloquial trends, which may be seen as precursors of change in the future, would be predicted based on this analysis. There does appear to be a colloquial tendency to lose the enclitic *l*, according to Rothe (1957: 38). Such an evolution would clarify the iconicity of the case system even more, since the resulting N/A case would then be totally unmarked ('featureless'), the G/D suffix constituting 'additive' morphology. The predominant iconic structure of the nominal inflection ranks as one of the *system defining structural properties* of Rumanian, a feature that could only degenerate due to extra-morphological factors.

---

1. For a more developed classification of direct vs. oblique cases, cf. Battistella (1990: 72).

4.1.2 *Historical evolution*

4.1.2.1 *Inflectional endings*

For the development of the two nominal suffixes of Rumanian, the following historical reconstruction seems to be valid and plausible.[2] (CL = Classical Latin, SL = Spoken Latin)

I. Noun suffixes
Masculine A

	CL (2nd decl.)		SL		Rum.	
	SG	PL	SG	PL	SG	PL
NOM	-ŭs	-ī	-o/u	-i	-u/Ø	-i
ACC	-ŭm	-ōs				
GEN	-ī	-ōrum				
DAT	-ō	-īs	-o	-i	-u/Ø	-i

Masculine B

	CL (3rd decl.)		SL		Rum.	
	SG	PL	SG	PL	SG	PL
NOM	-ĭs	-ēs	-e	-i	-e	-i
ACC	-ĕm	-ēs				
GEN	-ĭs	-(i)um	-e		-e	
DAT	-ī	-ĭbus		-i		-i

Feminine

	CL (1st decl.)		SL		Rum.	
	SG	PL	SG	PL	SG	PL
NOM	-ă	-ae	-a	-e	-a [ə]	-e
ACC	-ăm	-ās				
GEN	-ae	-ārum				
DAT	-ae	-īs	-e	-e	-e	-e

---

2. Only the relevant Latin cases are included, cf. Rothe (1957: 64).

Neuter

	CL (3rd decl.)		SL		Rum.	
	SG	PL	SG	PL	SG	PL
NOM	-ĕ	-(i)a	-e	-e	-e	-e
ACC	-ĕ	-(i)a				
GEN	-ĕs	-(i)um	-e		-e	
DAT	-ī	-ībus		-i		-e

These changes call for a few comments. In the masculine A class of nouns, Latin final [o] or [u] underwent apocope, except after *muta cum liquida* clusters: Lat. *soc(e)rum* to Rum. *socru* (Rothe 1957: 64). In these nouns, the NOM and ACC of Classical Latin merged in Spoken Latin already, due to regular sound change. For the Rum. G/D case, one may assume the disappearance of the CL genitive, since the dative phonetically delivers the requisite endings only. The singular of the second masculine class may be derived phonetically, the N/A from either the NOM or ACC, the G/D from the genitive only. However, the plural forms are explainable entirely by analogical formation based on the first class, for both cases, a change-over to be assumed for Spoken Latin already. In the feminine evolution, the analogical transfer of the NOM -e to the G/D is evident in the plural, again probably as early as in Spoken Latin. The singular of the neuter can be explained phonetically, but the plural seems to derive directly from the feminine paradigm.

II. Definite article
Masculine

	CL (demonst.)		SL		Rum.	
	SG	PL	SG	PL	SG	PL
NOM	*ille*	*illī*	*ille*	*illi*	*-le*	*-i*
ACC	*illŭm*	*illōs*	*illo/u*	*illos*	*-l*	
GEN	*illius*	*illōrum*		*illorum*		*-lor*
DAT	*illī*	*illīs*	**illui*		*-lui*	

Feminine

	CL (demonst.)		SL		Rum.	
	SG	PL	SG	PL	SG	PL
NOM	*illă*	*illae*	*illa*	*illae*	*-a*	*-le*
ACC	*illăm*	*illās*				
GEN	*illius*	*illārum*		*illorum*		*-lor*
DAT	*illī*	*illīs*	**illaei*		*-i*	

The neuter definite article does not constitute a separate development. One assumes the evolution of the masculine type B in the singular, while the plural duplicates the history of the feminine. In the latter, the MASC Gen. PL *illorum* is borrowed. What does remain mysterious is the reason for the double MASC SING evolution, one from the NOM *ille*, one from the ACC *illum*, although vowel harmony may have been involved in the appearance of *-le*, following nouns ending in *-e* (Rothe 1957: 76).

4.1.2.2 *Synthesis*
The evolution of the definite article into a suffix, perhaps the most distinguishing characteristic of Rumanian within the Romance group, requires addressing two issues:
1. How did a word order consisting of the noun *followed* by the demonstrative *ille* become established in the spoken Latin which became Rumanian?
2. What were the mechanics of the synthesis of the two constituents?

Two hypotheses exist for responding to (1) (Rothe 1957: 75–76). On the one hand, a Balkan substratum/adstratum may be assumed, as Albanian and Modern Bulgarian show enclitic articles. On the other hand, post-position of *ille* may simply be considered one of the syntactic options for Latin word order. After a period of fluctuation between pre-position and post-position of the demonstrative to the noun, the norm became post-position. It is significant to add that post-posed adjectives fit perfectly into a typologically consistent VO language (Harris 1978: 6). Therefore, it may be claimed that Rumanian continues the (assumed) VO order of Spoken Latin in this respect, while in the other Romance languages the proclitic definite article "must be explained", in view of the generally accepted VO typology for these languages also.

For discussing (2), let us propose the following syntactic sequences in Spoken Latin as bases:

Masculine	SG	*dominu(m) illu(m)*	*domnul* (N/A)
		arbore ille	*arborele* (N/A)
		dominu illui	*domnului* (G/D)
	PL	*domini illi*	*domnii* (N/A)
		domini illorum	*domnilor* (G/D)
Feminine	SG	*casa illa*	*casa* (N/A)
		casae illaei	*casei* (G/D)
	PL	*casae illae*	*casele* (N/A)
		casae illorum	*caselor* (G/D)

One can plausibly assume that the synthesis of the post-posed Latin demonstrative *ille* and the host noun proceeded analogously to that of the general Romance future development of infinitive and auxiliary *habere*. Thus, essentially the same four steps outlined in Schwegler (1990: 132–133) apply here also, adapted in some details:

a. Semantic reanalysis of *ille*: the demonstrative sense of *ille* was lost, evolving by way of a type of 'bleaching', to definiteness (cf. Carrasquel 1995).
b. Loss of morphosyntactic freedom: as mentioned above, there was alternation between pre- and post-position of *ille* for a while. However, after a choice to the latter had been made, rigidity must have set in, and *ille* as a clitic lost its transportability and separability, although an interesting remnant of the latter may still be detected in the (fairly rare) *bunul om*, mentioned above.
c. Phonological binding of noun +*ille*: the whole unit became phonologically bound, carrying a single main stress on the noun. Various vowel mergers at the noun/*ille* contact points clearly must be posited for the eventual surface output.
d. Decrease in morphological variation of *ille*: although the reflexes of this pronoun signal the two Rumanian cases, this result is less complex than the usual (Romance) outcome for pronouns, for which generally three cases, subject, indirect object, and direct object functions, are extant, at least in the 3rd person.

The creation of the Rumanian enclitic article, of course, fits well into the typology of Latin inflectional suffixation, corroborating rather than restructuring the SDSPs of Latin. It is also a nice demonstration of the 'suffixing preference', most thoroughly discussed in Hall (1992), within a processing approach to historical change, since there is an apparent "dispreference" for affixation in the case of the proclitic article in the other Romance languages. The obvious parallel exists, then, between the synthesis of infinitive plus *habere* to make the future in Romance (except in Rumanian!) and the Rumanian definite article evolution, these changes being opposed to the remaining analytic structure of both the *habere* plus past participle construction and the definite article plus noun sequences in Romance. "Partial" synthesis, however, may be detected for both of the last two combinations, as all the factors crucial to synthesis seem to be fulfilled, in varying degrees, with the exception of (c), phonological binding. Such incomplete synthesis certainly shows all the signs of advanced grammaticalization, as understood in the frameworks of Heine et al. (1991), Hopper and Traugott (1993), Heine (1993), Bybee et al. (1994) and Lehmann (1995). In addition, the *caveat* concerning analysis/synthesis explanation, as discussed above, in 3.1.3, is fully applicable to the Rumanian evolution.

4.2 The Old French case system

4.2.1 Noun and adjective data

For the synchronic and diachronic analysis of the Old French nominal structure to be performed in this section, Rheinfelder (1967: 19, 50) supplies the following tabular summaries for nouns and adjectives, respectively. (CL = Classical Latin, VL = Vulgar Latin [= Spoken Latin], OF = Old French, MF = Modern French)

The Noun in Old French

			CL	VL	OF	MF
Masculine						
I	SG	NOM	*murŭs*	*muros*	*murs*	
		ACC	*murŭm*	*muro*	*mur*	*mur*
	PL	NOM	*murī*	*muri*	*mur*	
		ACC	*murōs*	*muros*	*murs*	*murs*
II	SG	NOM	*gener*	*gener*	*gendre(s)*	
		ACC	*generŭm*	*genero*	*gendre*	*gendre*
	PL	NOM	*generī*	*generi*	*gendre*	
		ACC	*generōs*	*generos*	*gendres*	*gendres*
III	SG	NOM	*cŏmes*	*comes*	*cuens*	
		ACC	*cŏmitĕm*	*comite*	*conte*	*comte*
	PL	NOM	*cŏmitēs*	*cometes*	*conte(s)*	
		ACC	*cŏmitēs*	*cometes*	*contes*	*comtes*
Feminine						
I	SG	NOM	*portă*	*porta*	*porte*	
		ACC	*portăm*	*porta*	*porte*	*porte*
	PL	NOM	*portae*	*portas*	*portes*	
		ACC	*portās*	*portas*	*portes*	*portes*
II	SG	NOM	*flōs*	*flores*	*flour(s)*	
		ACC	*flōrem*	*flore*	*flour*	*fleur*
	PL	NOM	*flōres*	*flores*	*flour(s)*	
		ACC	*flōres*	*flores*	*flours*	*fleurs*
III	SG	NOM	*soror*	*soror*	*suer*	*soeur*
		ACC	*sorōrem*	*sorore*	*serour*	
	PL	NOM	*sorōres*	*sorores*	*serours*	[*soeurs*]
		ACC	*sorōres*	*sorores*	*sorores*	

The Adjective in Old French

			CL	VL	OF	MF
1. Masculine						
	I	SG NOM	*durŭs*	*duros*	*durs*	
		ACC	*durŭm*	*duro*	*dur*	*dur*
		PL NOM	*durī*	*duri*	*dur*	
		ACC	*durōs*	*duros*	*durs*	*durs*
Feminine						
	I	SG NOM	*dură*	*dura*	*dure*	
		ACC	*durăm*	*dura*	*dure*	*dure*
		PL NOM	*durae*	*duras*	*dures*	
		ACC	*durās*	*duras*	*dures*	*dures*
2. Masculine						
	II	SG NOM	*tener*	*tener*	*tendre(s)*	
		ACC	*tenerŭm*	*tenero*	*tendre*	*tendre*
		PL NOM	*tenerī*	*teneri*	*tendre*	
		ACC	*tenerōs*	*teneros*	*tendres*	*tendres*
Feminine						
	I.	SG nom	*teneră*	*tenera*	*tendre*	
		ACC	*teneră m*	*tenera*	*tendre*	*tendre*
		PL NOM	*tenerae*	*teneras*	*tendres*	
		ACC	*tenerās*	*teneras*	*tendres*	*tendres*
3. Masculine						
	I	SG NOM	*grandĭs*	*grandes*	*granz*	
		ACC	*grandĕm*	*grande*	*grant*	*grand*
		PL NOM	*grandēs*	*grandes*	*grant(s)*	
		ACC	*grandēs*	*grandes*	*granz*	*grands*
Feminine						
	II	SG NOM	*grandĭs*	*grandes*	*grant(s)*	
		ACC	*grandĕm*	*grande*	*grant*	*grande*
		PL NOM	*grandēs*	*grandes*	*granz*	
		ACC	*grandēs*	*grandes*	*granz*	*grandes*
4. Masculine						
	III	SG NOM	*mĕlior*	*melior*	*mieldre(s)*	
		ACC	*meliōrĕm*	*meliore*	*meillour*	*meilleur*
		PL NOM	*meliōrēs*	*meliores*	*meillour(s)*	
		ACC	*meliōrēs*	*meliores*	*meillours*	*meilleurs*

Feminine

III	SG NOM	mĕlior	melior	mieldre	
	ACC	meliōrĕm	meliore	meillour	meilleure
	PL NOM	meliōrēs	meliores	meillours	
	ACC	mĕliōrēs	meliores	meillours	meilleures

Explanation and preliminary analysis of data

Old French noun paradigms are first subdivided by gender and then into three groups within the latter, a fairly conventional classification. The case system depended (almost) entirely on a Ø/s alternation of suffixes, the different distribution of which motivating the subdivisions for each gender. In addition, each category III represents imparisyllabic paradigms, whose stem alternations supplement the suffix oppositions by signaling case and number. The Old French suffix patterning extracted from the data appears as follows (cf. Klausenburger 1990: 327):

Masculine

	I:		II:		III:	
	-s		Ø		-s	
	Ø		Ø		Ø	
	Ø		Ø		-s	
	-s		-s		-s	

Feminine

	I:		II:		III:	
	Ø		-s		Ø	
	Ø		Ø		Ø	
	-s		-s		-s	
	-s		-s		-s	

Rheinfelder's global overview of Old French adjective classes stresses their direct tie to the noun structure. Four types are identified (the fourth being a comparative), each of which combining masculine and feminine forms derived from one of the three noun classes of each gender (in Roman numerals). This cross-reference integrates the two parts of Old French nominal morphology explicitly and therefore facilitates the common analysis for case and number. The adjective system, however, manifests additionally a gender marker, the suffix -e, overt and transparent in the first class only.

4.2.2 *A natural morphological analysis*

4.2.2.1 *Old French synchrony*

Our central concern will be to supply an adequate description of the suffix *-s*, crucial for an understanding of Old French inflectional structure.³ For the Old French nominal categories of case, number, and gender, *-s* manifests the following distribution:

		Masculine	**Feminine**
NOUN			
SG	NOM	*mur-s*	[*flour-(s)*]
	ACC		
PL	NOM	[*conte-s*]	*porte-s*
	ACC	*mur-s*	*porte-s*
ADJECTIVE			
SG	NOM	*dur-s*	[*grant-(s)*]
	ACC		
PL	nom	[*grant-s*]	*dure-s*
	ACC	*dur-s*	*dure-s*

Of the 16 possible slots available, only four are *never* filled by *-s*, the accusative case in both genders in the singular. A classification of the 12 extant occurrences of *-s* would label it a number and case marker in both genders, captured as follows:⁴

Masculine				Feminine			
SING		PL		SING		PL	
NOM	ACC	NOM	ACC	NOM	ACC	NOM	ACC
+		+	+	+		+	+

Restricting ourselves to the eight "stable" examples of *-s*, we obtain the (more useful) following sketch:

---

3. We limit ourselves to the nominal system here and cannot include its verbal role also.

4. The plus sign indicates presence of *-s*. This grid is based on a hierarchy of Gender > Number > Case, assumed to be operative for Old French by Walker (1987b: 175).

Masculine				Feminine			
SING		PL		SING		PL	
NOM	ACC	NOM	ACC	NOM	ACC	NOM	ACC
+			+			+	+

Such a schema makes overt the fact that -*s* serves as a number marker in the feminine, and as a case and number marker in the masculine, both in nouns and adjectives. More specifically, number marking by final -*s* is transparent for both cases in the feminine and for the accusative in the masculine. Thus, three-fourths of number marking in Old French constitutes iconic structure, as the semantically marked category of plural is matched by (additive) suffixation (cf. Mayerthaler 1981). We have now isolated the "anomaly" of Old French nominal inflection, the presence of the suffix -*s* in the MASC/SING/NOM. It marks number counter-iconically in the nominative case, since SING, of course, must be considered the default semantic value. More complex and controversial may be seen its status vis-à-vis case marking, since disagreement exists as to the markedness status of the two Old French cases.

Blake (1994: 197) proposes the universal case hierarchy *nom* > *acc/erg* >*gen* > *dat* >*loc* > *abl/instr*, and a subset of it for Latin (p. 90). This is but a refinement of Greenberg (1966), and his claim that direct cases (N/A) are less marked than the oblique ones (all the rest). However, "Indo-European languages are unusual in having a marked nom. in most paradigms" (Blake 1994: 31). "Marked" here means 'overt morphological marking' and it results in counter-iconic structure, a situation also found in Old French by Plank (1979: 633), who considers it an accusative type language

> ... of a rather unusual kind ... since in canonical accusative type languages the DO (non-agent) case is morphologically marked and the S case morphologically unmarked.

The question is now posed as to whether the Old French accusative/oblique/-*régime* may have become the (semantically) unmarked case, due to "... its frequency and of the variety of syntactic environments into which it may be inserted" (Walker 1987b: 186). Pensado (1986: 289) constructs, in fact, a scenario of "markedness reversal" as follows:

> Son point de départ aurait été la réinterprétation du cas sujet vis-à-vis du cas régime, devenu le cas non-marqué, d'abord par son évolution phonétique, [essentially the loss of Lat. final -*m*, Pensado (1986: 276)] qui a entraîné ensuite son comportement syntaxique.

The distribution of the -*s* in the MASC NOM paradigm constitutes counter-iconicity in number marking in the NOM case, as already pointed out. Such a state cannot be 'avoided' for case also, for the following reasons:
1. If we consider the NOM as unmarked, then the SING forms relate counter-iconically, but the plural ones iconically;
2. If we accept the ACC as the default case, then the SING forms show an iconic *rapport* while that of the plurals would be counter-iconic.

Let us also investigate the possible role of final -*s* for gender marking in Old French. The first adjective class outlined above is characterized clearly and iconically for gender, as the FEM adjective *dure* contains the suffix (pronounced in Old French) -*e* [ə], compared to zero in the MASC *dur*. The same cannot be said for the other three classes, however, or the gender opposition in nouns. For these data, two choices of analysis offer themselves:
1. We consider gender to be non-iconic, zero-marking obtaining throughout these examples;
2. we include the -*s* suffix in our analysis of gender, 'opposing' its occurrence in the NOM SING MASC to its absence in the NOM SING FEM: a third counter-iconic connection is then uncovered.

As can be seen, quite a "burden" is put on the suffix -*s* in the workings of the Old French nominal inflectional structure, especially if the counter-iconic aspects are taken into consideration. Yet it is quite apparent that Class I MASC in the nouns and the first adjectival class constitute the default *paradigm structure condition* (cf. Wurzel 1984) in Old French, as evidenced by the well-known analogical shifts, indicated in both the noun and the adjective data by the final -*s* in parenthesis. These are (cf. Klausenburger 1986: 339, 1990: 329):
1. -*s* is added to the NOM/SG/MASC (noun MASC II, adjective 2,4)
2. -*s* is removed from the NOM/PL/MASC (noun MASC III, adjective 3,4)
3. -*s* is removed from the NOM/SG/FEM (noun FEM II)
4. -*s* is removed from the NOM/SG/FEM (adjective 3)

By way of these replications of the dominant paradigms, the "anomalous" patterning of the suffix -*s*, therefore, was strengthened in Old French. Why and how did this system crumble, then?

4.2.2.2 *Diachrony: Before and after Old French*
Wurzel (1984: 82) outlines six *system defining structural properties (= SDSPs)*, which combine to construct *system congruity* in the morphology of a language. These were already outlined above, in Chapter 2, 2.2, in the analysis of the Latin

verb system. They are here exemplified by representative data from the history of French noun inflection (A), followed by a tabular overview of the structural changes (B).

A. Historical sketch of Noun Evolution

			Latin	Old French	Mod. French
I.	sg	N.	*porta*	*la porte*	
		G.	*portae, e*		
		D.	*portae, e*		
		Ac.	*porta(m)*	*la porte*	*la porte*
		Ab.	*porta*		
	pl	N.	*portae, as*	*les portes*	
		G.	*portarum*		
		D.	*portis*		
		Ac.	*portas*	*les portes*	*les portes*
		Ab.	*portis*		
II.	sg	N.	*murus*	*li murs*	
		G.	*muri*		
		D.	*muro*		
		Ac.	*muru(m)*	*le mur*	*le mur*
		Ab.	*muro*		
	pl	N.	*muri*	*li mur*	
		G.	*murorum*		
		D.	*muris*		
		Ac.	*muros*	*les murs*	*les murs*
		Ab.	*muris*		
III.	sg	N.	*panis*	*li pains*	
		G.	*panis*		
		D.	*pani*		
		Ac.	*pane(m)*	*le pain*	*le pain*
		Ab.	*pane*		
	pl	N.	*panes*	*li pain(s)*	
		G.	*panum*		
		D.	*panibus*		
		Ac.	*panes*	*les pains*	*les pains*
		Ab.	*panibus*		

B. Changes in SDSPs

	Latin	Old French	Mod. French
(a)	G, N, C (5–6 cases)	G, N, C (2 cases)	G, N
(b)	stem inflection	stem/base	base
(c)	cum. exponence	cum. exponence	cum. exponence
(d)	syncretism	syncretism	non-iconicity of N (G)
	(i) G/D sg I	(i) N/A sg/pl I	
	(ii) D/Ab sg II	(ii) N sg/Ac pl II, III	
		Ac sg/N pl II, III	
	(iii) N/G sg III	(iii) Nsg/Npl II, III	
	N/Ac pl III		
	(iv) D/Ab pl I, II, III		
(e)	suffixation	suffixation	def. article (preposed, prefix)
(f)	3 declensions (in given data)	2 classes	no declensional divisions

The data in A differ from Rheinfelder's overview in three ways, being both more and less detailed:

1. all Latin cases are shown, not just two;
2. the definite article is included for both the Old and Modern French stages;
3. no imparisyllabics are incorporated.

Both sets of examples place Old French in a diachronic context. However, Rheinfelder's (traditional) outline focuses on how the (surface) details of Old French evolved from their Latin sources and what Modern French forms were later produced. The selected items in A, on the other hand, serve as the bases for the determination of differences in the *system congruity* of the three historical stages, central to Wurzel's theory of natural morphology.

According to Wurzel, SDSPs resist morphological change and, in fact, they determine it (1984: 89). The change-overs indicated in B can only be explained extra-morphologically, by sound change and syntactic innovation (grammaticalization). Three major phonological changes occurred in the data involved:

1. Apocope (incl. /a/ → [ə]) (Latin to Old French)
2. Final -*s* deletion (OF to MF)
3. /ə/-deletion (OF to MF)

All the Latin singular noun etyma illustrated were reduced to their OF counterparts by apocope, and most plurals also. The grammaticalization of syntactic change, concerning prepositions and the definite article, completes the scenario.[5] The change-over in the specifics of each of the five system congruity parameters is, ultimately, directly relatable to conditions explained by these non-morphological transformations. The two sound changes from OF to MF are the principal factors in delivering non-iconic nominal inflection in the contemporary (spoken) language (cf. Klausenburger 1992a, b).

4.3 Life cycle of (other) Romance case structures

4.3.1 *Spanish and Italian developments*

One of the striking details of historical Romance linguistics must be seen in the different evolution of Spanish in contrast to Old French with respect to nominal inflection. The puzzling aspect of this difference lies in the fact that both languages had the same phonetic raw material which was maintained in their development from Latin, final [s]. However, in Old French, as was seen in 4.2, above, this final consonant played the key role in the (rudimentary) case system for several centuries, while in Spanish the same suffix did not serve to support case distinctions, not even in the earliest attestations of Old Spanish. Why not?

The two evolutions may be juxtaposed as follows, with their Latin sources in the center. For illustration, only the 2nd declension masculine noun will first be given:

Spanish	**Spoken Latin**	**Old French**	**Modern French**
*muros	muros	murs	
muro	muro	mur	(le) mur
*mur(i)	muri	mur	
muros	muros	murs	(les) murs

What is clear from the phonetic history of Spanish is that the retention of final /s/ could potentially have led to a case system à la Old French, a paradigm incorporating the two starred forms given in the first column. The only sound change that never occurred in the history of Spanish, but did in French, was apocope of /o/. This apparently minor difference must be considered the key to answering the question posed at the end of the last paragraph, since the presence

---

5. For the latter, see below, section 4.3.

of this vowel in Spanish, but its absence in French, must have led to divergent morphological interpretations. A possible analysis would go as follows (cf. Klausenburger 1993b).

The Latin noun contained the morphological categories of gender, number, and case. It is generally accepted that a hierarchy exists among these, with case presupposing number, and number presupposing gender. Accordingly, case would be "the first to go, gender the last", in a normal development of noun inflection. Now, since Spanish retained two desinential segments, a final vowel and a final consonant, they were morphologically interpreted as the two stronger categories, final /o/ as (masculine) gender, final /s/ as (plural) number, delivering the extant forms *muro* for the singular and *muros* for the plural. There was then no remaining segment to be assigned to the category of case. It is true that Latin maintained for a long time the cumulative exponence of case, number, and gender in the suffix of the noun. However, this cumulation was lost in the history into Romance and a transparent identification of gender and number occurred in Spanish.

In light of the discussion in the preceding section, the Spanish evolution seems clear-cut and in no need of explanation, and it is rather the Old French stage which counters expectation with its retention of cases in the masculine paradigm. How did this come about? Apocope of /o/ left French with but one segment, final /s/. We are assuming that at least gender, being strongest on the markedness scale, had to be signaled by means of this consonant in Old French. But such a marking *forced* the continuation of both number and case also, since they were *inseparably* included along with gender in that one suffix. Quite simply, loss of the vowel /o/ made separate assignment of gender (and number) impossible in Old French and thus "safe-guarded" the case system, at least temporarily.

We find an explanation of the no-case paradigm of the dominant feminine class in Old French along the same lines of analysis, again presenting French and Spanish developments on both sides of the Latin etyma:

Spanish	Spoken Latin	Old French	Modern French
*puerta	porta	porte	
puerta	porta	porte	(la) porte
*puertas	portas	portes	
puertas	portas	portes	(les) portes

As the 'Romance' plural with final /s/ is already given for Spoken Latin (in the nominative), the following morphological analysis really holds for all three columns: final /a/ becomes the unambiguous marker of feminine gender, final /s/ that of the plural, the only phonetic modification in Old French being the change of the vowel into final schwa. None of the feminine nouns "with a case system" in Old French (i.e. *nes, nef*) contained the final schwa, which could have been liable to identification with gender.

The further evolution of nominal inflection into Modern French supports the hypothesis proposed, in this sense: The late Old French sound change of final /s/-deletion, and final schwa deletion in the 16th century, have transferred the morphological markings in the noun to the preposed definite article. Significantly, it carries only gender and number, not case (cf. 4.3.2). Gender and number do present themselves cumulatively, but they do not have to "pull along" case, since the latter had never been incorporated "inseparably" in the form of the definite article remaining from Old French.

A case system existed in Old Provençal also, and it can be shown easily and briefly that it arose and was maintained for the same reason as in Old French. The following examples represent the dominant classes of nouns (Jensen 1976: 22,43):

	Spoken Latin	**Old Provençal**
Feminine	*filia* (N, SG)	*filha*
	filia (Ac, SG)	*filha*
	filias (N, PL)	*filhas*
	filias (Ac, PL)	*filhas*
Masculine	*muros* (N, SG)	*murs*
	muro (Ac, SG)	*mur*
	muri (N, PL)	*mur*
	muros (Ac, PL)	*murs*

One may conclude that this Romance language occupies, in a sense, a position intermediary between Old French and Spanish. The effect of apocope is apparent, like in Old French, but final /a/ did not change, like in Spanish. Crucial for the case evolution, of course, was apocope, and it delivered the same case system as in Old French.

According to Bossong (1985: 299), "selectional pressure", based on the equating of Ac = marked and N = unmarked, led to the loss of final /s/ in the history of Spanish, not sound change, removing a counter-iconic relationship. Penny (1991: 105), on the other hand, proposes a series of analogical shifts, as a result of which the "dominant" value of final /s/ as plural marker eliminated any potential case distinction, between *muros* and *muro* in the singular, between *muri* and *muros* in the plural.[6] Neither proposal, however, gives a satisfactory account of the extant systems in Old French and Old Provençal, as explained above.

An interesting connection is made by Müller (1971:503) between the lack of a N vs. Ac distinction in Spanish by way of suffixation and the emergence of the "prepositional accusative", the grammaticalization of the Latin preposition *ad* to Spanish *a* as a case marker, at least for animate direct objects. Three zones of development may be distinguished (1971:504):

1. Iberian peninsula (Spanish, Portuguese, Catalan): almost complete replacement of N by Ac;
2. Eastern Romance (Italian, Rumanian): replacement of N by Ac in singular, but retention of N in plural (= also Ac in plural);
3. Gaul (Old French, Old Provençal): N vs. Ac opposition preserved.

Only in Zone 1 is the use of the prepositional accusative productive. In Rumanian, the Latin preposition *per* grammaticalized into *pe* as an accusative marker, but there is complementary distribution between the use of *pe* and the ([+def]) N/A case: the direct object is expressed either by way of *pe* + [−def] noun, or without *pe* and the noun in [+def], i.e. containing the enclitic, case-bearing definite article, although the two versions apparently do not have semantic equivalence (Müller 1971:514).

Let us now look at the evolution of the Italian noun. Why did case structure not develop in this Romance dialect? A principal feature in the phonetic history of Italian, of course, was the deletion of final /s/, assigning it to the Eastern Romania. Thus, the phonetic reflexes of the sample nouns were the following:

Spoken Latin	**Italian**
muros	*muro*
muro	*muro*
muri	*muri*
muros	*muro
porta	*porta*
porta	*porta*
porte	*porte*
portas	*porta

---

6. See also Lahiri and Dresher (1984).

In Italian, one suffixal segment remains, like in Old French, but it is a vowel, and not the final /s/. However, why did this one segment not continue to carry gender, number, and case cumulatively, due to the same reasoning as given for the final /s/ in Old French? There is one important difference in these two histories. In Old French, the final /s/ *differentiated* the two forms of the singular of the masculine noun and therefore became a potential case marker. This final vowel may, nevertheless, take on morphological signaling, cumulative gender and number marking. It differs from Spanish, thus, but again there is a phonetic reason for this: all final vowels of Latin are retained in Italian and the final /i/ and /e/ in the plural are here available to "replace" the loss of final /s/, which was usable in Spanish as a plural marker.

Although the phonetic results in the singular noun cannot reveal whether the Latin N or Ac continues into the *système casuel* of Italian (cf. Dardel and Gaeng 1992: 108), the plural forms derive unambiguously from a Latin nominative. However, at first sight, such a continuation seems to be contradicted in examples like *nipote, monte,* and *dente,* with an apparent Ac source in Latin. On the other hand, singulars like *uomo, moglie,* and *ladro* clearly betray a Latin N origin again. The examples given belong to Latin imparisyllabics (of the 3rd declension), with the following singular paradigms:[7]

	Latin	**Italian**
Nom	*nepos*	
Gen	*nepotis* >	*nipote*
Dat	*nepoti*	
Acc	*nepote(m)*	
Abl	*nepote*	
Nom	*mons*	
Gen	*montis* >	*monte*
Dat	*monti*	
Acc	*monte(m)*	
Abl	*monte*	
Nom	*dens*	
Gen	*dentis* >	*dente*
Dat	*denti*	

---

7. Cf. Dardel and Wüest (1993).

| Acc | dente(m) | |
| Abl | dente | |

Nom	homo >	uomo
Gen	hominis	
Dat	homini	
Acc	hominem	
Abl	homine	

Nom	mulier >	moglie
Gen	mulieris	
Dat	mulieri	
Acc	muliere(m)	
Abl	muliere	

Nom	latro >	ladro
Gen	latronis	
Dat	latroni	
Acc	latrone(m)	
Abl	latrone	

According to the arrows given, these Italian nouns derive from both the genitive and the nominative. It is clear, however, that imparisyllabics tended toward parisyllabicity in Spoken Latin, as attested in the Appendix Probi (*pecten* non *pectinis*). Therefore, one may claim that *all* the examples given really have a spoken nominative source, the classical genitive having become a new nominative, underlining, according to Mayerthaler (1981: 67) that the N must be considered unmarked over the (marked) accusative case.

4.3.2 *The definite article and Romance nouns*

A distillation of some crucial details of Romance noun evolution may be given as in the following overview:

Latin/Romance Noun Inflection

Latin	Italian	Spanish	Old French	Mod. French
port-a	la port-a		la port-e	
port-a(m)		la puert-a	la port-e	[lapɔʀt]
port-ae, as	le port-e		les port-e-s	
port-as		las puert-a-s	les port-e-s	[lepɔʀt]
mur-us	il mur-o		li mur-s	
mur-u(m)		el mur-o	le mur	[ləmyʀ]
mur-i	i mur-i		li mur	
mur-os		los mur-o-s	les mur-s	[lemyʀ]
pan-is	il pan-e		li pain-s	
pan-e(m)		el pan	le pain	[ləpɛ̃]
pan-es	i pan-i		li pain-(s)	
pan-es		los pan-e-s	les pain-s	[lepɛ̃]

This table incorporates both suffixal morphemic cuts (as suggested in the previous sections) and the role of the definite article. In Italian, Spanish, and Modern French the DA clearly functions in the gender and number marking of the noun, in Old French also in the case morphology. Epstein (1995: 160) reproduces Greenberg's four stages of the grammaticalization of the DA, concluding that Old French (like English) is most plausibly assigned Stage I, when the original Latin demonstrative *ille* had acquired 'identifiability' function, while Modern French is probably to be placed between II and III, as the semantic-pragmatic motivation has been lost and the DA is becoming an obligatory noun marker (cf. Harris 1978). It would seem that the Italian and Spanish DA most appropriately compares to the level reached in Old French, Stage I. How would the Rumanian DA be classified in this schema?

As was demonstrated in 4.1, the DA creates the case structure of Rumanian, unquestionably having attained the most advanced degree of grammaticalization, from post-position to enclisis to suffixation. The preposed nature of the DA in the other Romance languages constituted the barrier against such a complete evolution, although Epstein (1995: 171) also claims that except for the "more objective" Stage 0 to I change-over, the grammaticalization of the DA typically proceeds at an extremely slow rate, because "highly subjective, discourse-based" transitions are involved. Now, it is important to add that the actual case suffix of the enclitic DA in Rumanian was *not* due to a new grammaticalization of case evolution, such as the one outlined in Blake (1994: 172):

	nom	acc/erg	gen	dat	SEMANTIC
marking of bound					
pronoun	x	x	x	x	
suffix on noun		x<	x<	x<	x
adposition		x<	x<	x<	prep
open lexical class					post
					verb
					noun
					adverb

Rather, the case suffix of the Latin demonstrative *ille* continues, thus an extension of Latin case marking, very comparable to that on the Old French noun. In Indo-European languages like Latin, however, with their cumulative exponence in the noun suffix, "the prospects for determining the origin of particular case markers are not too promising" (Blake 1994: 163). Therefore, the key difference between the Old French and Rumanian histories does not lie in the a grammaticalization of case but in the degree of grammaticalization of the DA. With respect to the latter, the crucial pre- vs. post-position of *ille* was decisive in opposing Old French (and Italian and Spanish) to Rumanian, joining the grammaticalization scenario as proposed in Chapter 3, above.

Let us return to the sketch on Latin/Romance noun inflection. For Modern French, a phonetic representation is given, apparently analyzing the article as a prefix. A strict adherence to the grammaticalization scenario of Chapter 3, of course, would require an asterisk in front of these forms, since such prefixation, presumably, will be ruled out and never realized. Whether the grammaticalization of the French DA is considered "complete" or not is not crucial for the present discussion, however. The only morphological difference established between singular and plural, and between masculine and feminine (in the spoken language) occurs by way of the preposed determiner (demonstrative and possessive adjective, in addition to both definite and indefinite articles). The following oppositions hold in this signaling (for the DA):

	Masculine	**Feminine**
singular	[lə]	[la]
plural	[le]	[le]

This is an incomplete picture, not showing, for instance, liaison variants. However, the main point is that no case system is carried by the DA (or other determiner). Interestingly, Müller (1971: 510) adduces evidence that "beim Artikel in statu nascendi ... ist der Kasuskollaps später als beim Nomen erfolgt".

Indeed, some modern DA allomorphs derive from different Latin cases, as Italian *il* from Latin nominative *ille*, and *lo* from the accusative *illum*, today specialized for other purposes. In addition, it was suggested in Chapter 3, in the study of French dislocated sentences, that a new "case system" may be developing on the verb, by means of both subject and object pronominal clitics. The latter, of course, grammaticalized out of the same Latin source, demonstrative *ille*. The fact remains, still, that only Rumanian operates with a case system based in the DA, and that in Italian and Spanish the redundant nature of the DA for gender and number emerges also. In these languages, the extant suffix morphology would seem to serve adequately for those purposes.

CHAPTER 5

Theoretical Issues in Grammaticalization

5.1 Grammaticalization and the 'invisible hand' in language change

5.1.1 From Mandeville's paradox to 'invisible hand' explanations

Bernard (de) Mandeville was an 18th century Dutch writer and social critic, who is best known for *Fable of the Bees* (first version of 1705), a satire of contemporary society in England, where Mandeville had settled in 1696. The contents are quickly told, but the moral of the story turned out to be extremely explosive and was too much for Mandeville's contemporaries, who accused him of being an immoral cynic, although he may simply have been a *paradoxographus* (Pinkus 1975: 200).

The beehive enjoyed great prosperity, as commerce, the arts, and sciences flourished, but among the citizens there was hardly one decent person. They were lazy, corrupt, and vain. The lawyers, the doctors, the soldiers, and the ministers were all scoundrels:

> *All Trades and Places knew some Cheat,*
> *No Calling was without Deceit.*

Still, the whole society of bees flourished:

> *Thus every Part was full of Vice,*
> *Yet the whole Mass a Paradise.*
> *The worst of all the Multitude*
> *Did something for the Common Good.*

The original form of Mandeville's paradox, succinctly summarized by the subtitle given to the fable in a second edition of 1714, *Private Vices, Publick Benefits*, was thus: "The prosperity of the community was not the result of the virtue of its citizens, but of their vices and wickedness" (Keller 1994: 33).

But the story goes on, as some of the citizens complained to the gods about the vices of their fellow bees. Jupiter agreed to rid the hive of all the crimes and dishonesty — with the startling result that this action sealed the downfall of the bee community! The lawyers had nothing to do anymore, the blacksmiths and executioners became unemployed, and the beehive was reduced to a miserable, but exemplary and pure life:

> *They flew into a hollow Tree,*
> *Blest with Content and Honesty.*

The *Fable* ends with this moral:

> *Bare Virtue can't make Nations live*
> *In Splendor; they, that would revive*
> *A golden Age, must be as free,*
> *For Acorns, as for Honesty.*

One may generalize Mandeville's paradox by saying that "the question about the *motives* of individual actions must be separated from the question about the *social effects* of these actions" (Keller 1994: 35). It is believed that the Scottish moral philosopher Adam Smith was influenced by Mandeville's ideas and it is he who first coined the metaphor of the *invisible hand* in his work *An inquiry into the Nature and Causes of the Wealth of Nations* (1776), in the following well-known passage (p. 400):

> But the annual revenue of every society is always precisely equal to the exchangeable value of the whole annual produce of its industry, or rather is precisely the same thing with that exchangeable value. As every individual, therefore, endeavors as much as he can both to employ his capital in the support of domestic industry, and so to direct that industry that its produce may be of the greatest value, every individual necessarily labours to render the annual revenue of the society as great as he can. He generally, indeed, neither intends to promote the public interest, nor knows how much he is promoting it. By preferring the support of domestic to that of foreign industry, he intends only his own security; and by directing that industry in such a manner as its produce may be of the greatest value, he intends only his own gain, and he is in this, as in many other cases, led by an *invisible hand* to promote an end which was not a part of his intention.

According to Keller (1994: 37),

> What we are dealing with her is, so to speak, a serious version of Mandeville's paradox. Whereas in *Fable of the Bees* the vices of the individual are painted in caricatured exaggeration as the motives generating the public good, this function is fulfilled in Adam Smith by selfishness and the urge towards 'personal security'.

Smith's explanation of the genesis of communal wealth has led to the 'invisible hand explanation' as a type, "a conjectural story of a phenomenon which is the result of human actions, but not the execution of any human design" (Keller 1994: 38).

Five distinguishing features of invisible hand explanations are given by Ullmann-Margalit (1978: 277–8):

1. the domain of explanation: the social domain;
2. the explained phenomena: well-structured social pattern that result from human actions and that look like the product of intentional design;
3. the nature of the explanation: a species within the genus of genetic explanations, it consists of a description of a special kind of process (= IH process), and is addressed to the question of the generation of the explained phenomenon;
4. the mode of explanation: displacing the intentional-design account that 'naturally suggests itself' with an account that specifies the working of a mechanism that aggregates the dispersed actions of individuals into the overall pattern (the *explanandum* phenomenon), subject to the assumption that the individuals concerned neither foresee this resultant of their actions nor intend to bring it about; and
5. idiosyncrasies of the explanation: its having both explanatory and explicatory import; its lending itself to be characterized as 'cogent' in addition to the usual categories of truth and falsity; its being a matter of degree (varying with the extent to the *explanandum* phenomenon is structured and with the complexity of the IH-process); the element of *surprise* attaching to it.

Keller (1994) builds a theory of language (change), which incorporates invisible hand explanation, "upon the generalized Mandevillean-Smithian idea that more or less homogeneous actions performed by a large group of individuals may cumulatively bring about social phenomena intended by no one" (Nyman 1994: 237). These are called "phenomena of the third kind" (Keller 1994: 57), among which is to be placed language, in an overview and outline such as the following:

1. Overview

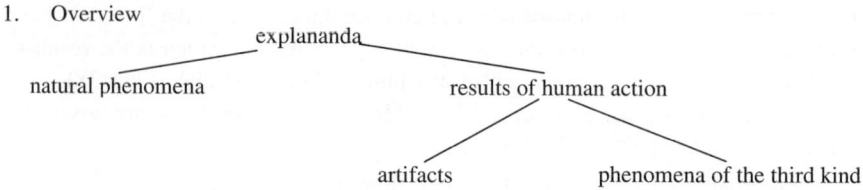

2. Outline

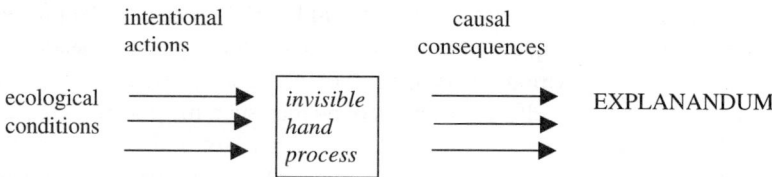

Keller (1994: 90) explains thus:

> On the left of the box is the micro-level, on the right the macro-level. The micro-level is the level at which one can situate the actions of the individuals involved, plus the relevant circumstances of their actions; the macro-level is the language in an hypostatised sense. The box itself represents the cumulative process which functions as a bridge between micro-level and macro-level.[1]

Nyman (1994) adds that "the macro-level explanation consists of identifying the LAWS that deterministically cause the EXPLANANDUM as an unintended, and possibly surprising, consequence of the IH-process", having *diagnostic*, not *prognostic*, value (p. 245). An example of an IH-phenomenon is described by Keller. It consists of four snapshots of a photographic series entitled "Ten minutes in front of the Pompidou Center". Curious onlookers form two circles on the square in order to watch two groups of street artists and traveling entertainers, shown in the last snap-shot. The first three pictures document the genesis of the two circles, never *planned* by anyone, but created spontaneously. None of the onlookers intended the emergence of this particular structure, and most of them probably never even noticed that their actions contributed to its formation.

A slightly different example of an IH-phenomenon, which highlights the distance between the *explanans* and the *explanandum* in terms of surprise and contradiction, is outlined by Nyman (1994: 243). It concerns a typical cocktail party scenario, in which one intends to be heard in a conversational setting

---

1. The 'ecological conditions' denote the totality of factors that influence the choice of an action.

involving background noise. In order to be heard, we raise our voices, but, as other people raise their voices also, the opposite of the desired effect is accomplished.

A brief taxonomy of the IH-situations referred to may be given as follows:

	unintended	surprising	paradoxical
Mandeville	+	+	+
Adam Smith	+	+	?
Pompidou	+	?	?
cocktail party	+	+	+?

The only common feature that is clear for all examples is the *sine qua non* for an IH-explanation, its unintended nature. Degrees of surprise and paradox may or may not be present.

5.1.2   Can grammaticalization be explained invisible-handedly?

As was mentioned in Chapter 3, 3.1.3, Bybee et al. (1994) give a rather "sober" assessment of the explanatory power of grammaticalization. They attribute no functional motivation to this process, since they "do not subscribe to the notion that languages develop grammatical categories because they NEED them" (p. 297). They take a purely mechanistic view (p. 298), claiming, rather, that "the processes that lead to grammaticalization occur in language use for their own sakes; it just happens that their cumulative effect is the development of grammar". Bybee et al. (1994: 300) add, however, that

> ... the push for grammaticization comes from below — it originates in the need to be more specific, in the tendency to infer as much as possible from the input, and the necessity of interpreting items in context.

I would like to claim that Bybee et al. actually supply the ingredients for an invisible hand explanation of grammaticalization, and will sketch briefly how the IH-schema can serve as a framework for this process.

It starts with the 'micro-world' of intentional actions, individual acts of communication by the most effective means available to the speaker, consisting, (a) on the *semantic* level, of concrete, or specific, concepts, and (b) on the *formal* level, of periphrastic, or syntactically 'robust', structures. The explananda, of course, are the grammaticalized forms, often affixes, most likely suffixes, if we accept the prefixation dispreference incorporated into grammaticalization, above, in Chapter 3. Following Keller's outline, we assume that the intentional actions of communication metamorphosed, by way of the invisible hand process, into the well-known causal consequences, captured by the so-called parallel reduction hypothesis (Bybee et al. 1994: 19), constituted by (a) semantic weakening ('bleaching'), or generalization, and (b) phonetic erosion. However, what has never been included in the sketching of grammaticalization before now becomes overt by way of the IH discussion: its *paradoxical* nature. I claim that the resulting generalized/grammaticalized form CONTRADICTS the concrete periphrasis existing at the outset, as it cannot any longer fulfill the goal of the intentional actions, that of communicating effectively. That leads to the well-known cycle of synthesis and analysis, or, equivalently, to the continuum of grammaticalization, the beginning of a new set of "intentional actions" — which, however, in turn are again "doomed", as if they were *programmed* for self-destruction.

Grammaticalization may, thus, be seen as the *unintended* and *paradoxical* consequence of efforts at effective communication, due to the invisible hand process. The PARADOX resides on two levels, as (a) effective communication becomes ineffective, needing compensation by new efforts, and (b) every grammaticalization continuum appears to be programmed for self-destruction. Of course, (b) actually captures the essence of the paradox, since the loss of effective communication must be due to the inexorable weakening or destructive evolution so characteristic during grammaticalization.[2]

Haspelmath (1997) also situates grammaticalization within an IH-explanation. He develops a detailed discussion of the components of Keller's outline (Ms., pp.10–11). Among the 'intentional actions', the notion of *extravagance* (= "Talk in such a way that you are noticed") is high-lighted, meant to replace and to rank above *expressivity* or 'most efficient means available', as mentioned above. The IH-process is then fleshed out by connecting three 'ecological conditions' with five 'maxims of action' in eight steps. This may be said to constitute another version of Bybee et al.'s (1994) parallel reduction hypothesis, Heine's (1993) four stages, and Lehmann's (1995) six parameters, but in a most explicit presentation and in terms of an invisible hand explanation. It may be summarized by Haspelmath's description of the culminating *explanandum* (1997: 11):

> An expression B-L, which was a lexical category at a certain stage of the language, has become a functional category B-F (with all sorts of accompanying phonological, semantic and syntactic changes).

---

2. See now also Ehala (1996), who considers language change to be due to 'self-organisation' having the 'goal' of a steady-state, or *homeostasis*, brought into existence by (teleological) processes "not designed to reach this state" (1996: 9).

Later, the beginning of the IH-process is pinpointed as "individual utterances of speakers who want to be noticed and who choose a new way of saying old things" (p. 14).

Haspelmath has succeeded in making the IH framework a most plausible one for an explanation of grammaticalization. In addition, he attempts to "derive irreversibility" in the lexical to functional change-over from such an explanation, an issue to be discussed in the following section.[3]

5.2 The explanatory potential of grammaticalization

5.2.1 *On the importance of irreversibility (unidirectionality)*

In a chapter entitled "Deconstructing grammaticalization", Newmeyer (1998) says that unidirectionality (of grammaticalization), if true, is "uninteresting" (1998: 262), unidirectionality is *not* true (1998: 263), and unidirectionality is *almost* true (1998: 275)! How can these seemingly contradictory statements be explained or reconciled? They point to a crucial miscommunication between "defenders" of grammaticalization (and thus of unidirectionality) and "opponents" to it. In the following, let us attempt to isolate the cause of this unfortunate state of affairs. It begins with the need to outline two distinct histories for grammaticalization:

a. the evolution of linguistic forms (= a 'physical' sequence or continuum, featuring the changeover from lexical to functional categories); and
b. the evolution of grammars (= a series of 'discontinuous' transmissions, or reanalyses, across generations).

Diagrammatically, we would be able to portray this contrast:

A. Lexical ⟶ Functional

B. Grammar x ⟶ Grammar $x+1$

An excellent case-study for this point of view is supplied by New Mexican Spanish *-nos*, as investigated in Janda (1995).

In New Mexican Spanish (and other regional dialects), the following first

---

3. Cf. Klausenburger (1998). Clements (1998: 16) proposes an intriguing view of grammaticalization within Chaos Theory: change in linguistic form is said to be predictable, but semantic change in grammaticalization, although regular, is claimed to be unpredictable and therefore chaotic.

person plural verb forms are heard (illustrated by *cantar* 'to sing'):

	I – *mos*		II – *nos*
PI	cantá<u>mos</u>	PS	cánte <u>nos</u>
Pret	cantá<u>mos</u>	II	cantába <u>nos</u>
F	cantaré<u>mos</u>	IS	cantára <u>nos</u>
		C	cantaría <u>nos</u>

(A stress mark is added to the spelling to show that Column I, signaling the 1PL by *-mos*, has penultimate stress, while there is antepenultimate stress in Column II, where *-nos* indicates 1PL).

Historically, this bifurcation of first person plurals no doubt looked like this:

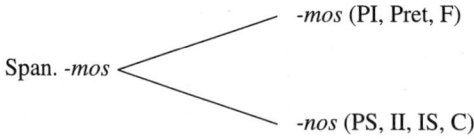

Span. *-mos* ⟨ *-mos* (PI, Pret, F) / *-nos* (PS, II, IS, C)

Janda (1995: 126) concludes that "… the switch from *-mos* to *-nos* involves the mutation of an agreement-affix into a subject-marking 'clitic' pronoun (or at least the acquisition of a subject-marking use by a former object-'clitic')". If we take this statement literally, it would confirm that an affix was "upgraded" to a clitic, a violation of unidirectionality in grammaticalization. However, Janda's use of "mutation" is inappropriate, since, by his own admission, there was no "purely phonological shift from /m/ to /n/" (p. 126). What he does mean, apparently, is that there occurred 'reanalysis' of the affix *-mos* by the clitic *nos*. His position would place the *nos*-evolution on Axis B, above, and could be fleshed out as follows:

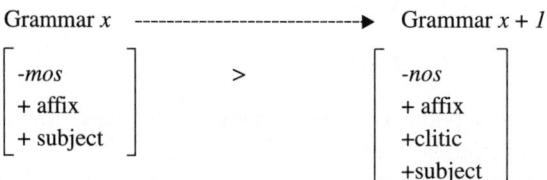

Grammar x ⟶ Grammar $x + 1$

$$\begin{bmatrix} \text{-}mos \\ + \text{affix} \\ + \text{subject} \end{bmatrix} > \begin{bmatrix} \text{-}nos \\ + \text{affix} \\ + \text{clitic} \\ + \text{subject} \end{bmatrix}$$

The shaft > is meant to symbolize the reanalysis having taken place. It constitutes, of course, a *replacement*: *-nos* has replaced *-mos* in the PS, II, IS, and C. However, the two grammars are discontinuous, and this schema misses the crucial *source* of the newly used *-nos*. Such a link will be supplied by Axis A:

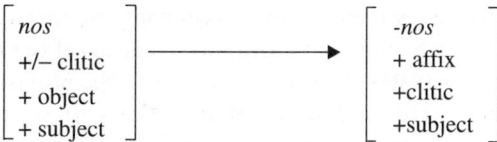

(The first *nos* describes the dative/accusative clitic *nos*, but also the *nos-* which is part of the (tonic) subject pronoun *nosotros*. The second *nos* captures the partially clitic status of *-nos* in New Mexican Spanish as the 1PL marker of the verb, made overt by the apparent stress shift to proparoxytonic in the PS).

In this evolution, the arrow means "actual linguistic change", and it does constitute a continuous sequence from a (more) lexical to a (more) functional unit, exactly as predicted in any definition of grammaticalization. Janda (1995: 120) argues that

> ... speakers simply do not have access to historical information that would be required in order to enforce unidirectionality directly ... [due to] phonological deformations which prevent speakers from (re)associating functional items with their lexical origins — due both to the unavailability of etymological information and the general arbitrariness of linguistic signs.

Although used by Janda as an argument *against* unidirectionality, this statement can plausibly be interpreted as favoring the latter, as long as the two axes of evolution, proposed above, are clearly kept distinct. Axis A reflects 'grammaticalization' as such, a continuum and inexorable evolution from lexical material to functional structure. Axis B, on the other hand, captures what speakers do from generation to generation. It is quite true that they have no access to previous historical stages. Therefore, their attempts at reanalysis may or *may not* reflect the (uni)directionality of the linguistic evolution understood as grammaticalization.[4]

---

4. The *nos/-mos* pair of New Mexican Spanish can be integrated into a long-term history from PIE as follows (based on Janda 1995: fn. 9):

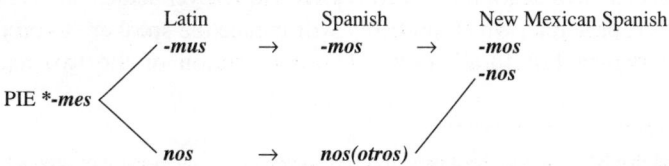

If this reconstruction is assumed to be correct, a first phase of grammaticalization took place from PIE to Latin, in the development of the suffix *-mus*. The second grammaticalization concerns the Spanish (clitic) pronoun evolving into a (clitic) affix in NMS. An interesting speculation complicates matters, however: since Spanish *-mos* and *nos* (by way of Latin) have the same source in PIE **mes*,

Let us return to Newmeyer's assessments of unidirectionality in grammaticalization. We can attempt to reconcile these contradictions by means of our two axes, above. When Newmeyer admits unidirectionality, it is with the proviso to "suppose that grammaticalization were, in fact, a distinct process. If so, then unidirectionality would be the most unremarkable fact imaginable" (Newmeyer 1998: 262). It is clear that the process characterization of grammaticalization becomes meaningful only in terms of Axis A in our depiction. Strong disagreement about how "unremarkable" unidirectionality would be in such a case has been expressed by Haspelmath (1997: 1):

> ... the irreversibility of the lexico-to-functional change is one of the most important constraints on possible language changes ...

Newmeyer dedicates the bulk of his discussion of unidirectionality to section 5.3 (1998: 263–75), in which it is declared *not true*. Here he presents capsule reviews of various cases of reversal found in the literature, always partials, never *complete* degrammaticalizations, agreeing that (1998: 263)

> ... it is certainly the case that complete reversals of grammaticalization are extremely rare, perhaps nonexistent. This should hardly be a cause of surprise ... it would be nothing less than a miracle if some aspect of the *precise* earlier stage of a language were recreated in degrammaticalization.

Like Janda (1995), Newmeyer actually makes a strong possible claim for unidirectionality as the essence or *raison d'être* of grammaticalization, if understood as Axis A, above. The (alleged) partial examples of bidirectional change include inflectional affix to clitic (like the NMS *-nos* discussed), affix to word, clitic to word, and syntactic changes, like hypotaxis to parataxis. I believe that they all fit on Axis B, constituting reanalyses in successive generations of speakers' grammars. Thus, they in no way violate the (inexorable) unidirectionality assumed on Axis A. Finally, Newmeyer, in Section 5.4, calls unidirectionality *almost* true. He stipulates this based on "a rough impression ... that downgradings have occurred at least ten times as often as upgradings" (275–276). As an explanation for such results, Newmeyer settles on a version of the least-effort principle, which probably will induce the speaker "to produce an affix rather than a full form" (276). In a conception of the two axes, this

---

could we claim that NMS *-nos* (at least partially) derives from *-mos*, an instance of reversal? Was the latter also involved in the uniform appearance of *-mos* in some other dialects, where it is not only the 1PL suffix of the verb (in all tenses) but the (clitic) pro as well, yielding also *mosotros*? Heath (1998: 751)'s hermit crab metaphor may also be relevant in this affix/clitic substitution.

scenario would mean that the speaker's reanalysis *coincides* with the (unidirectional) linguistic sequence on Axis A. Therefore, the two axes may evolve identically in a ratio of 10:1 over non-identity. However, this does not vitiate the valid distinction made in terms of language change vs. grammar change.[5]

Newmeyer is willing to grant to grammaticalization the status of "no more than a cover term for a conjunction of familiar developments from different spheres of language, none of which require or entail any of the others" (1998: 295).[6]

In a posting of the *Linguist List* of August 18, 1996, Dahl reacts to Newmeyer's assessment as follows:

> This to me seems like saying that since love and sex can occur without each other, they are totally different phenomena. For [Newmeyer's] argument to go through, he would have to show not only that the processes can occur independently but also that they are unrelated even in the well-documented cases when they show up together.

Interestingly, Newmeyer favorably reviews Roberts (1993), who considers grammaticalization an *explanandum*, not an *explanans* (1998: 292–4). Such a point of view, of course, implies that there is "something to be explained" in grammaticalization, and it is, in fact, *not* just a disparate set of individual changes which are involved.

If unidirectionality (irreversibility) is seen as the essence of grammaticalization, an explanatory framework for the latter would, by definition, also derive irreversibility. This is the exact position taken by Haspelmath (1997), employing the IH framework. He outlines two reasons why speakers do not "reverse" the order L > F (pp. 11–12):

1. To do so would require the opposite of *extravagance*, "a constant desire for understatement, a general predilection for litotes. Human speakers apparently are not like this" (Lehmann 1985: 315)
2. "Lexical elements are freely manipulable by speakers and ... accessible to consciousness, whereas functional elements are processed automatically and unconsciously".

The IH explanation seems to be able to bridge Axes A and B, proposed above.

---

5. An obviously close interaction of Axes A and B is envisaged, and the proposed alternate paths must not be interpreted as endorsing Lass' (rather depressing) concept of a "Ablösung der Sprache von der Menschenwelt" (1997: 388).
6. Similarly, Campbell (1998: 242) calls grammaticalization "derivative".

It connects human behavior directly to Axis A, causing actual language change. But the same "human factor" also is involved on Axis B, here in its capacity as grammar creator, or 'reanalysis maker'. This is then the true sense in which the IH structure constitutes the "overarching explanatory framework for this macrotendency" (i.e. unidirectionality) (Haspelmath 1997: 1).[7]

5.2.2 Morphocentricity

Unidirectionality is anchored crucially within "a conception of language in which grammar ... is morphocentric ..."(Joseph and Janda 1988: 196). For these authors, *morphologization* "describes any transition (via dephonologization or desyntacticization) from a state in which the corresponding generalization is nonmorphological in nature to a state in which the corresponding generalization is morphological in nature" (1988: 195). Therefore, grammaticalization, as defined currently, equates to *desyntacticization*, a subpart of two-pronged *morphologization* in Joseph and Janda's proposal. The 'norm', then, for all of morphologization must be unidirectionality, given the assumed *morphocentricity* of language, and the "centrality of morphology ... can ... be overcome, via demorphologization, only by massive accidental convergences of linguistic circumstances" (1988: 207, fn. 15).

Joseph and Janda's position finds corroboration and motivation by way of the semiotic framework advocated in Dressler (1985a). Making use of the Peircian triad of signs (symbols, indices, and icons), Dressler considers morphologization [here understood only as the change-over from phonology to morphology, the more conventional definition] to be the process of *de-iconization*, unidirectional because the only evolution possible among the three types of signs is icons > indices > symbols (1985a: 149).[8] Morphological signs are intrinsically indexical and one may establish, as a consequence, a "semiotic priority of morphology over phonology" (1985a: 303), because "morphological indexicality is higher valued than phonological indexicality" (p. 311). Two factors motivate morphologization: (a) the hierarchy of indexicality and (b) the efficiency of the change, in that there is an improvement in indexicality when phonology moves to

---

7. Lightfoot (1997: 358), in his reply to Bauer (1997), underlines that the change-over from *left-branching* to *right-branching*, proposed in Bauer 1995, "invokes the EVOLUTIONARY CONCEPT, in which general, linear, irreversible, and unidirectional changes are due to a natural selection process," a view which he, however, does not find plausible (cf. Lightfoot 1996).

8. McMahon (1994: 172) similarly considers grammaticalization as the "gradual fusion of icons into symbols".

morphology. The reverse development would, as a consequence, be unmotivatable.

In the face of such arguments, Morin et al. (1990) contend that the *phonologization* of an erstwhile morphophonological rule is not only possible, but they attempt to show that it may be the only plausible way to explain a change. Their example involves the change from a morphophonological rule of plur. tensing, O → [+tense] / __] N,A [+PL], to a phonological rule of word-final tensing, O → [+tense] / __], in the history of French (1990: 523). Morin et al. reconstruct the origin of the MP stage as due to the interaction of three post-Old French sound changes: (1) lengthening of stressed vowels in the plural, (2) loss of word-final consonants, and (3) tensing of long nonhigh vowels (p. 510). These deliver the singular/plural noun-adjective alternations attested in the early 18th century, exemplified by *gigot* [ʒigɔ] (SG) and *gigots* [ʒigo] (PL), a pair which has also incorporated a further phonetic change, one of word-final length neutralization (p. 511). One can say that the resulting MP rule constitutes a classic case of morphologization, as both phonetic and morphological conditionings may be said to play a role. It is also quite unexceptional in its next stage, the occurrence of paradigmatic leveling in the direction of one alternant, the plural, thus arriving at [ʒigo]–[ʒigo]. Until this point, the analysis has thus included two major phases, (a) morphologization of various phonetic changes into an MP rule of plural tensing in the beginning of the 18th century, and (b) the loss of this rule, visible in the paradigmatic regularization given. From this point on, Morin et al.'s examination becomes more controversial. They first reject one possible account of the leveling in question, one which would posit a rule inversion, something like O → [–tense] / __]N,A[+SG], and its subsequent loss, mainly because it would require the assumption of unmotivated markedness reversal, as the inversion would establish the plural an underlying category as concerns the singular (p. 515). Instead, they interpret the loss of the MP alternation as a case of generalization, leading to a rule like O → [+tense] / __]N,A. Actually, this alternative would also be acceptable, conventionally, accounting for the MP leveling of the original SG/PL alternation. For most theorists on morphologization, a sort of *Endstation* has now been reached: the paradigmatic leveling has put an end to the MP story — it can have no further evolution. However, Morin et al. claim that this story continues and the Modern French phonological rule of tensing derives *directly* from the previous MP rule of plural tensing, proceeding through various stages in which it is "progressively stripped of its morphological and lexical conditioning, so as to become maximally general ..." (p. 525). Morin et al.'s reasoning is the following (p. 520): "The first words affected were those to which rule (5) of plural O-Tensing had also applied; ergo, word-final O-Tensing is best explained as a generalization of plural O-Tensing". There is a *non sequitur* here, however. Although the authors have demonstrated the gradual spread of final O-Tensing throughout the French vocabulary, this does not prove it to be a *continuation*, a *phonologization*, of the original MP rule. Rather, it is reasonable to claim that the MP story has been completed. It has left the 'phonetic reality' of tense /o/ in final position in both members of the pair. Now, this phonetic/phonotactic fact of French pronunciation becomes generalized, *not* the MP 'non-alternation'. In this way, one is able to divorce the two evolutions, to insert a break between them, since *functionally* the phonological rule of today has nothing to do with the former morphophonological rule, schematically as follows:

Plural O-Tensing: O → [+tense] / __] N, A [+pl]
'General' Morphological Tensing: O → [+tense] / __] N, A, V

End of MP story

Generalization of phonetic/phonotactic residue of leveling
Phonological Rule of Tensing: O → [+tense] / __]

The proposed alternative to Morin et al.'s phonologization (a subcase of Joseph and Janda's *demorphologization*) is reminiscent of the cyclic view usually attributed to grammaticalization: a grammaticalized continuum (or cline) comes to an end (potentially constituted by zero), and a new one begins. Similarly, the loss of an MP-alternation leads to 'zero', or no rule. The P-residue may then phonologize, and (very likely) eventually morphologize in a *new* evolution. However, it is crucial to keep these histories distinct, just like it is clear that the starting point of a new grammaticalization continuum, the lexical (or syntactic) phase, cannot be considered a *genetic* evolution out of the previous grammaticalized affix (functional) state.[9]

The concept of morphocentricity, then, squarely puts the burden on unidirectionality's existence. As it supplies both origins of morphology, in the phonology and in the syntax, it doubly requires irreversibility. The fact that this can be demonstrated in the P > M evolution, i.e. in morphologization, as well as in the S > M evolution, i.e. grammaticalization, strengthens the position in favor

---

9. As pointed out by Haspelmath (1997: 5, fn. 2), Lightfoot (1979: 224–5) incorrectly portrays the classic synthesis/analysis cycle as an example of changes going in either direction, "moving at one stage from 'synthetic' to 'analytic' morphology, and at another stage in the reverse direction." The concept of *morphocentricity* remains to be worked out. It is likely that morphology must be considered, in some sense, *minimal* linguistic structure, to which (more) specific features are added in both phonology and syntax. Morphologization and grammaticalization would then consist of the "stripping", or removal, of such features, or conditionings.

of unidirectionality. The entire complex involved in morphocentricity receives the following schematization:

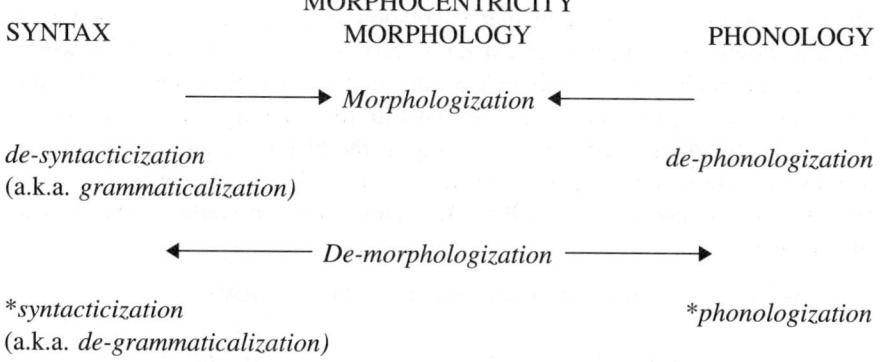

5.2.3 *Exaptation, regrammaticalization, degrammaticalization*

Lass (1990: 80) introduced the concept of *exaptation* into the literature on linguistic change, defining it as "opportunistic co-optation of a feature whose origin is unrelated or only marginally related to its later use." Vincent (1995: 437) compares and contrasts exaptation with grammaticalization as follows:

	Form	Content or Function
grammaticalization	NEW	NEW
exaptation	OLD	NEW

I would like to add two points to this schema. First, our analysis of Romance verbal grammaticalizations actually may question whether the function of a grammaticalized form is always new. As Vincent (1987) himself pointed out, there is a tight interaction between periphrasis and inflection in the history from Latin to the Romance languages, in the following ways:

a. In the evolution of the Romance future and past, there occurred not so much the creation of a new function but rather the "matching" of the Latin predecessors, since in the latter the future and past (perfect), of course, existed, the new structures entering as "replacements" of lost ones inherited from Latin. This is very clear in the case of the future, less so for the past, where it varies greatly from language to language.

b. The source of the grammaticalized forms in these evolutions, the Latin verb *habere*, by itself seems to perpetuate the (old) Latin function or content, certainly with respect to person and number marking.

Second, I would like to claim that exaptation may best be understood as a potential extension to a grammaticalization continuum, a development in which the affix, probably suffix, delivered as the end-point would not atrophy but would *undergo regrammaticalization,* an old form taking on new meaning. Vincent illustrates this very clearly by way of the history of the Italian clitic *li,* "a pronoun whose unambiguous function is to spell out objective case [but] derives from the nominative" (1995: 443). This evolution could be sketched in this manner:

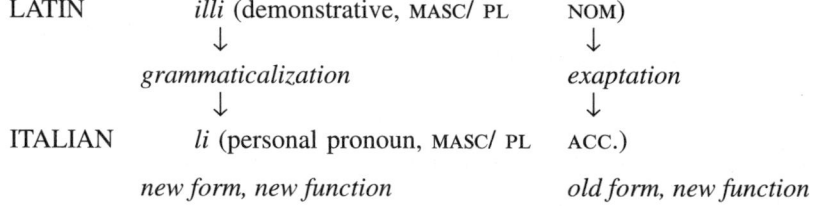

LATIN	*illi* (demonstrative, MASC/ PL	NOM)
	↓	↓
	grammaticalization	*exaptation*
	↓	↓
ITALIAN	*li* (personal pronoun, MASC/ PL	ACC.)
	new form, new function	*old form, new function*

The underlying cause for the exaptation in the clitic parallels that of the noun in Italian, in which the Latin nominative continues, not the accusative, due to the disappearance of the final /s/ in Eastern Romance. Here, however, no case distinction is signaled by the suffix, only gender and number. (See Chapter 4, 4.3).

Allen (1995) claims that the history of the suffix traditionally known as 'inchoative' from PIE via Latin to the Romance languages manifested grammaticalization, regrammaticalization, and degrammaticalization (p. 1). It can be demonstrated that the change from PIE *-sk-* to Latin *-sc-* constituted grammaticalization, in that there seems to have occurred a shift from derivational meaning (still evidenced in some older IE languages) to inflectional meaning, visible in a Latin inchoative like *senescere* "grow old" (from de-adjectival *senere* "be old", *senex* "old"). However, such an evolution is (almost) indistinguishable from what could be called regrammaticalization, since, in the Romance languages, if not already in Latin, this suffix also shows causative and transitive functions. Thus, while French 3PL *verdissent* "they become green" is inchoative, *blanchissent* "they whitewash, bleach" appears as a clear causative. In addition, the *-iss-* in *finissent* no longer seems to carry any kind of grammatical signal, and it has, according to Allen, therefore "degrammaticalized" (p. 5). He grants that this French example, along with Italian verbs like *finisco* and *capisco,* may also be considered regrammaticalizations, since the (erstwhile) inchoative could here be reinterpreted as an inflectional suffix of person and number. Furthermore, he notes that Rumanian has proliferated the inchoative (found in ca. 2800 verbs), but "the suffix *-esc-* serves as a buffer to prevent variation in the stem of many Romanian verbs ..." (p. 6). For him this result, which could be labeled the 'morphophonemic' function of the old inchoative, constitutes evidence of the strongest kind for degrammaticalization. Actually, Allen equates the degrammaticalization analysis of the inchoative to 'lexicalization' and believes that either concept would equal the *opposite* of grammaticalization, thus proving that the latter must not be seen as unidirectional (p. 1). Lexicalization in this sense had been called *demorphologization* in Klausenburger (1976, 1979), applied to Latin nasal infixation, a history very similar to that of the inchoative. As Joseph and Janda (1988) point out, however, it is preferable to consider such lexicalization as a further evolution in (their) *morphologization* (which includes grammaticalization), rather than demorphologization (which would incorporate degrammaticalization). In any case, even if Allen's degrammaticalization label is kept (cf. also Ramat 1992), this in no way can serve as proof for the absence of unidirectionality in grammaticalization, as discussed in the previous section, since no obvious *reversal* of an earlier grammaticalization cline has occurred. Therefore, Allen's inchoative example simply constitutes an idiosyncratic combination of grammaticalization, regrammaticalization, and degrammaticalization, as defined in this context. It does illustrate the (uncontroversial) concept of regrammaticalization, understood as a continuation of grammaticalization. However, degrammaticalization, in spite of its name, is best seen as an extension of grammaticalization also. Reduced to its essence, then, Allen (1995) deals with various aspects of the grammaticalization of the 'inchoative' suffix in Latin and the Romance languages.[10]

5.2.4 *Are grammatical categories discrete?*

Grammaticalization studies seem to challenge the notion of *categoriality*, since the latter must be replaced, according to Traugott & König (1991: 189), by

> ... the concept of a continuum of boundedness from independent units occurring in syntactically relatively free constructions at one end of the

---

10. According to Heath (1998: 732–3), grammaticalization is "... tightly controlled by system-internal considerations, including both the gross morphosyntactic form of the language (inflected, analytic, etc.) and a strong tendency to maintain preexisting categories (whether universal or language specific) whose prior expression had become unsatisfactory in one way or another".

continuum to less independent units such as clitics, connectives, particles, or auxiliaries, to fused agglutinative constructions, inflections and finally zero.

Similarly, Heine (1993: 116) refers to grammaticalization chains as "family resemblance categories", a notion which Steele (1994: 820) considers

> ... a reductio of the idea of grammaticalization. If all the points on a grammaticalization chain are associated with members of the same category, no line separates grammatical elements from lexical elements. Each member of the chain is grammatical to X extent and lexical to Y extent.

Steele raises an important point, and it is incumbent upon grammaticalization proponents to respond to such criticism. It turns out that a clarification on the (non)discreteness of grammatical categories will parallel the discussion on unidirectionality, above, in 5.2.1, making use of the same two axes. Let us return to the grammaticalization account of the Romance future given by Roberts (1993), first mentioned in Chapter 3, 3.1.3, as it will supply the most appropriate context for the issue to be resolved here.

Roberts' analysis is the only one extant which is positioned inside a "formal" framework, specifically the theory of Principles and Parameters syntax. Within this approach, grammaticalization, the change from lexical to functional category, is seen as "natural", in that a "category change from V to I takes place when a structure where V has moved to I is reanalyzed as one where the verbal element is base-generated in I" (1993: 227), due to a general mechanism of syntactic change, *diachronic reanalysis*. For the evolution of the Romance future from Latin, the grammaticalization of the verb *habere* occurred, or, in Roberts' terms, the movement of *habere* to I has been eliminated in favor of base generation of the verb in I. In this (limited) instance of grammaticalization, Roberts has been able to frame the change in terms of "a relationship between the grammars of successive generations" (p. 228), yielding *discrete* categories before and after the transition, (lexical) 'verb' to (functional) category of the future. However, as Haspelmath (1997: 9) has correctly noted, "Roberts' explanation can be made to work only because V-to-Infl has been motivated independently and has been widely adopted in Chomskyan linguistics". Thus, Roberts' implicit claim that his analysis would explain grammaticalization *in general* will receive confirmation only if he were "to assume N-to-P movement, Num-to-Det movement, and NP-to-Agr movement" (Haspelmath 1997: 9). Clearly, this is a partial explanation of grammaticalization at best, and it fails to account for the bulk of the historical changes that have been called instances of grammaticalization.

How can we relate the preceding discussion to the two axes representation offered in 5.2.1, above? It is apparent that Roberts' account situates itself on

Axis B, as it deals with the (discontinuous) transmission of grammars across generations. As such, *discrete* categories are involved, the type needed to "write a grammar", by definition. This conceptualization captures part of grammaticalization, but will, in all likelihood, it seems, never do justice to it completely.[11] For an exhaustive portrayal of the changes subsumed under "grammaticalization", we have to turn to Axis A, of course. Here, the continuum posited, again by definition, requires to be fleshed out by *nondiscrete* grammatical categories, a specific characteristic of the essence of grammaticalization. Simply put, if one desires to write grammars, one needs discrete categories, but if one focuses on historical evolution (a.k.a. grammaticalization), then one cannot (except arbitrarily) interrupt the continuous flow from lexical to functional categories. Far from being a *reductio* of grammaticalization, as Steele believes, such a state captures the *essence* of this process.[12]

The "complementary distribution" aspect ascribed to *discrete* vs. *nondiscrete* grammatical categories may also be relevant to a classification of functionalist vs. generative grammar in their interest in, or compatibility with, grammaticalization, as expressed by Trask, in a Linguist List posting of 8/26/96:

> The study of grammaticalization has seemingly revealed powerful regularities in the way speakers use languages, and, at the very least, the Chomskyan approach simply has nothing to say about these regularities. Grammaticalization proceeds in a manner which is inconsistent with a fundamental Chomskyan assumption (well-defined grammars), and it proceeds in identifiable directions which are inexplicable in Chomskyan terms.

Croft, in a posting of the same date, adds that "it is possible that the regularity and potential explanatory significance of grammaticalization is in itself perceived as a challenge to generative grammar".

---

11. Cf. Battye and Roberts (1995: 11), who state that "language change is essentially a random 'walk' through the space of possible parameter settings".

12. Although the "family resemblance categories" attributed to grammaticalization by Heine (1993) may at first glance seem to approach "prototype categories", they are crucially distinguished, as the following statement by Taylor (1995: 53) makes clear: "Prototype categories have a flexibility, unknown to Aristotelian categories, in being able to accommodate new, hitherto unfamiliar data. With only Aristotelian categories at our disposal, new data would often demand, for their categorization, the creation of new categories, or a redefinition of existing categories. On the other hand, new entities and new experiences can be readily associated, perhaps as peripheral members, to a prototype category, without necessarily causing any fundamental restructuring of the category system". One can immediately appreciate that such a description of prototype categories in no way would duplicate, or even come close to, the stages in the grammaticalization continuum.

CHAPTER 6

Conclusions

6.1 Results of this study

6.1.1 *Inflectional morphology*

6.1.1.1 *Verbal inflections*

In Chapter 2, the Latin verb and its evolution into French and Italian were cast into the framework of Natural Morphology, both of the "universal" variety (represented by Mayerthaler 1981, 1988) and of the "system dependent" approach (advocated in Wurzel 1984, 1989). The Latin structure turned out to be a highly iconic one, and the *system congruity* (SC) of this period was fleshed out in terms of *system defining structural properties* (SDSPs), their existence, along with that of (default) *paradigm structure conditions,* being verified by Late Latin developments. It was discovered, however, that the well-known "analytic" tendency in post-Classical Latin verbal changes could not be reconciled with the parameter of SC, an apparent instance of "Wurzel's problem" (to be 'solved' within the grammaticalization proposal of Chapter 3), while it did confirm the prediction in the direction of "more iconicity". Selected analogies in the evolution of the French and Italian verb were also subjected to a 'natural' analysis. This study reinforced the major role played by *schwa generalization,* which led to uniform coding, or paradigmatic leveling, delivering the default PSC and unmarked SDSP of Modern French verbs, non-iconicity, or invariance. In addition, long standing issues concerning the evolution of three Italian verbal suffixes were given satisfactory solutions by way of universal and language specific parameters of naturalness.

6.1.1.2 *Nominal inflections*
The most revealing histories in this domain were constituted by Old French and Rumanian, the best illustrations of a continuation of the Latin case system (Chapter 4). Modern Rumanian case structure manifests clear-cut iconicity,

arguably the principal characteristic of its SC and lending stability to the structure. A natural morphological analysis of Old French nouns and adjectives revolves around the role played by the suffix -*s*. The already existing counter-iconicity in the NOM.SG.MASC due to this /s/ is augmented by the well-known analogical shifts visible in Old French texts, in which we find non-etymological -*s* in both masculine and feminine nouns. Such additions can only be motivated on the model of a default PSC and they, obviously, contradict iconicity factors. Nominal evolution also underwent changes in SDSPs, caused by extra-morphological features, such as sound change, according to Wurzel's theory. These are also sketched in this study, focusing on resultant non-iconicity in Modern French. The latter joins a structure reached by the verb, permitting a clear global characterization of French inflectional morphology. Chapter 4 also briefly speculates on the history of the Latin noun in other Romance languages, making use of natural methodology in an attempt to shed light on recalcitrant questions in Romance linguistics.

6.1.2 *Grammaticalization*

This study hinges on Chapter 3, in which a theory of grammaticalization is constructed, consisting of diverse elements. It is based in Heine (1993), but it is supplemented by a perception/production model (Hall 1992), and by typological concerns (Bauer 1995). This theoretical structure aims to do two things, (1) serve as a vehicle for the analysis of significant Romance developments ('periphrastic' verbs, French subject pronouns, Romance object clitics, Romance definite article), and (2) integrate inflectional morphology into a (more) comprehensive framework. Parameters of grammaticalization are shown to allow the phasing out of the traditional synthesis/analysis cycle, supplying a much more systematic consideration of the development of auxiliaries of Romance past tenses vs. that of the future and conditional. The work on syntactic branching by Bauer and that of Hall on linguistic processing, crucial components of the grammaticalization proposal of Chapter 3, contribute promising avenues of explanation for the suffixation (future/conditional) vs. non-affixation (past tenses) conundrum in the history of Romance, as they do for an evaluation of the status of the French subject pronoun, Romance object clitics, and the Rumanian definite article vs. that of the other Romance languages on the word/clitic/affix continuum.

The grammaticalization proposal also supplies a direct link to the inflectional morphological details discussed. Specifically, all inflection is claimed to be subordinated to grammaticalization, as only one (late) stage in a grammaticalization cline or chain. For the Romance field, this means (roughly) two continua:

1. Grammaticalization delivering the Latin inflectional system. This would necessitate a reconstruction from PIE to Latin, an evolution recapitulated in many historical grammars, but not repeated here. A part of this cline, its continuation from Latin to the Romance languages, does appear in this study, mainly in Chapter 2. It constitutes evidence that the inflectional stage of the grammaticalization continuum may evolve further, potentially to zero, as illustrated in the atrophying of French P/N suffixes.
2. Grammaticalization delivering Romance suffixes and "non-affixation". Here, the Romance future/conditional history and the Rumanian definite article are obvious examples of suffixation and the rest of the material illustrates "non-affixation". The reasons for this non-affixation as a (probable) end-point are outlined in Chapter 3 and, limited to the Romance definite article, in Chapter 4.

It can be said that the irreversibility of grammaticalization, fully motivated in Chapter 5, implying the morphocentricity of language structure/evolution, renders a final verdict against the autonomy of inflections. One may state without hesitation, therefore, that "a theory of inflectional morphology must be a theory of grammaticalization".

6.2 Grammaticalization and naturalness

Heine et al. (1991: 121) conclude that "naturalness theory and grammaticalization deal with drastically different perspectives of linguistic behavior". This is a surprising assessment, since they had supplied (on the preceding page) "some striking parallels between the two". Such parallelism concerns in particular the unidirectionality principle. It is an integral part of grammaticalization, perhaps its *explanans*,[1] but it is equally essential for natural morphology, as "adherents of naturalness theory argue that linguistic change leads from 'non-preferential' marked phenomena to 'preferential' unmarked phenomena, not vice-versa" (Heine et al.1991: 120). Throughout this study, we have made reference to changes of this type, both within system-independent natural morphology, where

---

1. Heine (1997: 232) states: "Explanation is closely related to prediction ... [which relates] ... not only to future situations but also to unknown synchronic states and reconstructed past situations ... when derived from regularities of diachronic evolution." The question arises whether such a definition of explanation surpasses Lass' "feeble relativism": "Loosely, some phenomenon X is explained when our puzzlement about it is diminished, in some way and to some degree consonant with our expectations" (1997: 326). The answer should be in the affirmative ...

a reduction of markedness and a movement toward 'more iconicity' are predicted, and within system-dependent natural morphology, in which developments triggered by (unmarked) system congruity and default paradigm structure conditions are expected.

The last section concluded that a theory of inflectional morphology (such as natural morphology) must also be a theory of grammaticalization. The reverse can also be maintained: "Principles of grammaticalization are also principles of naturalness". They constitute but one field of inquiry in linguistics, one which Lightfoot (1997: 358) has called the "realist tradition".[2]

Specific features of the overlap between parameters of natural morphology and grammaticalization are the following:[3]

1. the 'iconicity' of robust linguistic form coinciding with concrete meaning vs. the coincidence of reduced phonological shape with abstract/functional meaning; and
2. the rise of 'marked' structures to take over the function of atrophied devices, as at the outset of a new cline of grammaticalization (cf. above, Chapter 5, the explanation of grammaticalization as an invisible hand process), finds a parallel in the changeover from one SDSP to another within Wurzel's version of natural morphology.

Both of these aspects were best illustrated in the examination of the occurrence of periphrasis in the evolution of the Latin verb into the Romance languages (Chapter 3). In the final analysis, it serves as the strongest evidence for the intimate tie-in between grammaticalization and natural morphology.

This evolution was dealt with, specifically, in terms of "the grammaticalization of auxiliaries" in Chapter 3, 3.1.3, and it qualifies to go under the rubric of an invisible hand explanation (Chapter 5, 5.1.2), which, in turn, would lead to an exemplification of irreversibility, or unidirectionality, discussed in 5.2.1. Let us recapitulate its essence by way of the following data:

---

2. Lightfoot claims that there has always existed a tension between such an approach and the "autonomous" way of doing linguistics. This division has also been framed in a functionalist vs. (formal) generativist dichotomy.

3. These are assumed to be more significant than the differences between the two, as summarized by Heine et al. (1991:121): "The former [i.e. naturalness] is concerned with factors such as co-occurrence and compatibility conditions holding between different linguistic structures both within a given language and between languages, while the latter [i.e. grammaticalization] is essentially concerned with the creative manipulation of language". In addition, of course, the very essence of grammaticalization disallows the "one form one meaning" principle, which does play a major role in natural morphology, in particular in the "universal" version.

Latin Compound Verb Structures in Romance

Latin	French	Spanish	Italian
HABEO CANTATUM	j'ai chanté	he cantado	ho cantato
HABEBAM CANTATUM	j'avais chanté	había cantado	avevo cantato
CANTARE HABEO	je chanterai	cantaré	canterò
CANTARE HABEBAM	je chanterais	cantaría	canterei
HABERE HABEO CANTATUM	j'aurai chanté	habré cantado	avrò cantato
HABERE HABEBAM CANTATUM	j'aurais chanté	habría cantado	avrei cantato

Such verbal evolutions contain all the crucial aspects of this study:

1. Right-branching HABEO CANTATUM and HABEBAM CANTATUM delivered the Romance compound past and pluperfect with the auxiliary "to have" remaining pre-posed, as a proclitic, incompletely grammaticalized in not reaching affix (i.e., prefix) status.
2. Left-branching CANTARE HABEO and CANTARE HABEBAM, on the other hand, resulted in the Romance future and conditional, the same auxiliary turning into suffixes, as predicted by the *suffixing preference*, constituting complete grammaticalization.
3. The remaining two transformations combine both the right-branching and left branching structures and, as a consequence, deliver both preposed proclitics of the auxiliary in the future perfect and past conditional and suffixation of the auxiliary itself: the "second" auxiliary HABEO and HABEBAM became the suffix to the "first" auxiliary HABERE.

These specific formal changes fit the invisible hand scenario outlined in 5.1.2, above, not repeated here, which also supplies the semantic side of the developments. Both parts were also discussed in much detail in Chapter 3, 3.1.3. In addition, the irreversibility of the lexical to functional change-over is derivable from the IH framework. This means that the evolution of the various Latin periphrases shown takes place on Axis A of the two possible grammaticalization axes proposed in 5.2.1, above.

The rise of periphrastic structures in Late Latin may be clearly motivated within the invisible hand schema and their "partial" and "complete" grammaticalization in the Romance languages follows the expected unidirectionality of this process. However, it was pointed out at the outset of this chapter that such an evolution is apparently not reconcilable within the system-dependent version of Natural Morphology of Wurzel's (cf. Chapter 1, 1.1.2), since inflectional suffixation was 'system defining' in Latin, not right-branching periphrasis. Periphrasis, on the other hand, may be said to be more iconic than suffixation, and its existence would then be predicted within system-independent, or universal Natural Morphology, as proposed by Mayerthaler (cf. Chapter 1, 1.1.1). Of course, changes in SDSPs are envisaged by Wurzel, caused by extra-morphological factors, either phonological or syntactic. A combination of the two is traditionally assumed for the beginning of so-called analytic structure in Late Latin. This assumption is now theoretically fleshed out by means of the grammaticalization/natural morphology interface.[4]

---

4. For the most current and recent review of issues in grammaticalization, see now Giacalone Ramat (1998).

Appendix

Latin and Romance verbs

I make use of ten tense–mood abbreviations (cf. the analysis of Chapter 2):

- PI present indicative
- PS present subjunctive
- II imperfect indicative
- IS imperfect subjunctive
- PeI perfect indicative
- PeS perfect subjunctive
- PPI pluperfect indicative
- PPS pluperfect subjunctive
- F future indicative
- FP future perfect indicative

The Romance forms marked with + indicate analogical changes, and they are discussed in 2.4, above.

ACTIVE

	French	Latin	Italian
PI	*(je) chante* +	*canto*	*cant o*
	chantes	*cantas*	*canti* +
	chante	*cantat*	*canta*
	chantons +	*cantamus*	*cantiamo* +
	chantez	*cantatis*	*cantate*
	chantent	*cantant*	*cantano* +
PS	*(je) chante* +	*cantem*	*canti* +
	chantes +	*cantes*	*canti* +
	chante +	*cantet*	*canti* +
	chantions +	*cantemus*	*cantiamo* +
	chantiez +	*cantetis*	*cantiate* +
	chantent	*cantent*	*cantino* +

APPENDIX

II	*(je) chantais +*	*cantabam*	*cantavo +*
	chantais +	*cantabas*	*cantavi +*
	chantait +	*cantabat*	*cantava*
	chantions +	*cantabamus*	*cantavamo*
	chantiez +	*cantabatis*	*cantavate*
	chantaient +	*cantabant*	*cantavano*
IS		*cantarem*	
		cantares	
		cantaret	
		cantaremus	
		cantaretis	
		cantarent	
PeI	*(je) chantai*	*cantavi*	*cantai*
	chantas +	*cantavisti*	*cantasti +*
	chanta	*cantavit*	*cantò*
	chantâmes +	*cantavimus*	*cantammo*
	chantâtes +	*cantavistis*	*cantaste +*
	chantèrent +	*cantaverunt*	*cantarono +*
PeS		*cantaverim*	
		cantaveris	
		cantaverit	
		cantaverimus	
		cantaveritis	
		cantaverint	
PPI		*cantaveram*	
		cantaveras	
		cantaverat	
		cantaveramus	
		cantaveratis	
		cantaverant	
PPS	*(je) chantasse +*	*cantavissem*	*cantassi +*
	chantasses +	*cantavisses*	*cantassi +*
	chantât +	*cantavisset*	*cantasse +*
	chantassions +	*cantavissemus*	*cantassimo +*
	chantassiez +	*cantavissetis*	*cantaste +*
	chantassent +	*cantavissent*	*cantassero +*

APPENDIX

F   *cantabo*
           cantabis
           cantabit
           cantabimus
           cantabitis
           cantabunt

FP   *cantavero*
           cantaveris
           cantaverit
           cantaverimus
           cantaveritis
           cantaverint

		Old French	**Latin**	**Italian**
PI	*(j')aime*	*aim*	*amo*	*amo*
	aimes	*aimes*	*amas*	*ami*
	aime	*aime*	*amat*	*ama*
	aimons +	*amons*	*amamus*	*amiamo*
	aimez +	*amez*	*amatis*	*amate*
	aiment	*aiment*	*amant*	*amano*
PS	*(j')aime*	*aim*	*amem*	*ami*
	aimes	*ains*	*ames*	*ami*
	aime	*aint*	*amet*	*ami*
	aimions +	*amons*	*amemus*	*amiamo*
	aimiez +	*amez*	*ametis*	*amiate*
	aiment	*aiment*	*ament*	*amino*

PASSIVE

	French	**Latin**	**Italian**
PI		*laudor*	
		laudaris	
		laudatur	
		laudamur	
		laudamini	
		laudantur	

PS		*lauder*	
		lauderis	
		laudetur	
		laudemur	
		laudemini	
		laudentur	
II		*laudabar*	
		laudabaris	
		laudabatur	
		laudabamur	
		laudabamini	
		laudabantur	
IS		*laudarer*	
		laudareris	
		laudaretur	
		laudaremur	
		laudaremini	
		laudarentur	
PeI	*(je) suis loué +*	*laudatus sum*	*sono lodato +*
	es loué	*laudatus es*	*sei lodato +*
	est loué	*laudatus est*	*è lodato*
	sommes loués +	*laudati sumus*	*siamo lodati +*
	êtes loués +	*laudati estis*	*siete lodati +*
	sont loués	*laudati sunt*	*sono lodati +*
PeS	*(je) sois loué +*	*laudatus sim*	*sia lodato +*
	sois loué +	*laudatus sis*	*sia lodato +*
	soit loué +	*laudatus sit*	*sia lodato +*
	soyons loués +	*laudati simus*	*siamo lodati +*
	soyez loués +	*laudati sitis*	*siate lodati +*
	soient loués +	*laudati sint*	*siano lodati +*
PPI	*(j')étais loué +*	*laudatus eram*	*ero lodato +*
	étais loué +	*laudatus eras*	*eri lodato +*
	était loué +	*laudatus erat*	*era lodato*
	étions loués +	*laudati eramus*	*eravamo lodati +*
	étiez loués +	*laudati eratis*	*eravate lodati +*
	étaient loués +	*laudati erant*	*erano lodati +*

PPS	*laudatus essem*
	laudatus esses
	laudatus esset
	laudati essemus
	laudati essetis
	laudati essent
F	*laudabor*
	laudaberis
	laudabitur
	laudabimur
	laudabimini
	laudabuntur
FP	*laudatus ero*
	laudatis eris
	laudatus erit
	laudati erimus
	laudati eritis
	laudati erunt

References

Adams, Marianne. 1987a. "From Old French to the Theory of Pro-Drop". *Natural Language and Linguistic Theory* 5.1–32.
———. 1987b. *Old French, Null Subjects, and Verb Second Phenomena*. Unpub. Ph.D. Dissertation, UCLA.
Allen, Andrew. 1995."Regrammaticalization and Degrammaticalization of the Inchoative Suffix". *Historical linguistics 1993*, ed. by Henning Andersen, 1–8. Amsterdam & Philadelphia: John Benjamins.
Anderson, Stephen. 1992. *A-morphous Morphology*. Cambridge: Cambridge Univ. Press.
Ashby, William. 1977. *Clitic Inflection in French: An Historical Perspective*. Amsterdam: Rodopi.
———. 1980. "Prefixed Inflection in Parisian French". *Italic and Romance. Linguistic Studies in Honor of Ernst Pulgram*, ed. by Herbert Izzo, 195–207. Amsterdam & Philadelphia: John Benjamins.
———. 1982. "The Drift of French Syntax". *Lingua* 57.29–46.
———. 1988. "The Syntax, Pragmatics, and Sociolinguistics of Left- and Right-Dislocations in French". *Lingua* 75.203–229.
Auger, Julie. 1993. "More Evidence for Verbal Agreement-Marking in Colloquial French". *Linguistic Perspectives on the Romance Languages*, ed. by William Ashby et al., 177–198. Amsterdam & Philadelphia: John Benjamins.
Baldinger, Kurt. 1968. "Post- und Prädeterminierung im Französischen". *Festschrift Walther von Wartburg*, ed. by Kurt Baldinger, 87–106. Tübingen: Niemeyer.
Barnes, Betsy. 1985. *The Pragmatics of Left Detachment in Spoken Standard French*. Amsterdam & Philadelphia: John Benjamins.
Battistella, Edwin. 1990. *Markedness. The Evaluative Superstructure of Language*. Albany: SUNY.
Battye, Adrian & Ian Roberts, eds.1995. *Clause Structure and Language Change*. Oxford: Oxford Univ. Press.
Bauer, Brigitte. 1995. *The Emergence and Development of SVO Patterning in Latin and French. Diachronic and Psycholinguistic Perspectives*. Oxford: Oxford Univ. Press.
———. 1997. Response to Lightfoot's Review of Bauer 1995. *Language* 73.352–358.
Blake, Barry. 1994. *Case*. Cambridge: Cambridge Univ. Press.
Blasco, Mylene. 1997. "Pour une approche syntaxique des dislocations". *French Language Studies* 7.1–21.

REFERENCES

Bossong, Georg. 1985. "Zur Entwicklungsdynamik von Kasussystemen". *Folia Linguistica Historica* 6.285–321.
Brandi, Luciana & P. Cordin. 1989. "Two Italian Dialects and the Null Subject Parameter". *The Null Subject Parameter*, ed. by Osvaldo Jaeggli & Kenneth Safir, 111–142. Dordrecht: Kluwer.
Bybee, Joan. 1985. *Morphology. A Study of the Relation Between Meaning and Form.* Amsterdam & Philadelphia: John Benjamins.
—————. 1988. "The Diachronic Dimension in Explanation". *Explaining Language Universals*, ed. by John Hawkins, 350–379. Oxford: Blackwell.
—————, Revere Perkins & W. Pagliuca. 1994. *The Evolution of Grammar. Tense, Aspect, and Modality in the Languages of the World.* Chicago: University of Chicago Press.
Campbell, Lyle. 1998. *Historical Linguistics. An Introduction.* Cambridge, Mass.: MIT Press.
Carrasquel, José. 1995. *The Evolution of Demonstrative* **ille** *from Latin to Modern Spanish: a Grammaticalization Analysis.* Unpub. PhD. Dissertation, Univ. of Washington, Seattle.
Carstairs, Andrew. 1987. *Allomorphy in Inflexion.* London: Croom Helm.
Carstairs-McCarthy, Andrew. 1992. *Current Morphology.* London: Routledge.
Clements, J. Clancy. 1998."A Creole Contribution to the Notion of Grammaticalization". Ms., Indiana University.
Corbett, Noel. 1969. "The French Verbal Flexion *-ons* as a Result of Homonymy". *Romance Philology* 22.421–431.
Croft, William. 1996. Posting on *Linguist List.* 8/26/96.
Cutler, Ann, et al. 1985. "The Suffixing Preference: a Processing Explanation". *Linguistics* 23.723–758.
Dahl, Östen. 1996. Posting on *Linguist List.* 8/18/96.
Dardel, Robert de & Paul Gaeng. 1992. "La déclinaison nominale du latin non-classique: essai d'une méthode de synthèse". *Probus* 4.91–125.
————— & Jakob Wüest. 1993. "Les systèmes casuels du protoroman. Les deux cycles de simplification". *Vox Romanica* 52.25–65.
Dees, A. et al. 1980. "Un cas d'analogie: l'introduction de *-e* à la première personne du singulier de l'indicatif présent des verbes en *-er* en ancien français". *Rapports / Het Franse Boek* 50.105–110.
De Poerck, Guy. 1963. "Les plus anciens textes de la langue française comme témoins de l'époque". *Revue de Linguistique Romane* 27.1–34.
D'Ovidio, F. 1899. "Ancora sulla etimologia delle forme grammaticali italiane *amano, dicono* ecc.". *Zeitschrift für romanische Philologie* 23.313–320.
Dressler, Wolfgang. 1985a. *Morphonology: the Dynamics of Derivation.* Ann Arbor: Karoma.
—————. 1985b. "On the Predictiveness of Natural Morphology". *Journal of Linguistics* 21.321–337.

————— ed. 1987. *Leitmotifs in Natural Morphology*. Amsterdam & Philadelphia: John Benjamins.
Dufresne, Monique & Fernande Dupuis. 1994. "Modularity and Reanalysis of the French Subject Pronoun". *Probus* 6.103–123.
Ehala, Martin. 1996. "Self-Organisation and Language Change". *Diachronica* 13.1–28.
Einhorn, E. 1974. *Old French. A Concise Handbook*. Cambridge: Cambridge Univ. Press.
Epstein, Richard. 1995. "The Later Stages in the Development of the Definite Article: Evidence from French". *Historical linguistics 1993*, ed. by Henning Andersen, 159–175. Amsterdam & Philadelphia: John Benjamins.
Everett, Daniel. 1996. *Why There Are No Clitics. An Alternative Perspective on Pronominal Allomorphy*. Summer Institute of Linguistics, Publications in Linguistics 123. The University of Texas at Arlington.
Fertig, David. 1998. "Suppletion, Natural Morphology, and Diagrammaticity". *Linguistics* 36.1065–1091.
Fleischman, Suzanne. 1982. *The Future in Thought and Language*. Cambridge: Cambridge Univ. Press.
—————. 1983. "From Pragmatics to Grammar: Diachronic Reflections on Complex Pasts and Futures in Romance". *Lingua* 60.183–214.
Foerster, W. 1898. "Die toskanische Endung *a/ono* der 3.Pluralis Praesentis". *Zeitschrift für romanische Philologie* 22.521–525.
Geisler, Hans. 1982. *Studien zur typologischen Entwicklung. Latein — Altfranzösisch — Neufranzösisch*. Munich: Fink.
Giacalone-Ramat, Anna. 1995. "Iconicity in Grammaticalization Processes". *Iconicity in Languages*, ed. by R. Simone, 119–139. Amsterdam & Philadelphia: John Benjamins.
—————. 1998. "Testing the Boundaries of Grammaticalization". *The Limits of Grammaticalization*, ed. by Anna Giacalone-Ramat & Paul J. Hopper, 107–127. Amsterdam & Philadelphia: John Benjamins.
Grandgent, Charles. 1927. *From Latin to Italian*. Cambridge, Mass.: Harvard University.
Green, John. 1987. "The evolution of Romance Auxiliaries: Criteria and Chronology". *The Historical Development of Auxiliaries*, ed. by Martin Harris & Paolo Ramat, 257–267. Berlin: Mouton de Gruyter.
Greenberg, Joseph. 1966. *Language Universals*. The Hague: Mouton.
Hall, Christopher. 1992. *Morphology and Mind. A Unified Approach to Explanation in Linguistics*. London: Routledge.
Halpern, Aaron. 1995. *On the Placement and Morphology of Clitics*. Stanford: CSLI Publications.
Harris, Martin. 1978. *The Evolution of French Syntax: A Comparative Approach*. London: Longman.
————— & Nigel Vincent, eds. 1988. *The Romance Languages*. Oxford: Oxford Univ. Press.

Haspelmath, Martin. 1997. "Why is the Change From Lexical to Functional Categories Irreversible"? Paper Read at the 13th ICHL, Düsseldorf, August 1997.
Heath, Jeffrey. 1998. "Hermit Crabs: Formal Renewal of Morphology by Phonologically Mediated Affix Substitution". *Language* 74.728–759.
Heine, Bernd. 1993. *Auxiliaries. Cognitive Forces and Grammaticalization*. Oxford: Oxford Univ. Press.
———. 1994. "Grammaticalization as an Explanatory Parameter". *Perspectives on Grammaticalization*, ed. by William Pagliuca, 255–287. Amsterdam & Philadelphia: John Benjamins.
———. 1997. *Possession. Cognitive Sources, Forces, and Grammaticalization*. Cambridge: Cambridge Univ. Press.
———, Ulrike Claudi & Friederike Hünnemeyer. 1991. *Grammaticalization. A Conceptual Framework*. Chicago: University of Chicago Press.
Herschensohn, Julia. 1993. "Applying Linguistics to Teach Morphology: Verb and Adjective Inflection in French". *International Review of Applied Linguistics* 31.97–112.
Hopper, Paul & Elizabeth Traugott. 1993. *Grammaticalization*. Cambridge: Cambridge Univ. Press.
Horne, Merle. 1990. "The Clitic Group as a Prosodic Category in Old French". *Lingua* 82.1–13.
Hunnius, Klaus. 1977. "Frz. *je*: ein präfigiertes Konjugationsmorphem"? *Archiv für das Studium der neueren Sprachen* 214.37–48.
———. 1991. "*T'as vu*? — Die Deklination der klitischen Personalpronomina im Französischen". *Zeitschrift für französische Sprache und Literatur* 101.113–124.
Jacob, Daniel. 1990. *Markierung von Aktantenfunktionen und "Prädetermination" im Französischen*. Tübingen: Niemeyer.
Jaeggli, Osvaldo & Kenneth Safir. 1989. "The Null Subject Parameter and Parametric Theory". *The Null Subject Parameter*, ed. by Osvaldo Jaeggli & Kenneth Safir, 1–44. Dordrecht: Kluwer.
Janda, Richard. 1995. "From Agreement Suffix to Subject 'Clitic'- and Bound Root: *-mos >-nos* vs.(-)*nos*(-) and *nos-otros* in New Mexican and Other Regional Spanish Dialects". *CLS 31: Papers From the 31st Regional Meeting of the Chicago Linguistics Society, 1995, Volume 2: The Parasession on Clitics*, ed. by A. Dainora et al.,118–139. Chicago: Chicago Linguistic Society.
Jensen, Frede. 1971. *The Italian Verb. A Morphological Study*. Chapel Hill: University of North Carolina Press.
———. 1976. *The Old Provençal Noun and Adjective Declension*. Odense: University of Odense Press.
Joseph, Brian & Richard Janda. 1988. "The How and Why of Diachronic Morphologization and Demorphologization". *Theoretical Morphology*, ed. by Michael Hammond & Michael Noonan, 193–210. New York: Academic Press.

Joseph, John. 1988. "Inflection and Periphrastic Structures in Romance". *Studies in Romance Linguistics*, ed. by Carl Kirschner and Janet De Cesaris, 195–208. Amsterdam & Philadelphia: John Benjamins.

Kaiser, Georg. 1992. *Die klitischen Personalpronomina im Französischen und Portugiesischen. Eine synchronische und diachronische Analyse*. Frankfurt: Vervuert.

Kefer, Michel. 1985. "What Syntax Can Be Reconstructed From Morphology"? *Lingua* 66.151–175.

Keller, Rudi. 1994. *On Language Change. The Invisible Hand in Language*. London and New York: Routledge.

Kilani-Schoch, Marianne. 1988. *Introduction à la morphologie naturelle*. Berne: Lang.

Klausenburger, Jurgen. 1970. *French Prosodics and Phonotactics. An Historical Typology*. Tübingen: Niemeyer.

———. 1976. "(De)-morphologization in Latin". *Lingua* 40.305–320.

———.1979. *Morphologization. Studies in Latin and Romance Morphophonology*. Tübingen: Niemeyer.

———. 1986. "Two Aspects of Morphological Naturalness". *Canadian Journal of Linguistics* 31.327–342.

———. 1989. "Abstractness, Iconicity, Redundancy: Reflections on French Inflections". *Zeitschrift für französische Sprache und Literatur* 99.225–33.

———. 1990. "Geometry in Morphology: The Old French Case System". *Zeitschrift für Phonetik, Sprachwissenschaft, und Kommunikationsforschung* 43.327–333.

———. 1992a. "Explaining French Morphology 'Naturally'". *Romance Philology* 45. 410–422.

———. 1992b. "The Morphology of Schwa in the History of French". *Lingua* 86.223–233.

———. 1992c. "Three problems in Italian Inflectional Morphology". *Romance Languages and Modern Linguistic Theory*, ed. by Paul Hirschbühler & Konrad Koerner, 151–159. Amsterdam & Philadelphia: John Benjamins.

———. 1993a. "On the Evolution of Latin Verbal Inflection into Romance: Change in Parameter Setting"? *Linguistic Perspectives on the Romance Languages*, ed. by William Ashby et al., 165–173. Amsterdam & Philadelphia: John Benjamins.

———. 1993b. "Quelques remarques sur l'histoire de la déclinaison latine en roman". *Du lexique à la morphologie: du côté de chez Zwaan*, ed. by Afke Hulk et al., 173–178. Amsterdam: Rodopi.

———. 1994. "The Cycle Revisited". *Canadian Journal of Linguistics* 39.217–223.

———. 1998. "Can Grammaticalization Be Explained Invisible-Handedly"? *Historical Linguistics 1997*, ed. by Monika Schmid et al., 191–200. Amsterdam & Philadelphia: John Benjamins.

Lahiri, Aditi & Elan Dresher. 1984. "Diachronic and Synchronic Implications of Declension Shifts". *The Linguistic Review* 3.141–163.

Lambrecht, Knut. 1981. *Topic, Antitopic and Verb Agreement in Non-Standard French*. Amsterdam & Philadelphia: John Benjamins.

Lass, Roger. 1990. "How to Do Things With Junk: Exaptation in Language Evolution". *Journal of Linguistics* 26.79–102.
———. 1997. *Historical Linguistics and Language Change*. Cambridge: Cambridge Univ. Press.
Lehmann, Christian. 1985. "Grammaticalization: Synchronic Variation and Diachronic Change". *Lingua e stile* 20.303–318.
———. 1995. *Thoughts on Grammaticalization*. Munich: Lincom Europa.
Lightfoot, David. 1979. *Principles of Diachronic Syntax*. Cambridge: Cambridge Univ. Press.
———. 1991. *How to Set Parameters. Arguments From Language Change*. Cambridge, Mass.: MIT Press.
———. 1996. Review of Bauer 1995. *Language* 72.156–159.
———. 1997. Reply to Bauer 1997. *Language* 73.358.
Lüdtke, Helmut. 1980. "The Place of Morphology in a Universal Cybernetic Theory of Language Change". *Historical Morphology*, ed. by Jacek Fisiak, 273–281. The Hague: Mouton.
Mallinson, Graham. 1986. *Rumanian*. London: Croom Helm.
Manczak, Witold. 1980. "Frequenz und Sprachwandel". *Kommunikationstheoretische Grundlagen des Sprachwandels*, ed. by Helmut Lüdtke, 37–79. Berlin: de Gruyter.
Mandeville, Bernard (de). 1732 / 1924. *The Fable of the Bees: Or, Private Vices, Publick Benefits*. 2 vols. Oxford.
Marchello-Nizia, Christiane. 1995. *L'évolution du français. Ordre des mots, démonstratifs, accent tonique*. Paris: Armand Colin.
Matthews, Peter. 1972. *Inflectional Morphology*. Cambridge: Cambridge Univ. Press.
———. 1991. *Morphology*. 2nd ed. Cambridge: Cambridge Univ. Press.
Mayerthaler, Willi. 1972. "Zur Diachronie von französisch *-ons*: eine generativ- transformationelle Analyse". *Zeitschrift für französische Sprache und Literatur* 82.289–335.
———. 1981. *Morphologische Natürlichkeit*. Wiesbaden: Athenaion.
———. 1988. *Morphological Naturalness*. Ann Arbor: Karoma.
McCray, Stanley. 1979. *Proto-IE to Romance: Aspects of Verbal Morpho-Syntax*. Unpub. PhD. Dissertation, Univ. of Michigan.
McMahon, April. 1994. *Understanding Language Change*. Cambridge: Cambridge Univ. Press.
Meyer-Lübke, Wilhelm. 1967. *Grammatica storica della lingua italiana e dei dialetti toscani*. Torino: Loeschner.
Morin, Yves-Charles, M.C. Langlois & M.E. Varin. 1990. "Tensing of Word-Final [ɔ] to [o] in French: The Phonologization of a Morphophonological Rule". *Romance Philology* 43.507–528.

Müller, Bodo. 1971. "Das morphemmarkierte Satzobjekt der romanischen Sprachen (Der sogenannte präpositionale Akkusativ)". *Zeitschrift für romanische Philologie* 87.477–519.
Nevis, Joel, ed. 1994. *Clitics. A Comprehensive Bibliography 1892–1991*. Amsterdam & Philadelphia: John Benjamins.
Newmeyer, Frederick. 1998. *Language Form and Language Function*. Cambridge, Mass.: MIT Press.
Nyman, Martti. 1982. "Pragmatics and Morphological Change". Ms., University of Helsinki.
———. 1994. "Language Change and the 'Invisible Hand'". *Diachronica* 11.231–258.
Penny, Ralph. 1991. *A History of the Spanish Language*. Cambridge: Cambridge Univ. Press.
Pensado, Carmen. 1985. "Inversion de marquage et perte du système casuel en ancien français". *Zeitschrift für romanische Philologie* 102.271–296.
Petruck, Christoph. 1996. Review of Kaiser 1992. *Zeitschrift für französische Sprache und Literatur* 106.78–83.
Pignatelli, Cinzia. 1988. "La grammaticalizzazione dei clitici francesi". *Archivio Glottologico Italiano* 73.25–49.
Pinkster, Harm. 1987. "The Strategy and Chronology of the Development of Future and Perfect Tense Auxiliaries in Latin". *The Historical Development of Auxiliaries*, ed. by Martin Harris and Paolo Ramat, 193–223. Berlin: Mouton de Gruyter.
Pinkus, Philip. 1975. "Mandeville's Paradox". *Mandeville Studies. New Explorations in the Art and Thought of Dr. Bernard Mandeville (1670–1733)*, ed. by I. Primer, 193–211. The Hague: Martinus Nijhoff.
Plank, Frans. 1979. "The Functional Basis of Case Systems and Declension Classes: From Latin to Old French". *Linguistics* 17.611–640.
Pulgram, Ernst. 1977. "Indo-European Passive Paradigms: Defects and Repairs". *Forum Linguisticum* 2.95–106.
———. 1987. "Latin-Romance, English, German Past Tenses and Aspects: Defects and Repairs". *Folia Linguistica Historica* 7.381–397.
Ramat, Paolo. 1992. "Thoughts on Degrammaticalization". *Linguistics* 30.549–560.
Rheinfelder, Hans. 1967. *Altfranzösische Grammatik. 2. Teil. Formenlehre*. München: Hueber.
Rini, Joel. 1990. "Dating the Grammaticalization of the Spanish Clitic Pronoun". *Zeitschrift für romanische Philologie* 106.354–370.
Roberge, Yves. 1990. *The Syntactic Recoverability of Null Arguments*. Kingston and Montreal: McGill-Queen's University Press.
Roberts, Ian. 1993. "A Formal Account of Grammaticalisation in the History of Romance Futures". *Folia Linguistica Historica* 13.219–258.
Rohlfs, Gerhard. 1968. *Grammatica storica della lingua italiana e dei suoi dialetti. Morfologia*. Torino: Einaudi.
Rothe, Wolfgang. 1957. *Einführung in die historische Laut- und Formenlehre des Rumänischen*. Halle: Niemeyer.

———. 1966. "Romanische Objektkonjugation". *Romanische Forschungen* 78.530–547.
Sánchez Miret, Fernando, A. Koliadis & W.U. Dressler. 1998. "Connectionism vs. Rules in Diachronic Morphology". *Folia Linguistica Historica* 18.149–182.
Schwegler, Armin. 1990. *Analyticity and Syntheticity. A Diachronic Perspective with Special Reference to Romance Languages*. Berlin: Mouton de Gruyter.
———. 1993. Review of Jacob 1990. *Romance Philology* 47.91–99.
Seklaoui, Diana. 1989. *Change and Compensation*. Berne: Lang.
Skalička, Vladimir. 1979. *Typologische Studien*. Braunschweig: Vieweg.
Smith, Adam. 1776/1970. *The Wealth of Nations. Vol. 1, Reprint*. London and New York.
Smith, John Charles. 1995. "Perceptual Factors in the Disappearance of Agreement Between Past Participle and Direct Object in Romance". *Linguistic Theory and the Romance Languages*, ed. by John Charles Smith and Martin Maiden, 161–80. Amsterdam & Philadelphia: John Benjamins.
Steele, Susan. 1994. Review of Heine 1993. *Language* 70.811–817.
Steever, Sanford. 1993. *Analysis to Synthesis. The Development of Complex Verb Morphology in the Dravidian Languages*. Oxford: Oxford Univ. Press.
Stolz, Thomas. 1987. "Auf dem 'natürlichsten' Weg von der Synthese zur Analyse"? *Skandinavistik* 17.3–23.
———. 1992. "(Wieviel) verbale Objektflexion im Portugiesischen"? *Zeitschrift für Phonetik, Sprachwissenschaft, und Kommunikationsforschung* 45.437–457.
Taylor, John R. 1995. *Linguistic Categorization. Prototypes in Linguistic Theory*. Oxford: Clarendon.
Touratier, Christian. 1971. "Essai de morphologie synchronique du verbe latin". *Revue des études latines* 49.331–357.
Trask, Larry. 1996. Posting on *Linguist List*. 8/26/96.
Traugott, Elizabeth & Ekkehart König. 1991. "The Semantics-Pragmatics of Grammaticalization Revisited". *Approaches to Grammaticalization*, ed. by Elizabeth Traugott and Bernd Heine, 189–218. Amsterdam & Philadelphia: John Benjamins.
Ullmann-Margalit, Edna. 1978. "Invisible-Hand Explanations". *Synthese* 39.263–291.
Vance, Barbara. 1995. "On the Clitic Nature of Subject Pronouns in Mediaeval French". *CLS 31: Papers From the 3rd Regional Meeting of the Chicago Linguistics Society, 1995, Volume 2: The Parasession on Clitics*, ed. by A. Dainora et al., 300–315. Chicago: Chicago Linguistic Society.
Vincent, Nigel. 1980. "Words Versus Morphemes in Morphological Change: The Case of the Italian *-iamo*". *Historical Morphology*, ed. by Jacek Fisiak, 383–398. The Hague: Mouton.
———. 1987. "The Interaction of Periphrasis and Inflection: Some Romance Examples". *The Historical Development of Auxiliaries*, ed. by Martin Harris and Paolo Ramat, 237–256. Berlin: Mouton de Gruyter.
———. 1995. "Exaptation and Grammaticalization". *Historical Linguistics 1993*, ed. by Henning Andersen, 433–445. Amsterdam & Philadelphia: John Benjamins.
——— & Martin Harris, eds. 1982. *Studies in the Romance Verb*. London: Croom Helm.

Walker, Douglas. 1987a. "Patterns of Analogy in the Old French Verb System". *Lingua* 72.109–131.

———. 1987b. "Morphological Features and Markedness in the Old French Noun Declension". *Canadian Journal of Linguistics* 32.143–197.

———. 1995. "Patterns of Analogy in the Canadian French Verb System". *French Language Studies* 5.85–107.

Wanner, Dieter. 1975. "Die historische Motivierung der Endung -*iamo* im Italienischen". *Zeitschrift für romanische Philologie* 91.153–175.

———. 1981. "Clitic Placement From Old to Modern Italian: Morphologization of a Syntactic Rule". *Linguistic Symposium on Romance Languages: 9*, ed. by William Cressey & Donna Napoli, 331–348. Washington, D.C: Georgetown University Press.

Watson, Keith. 1997. "French Complement Clitic Sequences: A Template Approach". *French Language Studies* 7. 69–89.

Wheeler, Max. 1993. "On the Hierarchy of Naturalness Principles in Inflectional Morphology". *Journal of Linguistics* 29.95–111.

Wurzel, Wolfgang. 1984. *Flexionsmorphologie und Natürlichkeit*. Berlin: Akademie Verlag.

———. 1987. "Paradigmenstrukturbedingungen: Aufbau und Veränderung von Flexionsparadigmen". *Papers From the 7th ICHL*, ed. by Anna Giacalone-Ramat et al., 629–644. Amsterdam & Philadelphia: John Benjamins.

———. 1988. "Zur Erklärbarkeit sprachlichen Wandels". *Zeitschrift für Phonetik, Sprachwissenschaft, und Kommunikationsforschung* 41.488–510.

———. 1989. *Inflectional Morphology and Naturalness*. Dordrecht: Kluwer.

———. 1994. "Natural Morphology". *The Encyclopedia of Language and Linguistics, Volume 5*, ed. by R.E. Asher, 2590–2598. Oxford: Pergamon Press

Subject Index

A
A/S cycle 77
A/S dichotomy 75
accidental 16
accidental homonymy 61
adstratum 112
affix 73, 102, 138, 140, 144, 146, 155
affix/clitic 140
African 19
agglutinating 9, 17
agglutinative 10, 148
agreement-affix 138
Albanian 112
alinearity 102
allomorphic variation 15
allomorphs 130
allomorphy 14, 27
analogical 61, 111, 124, 152
analogy 49, 51, 57, 61
analysis 63, 65, 67, 71, 105
analysis/synthesis 113
analytic 17, 27, 38, 41, 44, 64, 65, 68-70, 102, 144, 147, 151, 156
analytic structure 65
analytically 44
Analyticity 24, 27, 46, 67, 68, 71-74, 77, 78
anteposition 65
anti-topic 96
Appendix Probi 127
auxiliary 155
auxiliation 76

B
base form inflection 5, 6
basic 13
bidirectional 140
biunique relationship 4
biuniqueness 10, 19
bleaching 75, 79, 80, 113
Brazilian Portuguese 101, 105

C
Canadian French 63
Castilian Spanish 24
Catalan 125
categoriality 147
central 3
chains of grammaticalization xii
Chanson de Roland 93
Chaos Theory 137
class stability 9, 11
Classical Aztec 100
Classical Latin 14, 29, 62, 68-71, 82, 110, 114, 151
Classical Latin (CL) 25, 26
cline 144, 153, 154
clitic 77, 97, 99, 100, 113, 138-140
clitic/affix 102, 104, 106
Cliticization 75, 77, 88, 95
clitics 101, 104, 130, 152
coding 8
coding pattern 7
cohort 88
Cohort Model 27
complement 30-32

conflict of naturalness 10
connectionism 11
constructional iconicity 2, 9, 11, 49, 62, 73
continuum 21, 139, 144, 146, 147, 149, 153
counter-iconic 1, 4, 48, 118, 124
counter-iconically 118
Counter-iconicity 2, 49, 64, 119, 152
cumulative 5, 10, 126
cumulative exponence 14, 121, 129
cumulatively 124, 126
cycle of grammaticalization 20

D

de-grammaticalization 145
de-iconization 142
De-morphologization 145
de-phonologization 145
de-syntacticization 145
Decategorialization 75, 77, 88
decoding 73, 74
decoding/encoding 105
default 7, 57, 60, 61, 119
default paradigm structure conditions 154
default PSC 41, 52, 54, 55, 60, 151, 152
degrammaticalization 140, 146, 147
demorphologization 142, 144, 147
dependence 78, 79
dephonologization 142
deponent verbs 40
deponents 41
derivational 146
derivational morphology 13
derived 13
Desemanticization 75, 77, 88
Desyntacticization 96, 142
desyntacticized 96
diachronic reanalysis 148
Diachronic Reanalysis (DR) 80
Diagrammaticity 10, 73

diagrams 13
direct cases 109
discrete categories 149
dislocated 130
Displaceability 24, 74
dominant PSC 62
downgradings 140

E

e-caduc 101
Eastern Romance 146
elision 101
enclisis 100, 101, 128
enclitic 109
enclitic article 113
encoding 73, 74
English 2, 3, 6, 7, 78, 128
English Creole Tok Pisin 23
Erklärbarkeitsbehauptungen 79
Erosion 75, 77, 88
erosion/fusion 105
eurythmy 94
Ewe 19
exaptation 145, 146
explananda 135
explanandum 133, 134, 136, 141
explanans 90, 134, 141, 153
exponents 14
expressivity 136
extended exponence 14
extended inflection 104
extra-morphological 5, 152, 156
extra-morphologically 121
extravagance 136, 141

F

Fable of the Bees 131
family resemblance categories 148, 149
final devoicing 50
Fiorentino 95
flirting 27, 28, 88-90, 95
flirting stage 28

SUBJECT INDEX

flirting/rebuffing 91
Francien dialect 54
French 2, 25-27, 30, 31, 37, 42-48,
  51, 52, 54, 55, 63, 65, 67, 68,
  71-74, 81, 86-88, 91-97,
  100-103, 105, 120, 123, 130,
  143, 144, 146, 151-153, 155,
  157, 159
French dislocations 99
French oxytonic stress 100
fusion 12, 13, 74, 78, 79
fusional 9, 10, 14, 17, 40
futur proche 64

G

Gallo-Romance 52
generality 12, 13, 22, 24, 74
generic 4
German 4, 6, 8, 16, 17, 62
Glossary of Reichenau 40
Glosses of Reichenau 41
go-future 64, 105
grammaticalization scenario xii
Grammaticalization chain 18
grammaticalization theory xi
Greek 7

H

Haplology 47
head 30-32
homeostasis 136
homonymies 16
Homonymy 14, 17, 52, 61
Homonymy conflict 51
Hungarian 15, 16, 98, 99
Hungarian paradigm 17
hypotaxis 140

I

iconic 2, 13, 43, 63, 65, 100, 109,
  118, 151, 156
iconically 119

iconicity 1, 3, 7, 8, 10, 14, 49, 53,
  64, 65, 100, 109, 151, 152, 154
icons 9, 142
IH-explanation 135, 136, 141
IH-process 137
imparisyllabic 116
imparisyllabics 121, 126, 127
implications 8
implicative structuring 5
inchoative 146, 147
index 10
indexical 142
indexicality 9, 10
indices 142
Indo-European 9, 32, 34, 70, 89, 90,
  118, 129
inflected 147
Inflected forms 31
inflecting languages 14
inflection 17, 84, 105, 122, 128, 129
inflectional 5, 8, 9, 11, 14, 24, 35, 65,
  72, 89, 95, 110, 146, 147, 151,
  152, 154
inflectional classes 6
inflectional morphology xii, 13, 63,
  66
inflectional prefix 88
inflectional prefixation 73
inflectional suffixation 34, 40, 92,
  113, 156
inflectionally 22
inflections 153
inflexional 73
Informal Spoken French (ISF) 25
invariance 63, 151
invisible hand xii, 131, 132, 136
invisible hand explanation 80, 133,
  135
invisible hand process 154
invisible hand scenario 155
invisible-handedly 135
inward sensitivity 39, 44

irreversibility xii, 79, 137, 140, 141, 144, 153, 155
ISF 26
Isolatedness 24, 74
Italian 3, 37, 42-48, 54, 55, 58, 59, 61-63, 65, 67, 69, 71, 81, 95, 99, 100, 102-104, 108, 122, 125-130, 146, 151, 155, 157, 159

K
Konjugationsthese 86

L
l-vocalization 50
language dependent xi
language independent naturalness xi
Late Latin 40, 49, 52, 54, 55, 151, 155
Latin 3, 8-10, 14, 15, 17, 23, 25, 27, 30, 31, 34, 37-41, 44-46, 48-56, 58, 59-64, 67-73, 76, 80, 81, 84-86, 88, 91, 94, 102, 103, 105, 106, 108, 110-113, 118, 120-123, 125, 126, 128-130, 145-148, 151, 152, 155-157, 159
Latin inflectional system 153
Latin nasal infixation 147
Latin suffixation 65
Latin word order 112
Latin-Romance 35
Latin/Romance 128, 129
Layering 22
LB 88
LB formations 92
LB structures 89, 90
LB-M 34
Least Effort Strategy (LES) 80
least-effort principle 140
Left Branching 30-32, 89, 91, 92, 97, 101, 105
left branching 'morphological' structure 34
left branching syntactic (LB-S) 34

left branching/suffixation 101
left dislocated 96
left dislocation 97
left vs. right branching 29, 104
left-branching 71, 93, 155
lexical conditioning 143
lexical to functional change-over 155
lexicalization 147
liaison 101, 129
Linearity 24, 25, 27, 74, 102, 103
linguistic processing 152

M
Mandeville's paradox 131, 132
Mandevillean-Smithian 133
marked 1, 4, 5, 8, 38-40, 49, 55, 58, 60, 68, 92, 100, 118, 124, 127, 154
markedness 1, 4, 5, 7, 8, 11, 17, 38, 39, 41, 53, 55, 60, 62, 73, 100, 109, 123, 154
markedness reversal 118, 143
markedness reversal (or inversion) 4
markerless 4
Markiertheitstheorie 4
Maximal iconicity 1
maximally iconic 1
maxims of action 136
medieval Italian 61
medio-passive voice 41
mesoclisis 100
metaphor 19, 21
Metaphorical abstraction 18
Metaphorical leaps 18
Metonymic links 18
metonymic-metaphorical 18, 20, 79
metonymy 19
Middle French 95
Minimal iconicity 1
minimal inflectional system 65
minimally iconic 1
Mod. French 120, 121, 128
Modern (Spoken) French 82, 92

SUBJECT INDEX

Modern Bulgarian 112
Modern French 23-25, 28, 29, 42, 48, 53, 55, 63-65, 82, 84-86, 90, 91, 95, 103, 104, 114, 124, 128, 129, 143, 151, 152
Modern German 5
Modern Greek 6
Modern High German 7
Modern Italian 58, 61, 62
Modern Spoken French 65, 97
Modern Swedish 7
morphemic proximity 12
morphocentric 142
Morphocentricity 142, 144, 145
morphological conditionings 143
morphological naturalness 5, 61
morphologization 99, 142-145, 147
Morphosemantic 10
morphosyntactic 5, 15, 147
morphosyntactic transparency 41
morphosyntax xii, 35
morphotactic 73
morphotactic stability 100
Morphotactic transparency 10
MP rule 143

N

natural 8, 9, 74
natural methodology 152
natural morphological analysis 117, 152
natural morphology xi, 1, 3, 8, 10, 11, 13, 14, 17, 18, 35, 37, 50, 52, 100, 121, 151, 154-156
natural morphology interface 156
natural parameters 71
natural analysis 151
naturalness xi, 4, 9, 92, 153, 154
naturalness parameters 17, 47, 49, 60, 63
naturalness theory 153
New Mexican Spanish 137, 139
non-generic 4

non-iconic 1, 63-65, 109, 119, 122
Non-iconicity 2, 49, 121, 151, 152
nondiscrete grammatical categories 149
null object language 97
null subject 65, 97

O

object case 4
object conjugation 97–99, 100
object-enclisis 105
obligatoriness 12, 13, 24-26, 74, 84
oblique 118
oblique cases 109
Old Florentine 59
Old French 25, 48-53, 55, 64, 92-95, 97, 109, 114, 116-126, 128, 129, 143, 151, 152, 159
Old French case system 4
Old High German 7
Old Italian 59, 60
Old Latin 62
Old Provençal 109, 124, 125
Old Spanish 122
Old Swedish 7
optimal word size 10
outward sensitivity 39, 55
oxytonic stress 94

P

paradigm 122
Paradigm Economy Principle (PEP) 14
paradigm structure condition (PSC) 40, 119
paradigm structure conditions (PSC) 5, 151
paradigmatic 3
paradigmatic leveling 143, 151
Paradigmatic structure 14
paradigmatic transparency 49, 50, 100
Paradigmenstrukturbedingungen 5
paradoxographus 131

parallel reduction 21
parallel reduction hypothesis 136
parameter (re)setting. 81
parameter of (diagrammatic) iconicity 79
parameter of naturalness 39, 55
parameter settings 81, 149
Parameters of grammaticalization 152
parameters of natural morphology 68, 73, 154
parameters of naturalness 10, 38, 54, 56, 58, 62, 151
parametric change 81
parataxis 140
PC 15, 17
Peircian 142
PEP 15, 17
perception/processing 105
perception/production 152
peripheral 3
peripherality constraint 3, 73
Peripherality Constraint (PC) 14, 39
periphrasis xi, 65, 66, 70, 105
periphrastic 24, 38, 41, 65, 71, 73, 75, 90, 152, 155
periphrastically 22
phonetic erosion 136
phonetic erosion parameter 101
phonetic iconicity 11
Phonological binding 113
Phonological bonding 24, 74
phonological markedness 43
phonological reduction 21
phonologization 143, 144
phonotactic 144
phonotactically 49
PIE 139, 146, 153
portmanteau 40, 84
portmanteau formations 39
Portuguese 98-102, 104, 125
Portuguese enclitic 103
prefix 85, 86, 97, 101, 105, 155

prefixation 32, 73, 91, 92, 95, 105, 129
prefixes 65, 81, 84
prefixing 28
prefixing dispreference 27, 89
Principles and Parameters syntax 148
procliticization 95
pro-drop 65, 92, 93, 95-97
processing/perception 101
proclisis 100
proclitic 113, 155
proclitics 65, 81, 84, 97, 102
productivity 9
prototype categories 149
Prototypical 4
PSC 63
PSC parameter 60
PSCs 8, 9, 17

Q
Queste del saint Graal 93

R
RB formations 90
RB position 88
RB structures 89
re-analyses 81, 140
re-iconization 79
reanalysis 72, 113, 138, 141, 142
rebuffed 88
rebuffing 90
regrammaticalization 146, 147
relevance 12-14, 17, 22, 24, 74
relevant 13, 14
replacement 138
reversal 140, 147
Rheme 73
rich agreement 95, 96
Right Branching 30-32, 89, 91, 92, 97, 101, 105, 106
right branching syntactic (RB-S) 34
Right branching/proclisis 101
right dislocated 96

SUBJECT INDEX

right dislocation 97
right dislocations 92
right-branching 71, 93, 155
right-branching periphrasis 156
Romance 17, 23, 24, 26, 37, 41, 45, 51, 62, 63, 65, 67-81, 87, 97, 99, 101, 102, 103, 105, 106, 108, 112, 113, 122-125, 145-148, 152, 153, 155, 157
Romance inflectional prefixation 101
Romance languages 14, 34
Romance prefixation 106
rule inversion 143
Rumanian 107-112, 113, 125, 128-130, 147, 151-153

S

S/A dichotomy 79
SC 45, 55, 152
Scenarios for grammaticalization 86
Schwa 47-50
Schwa generalization 47, 48, 50, 51, 151
schwa insertion rule 42
SDSP 58, 154
SDSPs 6, 9, 14, 45, 50, 55, 62, 113, 121, 152, 156
Semantic reduction 21
semantic relevance 74
semantic transparency 73
semiotic 142
semiotic priority 142
sensitivity 15
Separability 24, 25, 71, 72, 74, 113
SHC 17
shortness 78, 79
signans 1, 3, 4
signatum 1, 3, 4
signs 9, 142
Spanish 52, 65, 68, 70, 99, 100, 102-105, 122-126, 128-130, 155
spoken French 83, 90-92, 95

spoken Latin 54, 110-112, 114, 123, 125, 127
stability 8
stability-neutral inflectional 8
stable 8
stem inflection 5, 6, 39
Stratum 51
Structural transparency 103
Subj. conjugation 98
subject case 4
substratum 112
suffix 102, 105, 116, 117, 119, 129, 139, 146, 147
suffixal 126, 128
suffixation 32, 73, 89, 91, 100, 105, 118, 121, 128, 152
suffixes 88, 97, 101, 116, 153, 155
suffixing 28
suffixing preference 27, 113, 155
suppletion 14, 21
Suppletive 14, 84
symbols 9, 142
syncretic 40, 59
syncretism 11, 14, 16, 17, 40, 121
Syntactic branching 29, 32, 152
syntagmatic 3
syntagmatic iconicity 13, 17
synthesis 63, 65-67, 71-73, 112, 113
synthesis/analysis 20, 24, 29, 144
synthesis/analysis cycle xi, 152
synthesized 72, 73
synthetic 27, 38, 41, 42, 44, 46, 64, 69, 71, 74, 102, 103, 144
synthetic/analytic 46, 105
syntacticization 145
synthetically 45
syntheticity 73, 77, 78
system congruent 7, 14
system congruity 5, 7-9, 11, 41, 50, 65, 119, 121, 122, 154
system congruity (SC) 40, 151
system congruous 9
system defining 156

system defining structural properties
(= SDSPs) 5, 39, 92, 109, 119, 151
system incongruent 53
system-congruent 7
system-congruous 61, 68
system-definierende Struktureigenschaften 5
system-dependent 8, 9, 151
system-dependent natural morphology 154
System-dependent naturalness 5, 9, 11
system-independent 7, 9, 11, 156
system-independent natural morphology 153
System-independent naturalness 1
systematic homonymies 16, 17
systematic homonymy 51
Systematic Homonymy Claim (SHC) 14, 50

T
takeovers 17
teleological 65, 136
Theme 73
topic 96
topicalization 94
transderivational account 60
transparency 3, 9, 14, 17, 24, 26, 74, 102, 103
transportability 71, 72, 113
Trentino 95
Turkish 9, 10, 15
typological 14, 17, 152
typological adequacy 10
typological uniformity 5
typology 9, 112, 113

U
unidirectional 103, 141, 147
unidirectionality xii, 21, 79, 89, 137-140, 142, 144, 145, 148, 153

unidirectionally 19
uniform coding 3, 7, 14, 17, 151
uniform symbolization 55, 58
uniform transparent coding 4
uniformity 9
uniformity and transparency 11
universal xi, 2, 9, 151, 156
universal case hierarchy 118
universal naturalness 10, 14, 17
Universal paths 21
unmarked 1, 2, 5, 7, 8, 13, 38, 40, 58, 60, 93, 94, 100, 109, 118, 124, 127, 154
unmarked SDSP 151
unstable 8
unstable inflectional classes 9
upgradings 140

V
V-2 constraint 93
V-2 effects 94
valence 13
verb-second constraint 94
Vulgar Latin 114

W
Welsh 2
word order 92, 96, 97, 112
Wurzel's problem 151

Z
zero allomorph 85
zero expression 13
Zero marking 45, 63
zero morph 40
zero morpheme 43
zero suffix 84
zero-marking 64, 119
Zulu 15

Name Index

A
Adams 93-95
Allen 147
Anderson 104
Ashby 85, 86, 97
Auger 96

B
Baldinger 85, 86
Barnes 97
Battistella 2, 109
Battye 149
Bauer xii, 29, 30, 32, 34, 71, 86, 87, 89, 90, 93, 94, 152
Blake 118, 128, 129
Blasco 96
Bossong 124
Brandi 95
Bybee xi, 11-14, 17, 22, 69, 75
Bybee et al. xi, 21-24, 76, 78, 79, 89, 90, 103, 113, 135, 136

C
Campbell 141
Carrasquel 88, 113
Carstairs xi, 3, 11, 14-18, 39, 50, 51, 55, 61, 73
Carstairs-McCarthy 3, 4, 6, 7, 10
Charles Sanders Peirce 9
Claudi 79
Clements 137
Corbett 52
Cordin 95
Croft 149
Cutler et al. 27, 28, 73

D
d'Ovidio 61, 62
Dahl 141
Dardel 126
de Poerck 52
Dees et al. 50
Dresher 125
Dressler xi, 4, 9-11, 73, 142
Dufresne 94
Dupuis 94

E
Ehala 136
Einhorn 93
Epstein 128
Everett 104

F
Fleischman 68-70, 72
Foerster 62

G
Gaeng 126
Geisler 73, 94, 95, 105
Giacalone-Ramat 79, 156
Grandgent 61
Green 76
Greenberg 28, 109, 118, 128

H
Hall xii, 27-29, 34, 86, 88-90, 92, 113, 152
Halpern 104
Harris 64, 70, 74, 94, 97, 112, 128

NAME INDEX

Haspelmath 136, 137, 140-142, 144, 148
Heath 106, 140, 147
Heine 75-79, 86, 88, 89, 95, 113, 136, 148, 149, 152, 153
Heine et al. xi, 18–20, 21, 113, 153, 154
Herschensohn 63
Hopper 81, 113
Hopper & Traugott xi, 20
Horne 94
Hünnemeyer 79
Hunnius 86

J
Jacob 85, 86
Jaeggli 95
Janda 79, 137-140, 142, 144, 147
Jensen 57, 61, 124
Joseph, B. 79, 144, 147
Joseph, J. 72

K
Kaiser 97
Kefer 72
Keller 131-136
Kilani-Schoch xi, 10, 45, 65, 95
Klausenburger 49, 62-64, 71, 74, 94, 109, 116, 119, 122, 123, 137, 147
Koliadis 11
König 147

L
Lahiri 125
Lambrecht 83, 96, 101
Lass 141, 145, 153
Lehmann xi, 113, 136, 141
Lightfoot 32, 81, 142, 144, 154
Lüdtke 27, 74

M
Mallinson 107, 109

Manczak 37, 51, 52
Mandeville 131, 132, 135
Marchello-Nizia 92–94
Matthews 2, 3, 37, 39, 43, 65
Mayerthaler xi, 1-4, 51, 73, 118, 127, 151, 156
Mayerthaler 127
McCray 70
McMahon 142
Meyer-Lübke 56, 58
Morin et al. 143, 144
Müller 125, 129

N
Nevis et al. 97
Newmeyer 137, 140, 141
Nyman 60, 133, 134

P
Penny 124
Pensado 118
Petruck 97
Pignatelli 86
Pinkster 76
Pinkus 131
Plank 118
Pulgram 41, 70

R
Ramat 79, 147
Rheinfelder 52, 54, 114, 116, 121
Rini 99
Roberge 95, 97
Roberts 80, 81, 141, 148, 149
Rohlfs 57, 61
Rothe 98-101, 104, 109-112

S
Safir 95
Sánchez Miret 11
Schwegler xi, 20, 24-27, 71, 72, 74, 77, 85, 94, 95, 102, 103, 113
Seklaoui 57

Skalička 39
Smith 76
Smith, Adam 132
St. Léger 53
Steele 79, 148, 149
Steever 71
Stolz 71, 99-101

T
Taylor 149
Touratier 37, 39
Trask 149
Traugott 81, 113, 147

U
Ullmann-Margalit 133

V
Vance 94
Vincent 60, 70, 76, 145

W
Walker 49, 50, 53, 55, 117, 118
Wanner 59, 60, 99
Watson 104
Wheeler xi, 11, 63
Wüest 126
Wurzel xi, 2-8, 10, 39, 41, 121, 151, 152, 154, 155

The *Current Issues in Linguistics Theory* series (edited by E. F. Konrad Koerner, University of Ottawa) is a theory-oriented series which welcomes contributions from scholars who have significant proposals to make towards the advancement of our understanding of language, its structure, functioning and development.

Current Issues in Linguistics Theory (CILT) has been established in order to provide a forum for the presentation and discussion of linguistic opinions of scholars who do not necessarily accept the prevailing mode of thought in linguistic science. It offers an alternative outlet for meaningful contributions to the current linguistic debate, and furnishes the diversity of opinion which a healthy discipline must have. In this series the following volumes have been published thus far or are scheduled for publication:

1. KOERNER, Konrad (ed.): *The Transformational-Generative Paradigm and Modern Linguistic Theory*. 1975.
2. WEIDERT, Alfons: *Componential Analysis of Lushai Phonology*. 1975.
3. MAHER, J. Peter: *Papers on Language Theory and History I: Creation and Tradition in Language. Foreword by Raimo Anttila*. 1979.
4. HOPPER, Paul J. (ed.): *Studies in Descriptive and Historical Linguistics. Festschrift for Winfred P. Lehmann*. 1977.
5. ITKONEN, Esa: *Grammatical Theory and Metascience: A critical investigation into the methodological and philosophical foundations of 'autonomous' linguistics*. 1978.
6. ANTTILA, Raimo: *Historical and Comparative Linguistics*. 1989.
7. MEISEL, Jürgen M. & Martin D. PAM (eds): *Linear Order and Generative Theory*. 1979.
8. WILBUR, Terence H.: *Prolegomena to a Grammar of Basque*. 1979.
9. HOLLIEN, Harry & Patricia (eds): *Current Issues in the Phonetic Sciences. Proceedings of the IPS-77 Congress, Miami Beach, Florida, 17-19 December 1977*. 1979.
10. PRIDEAUX, Gary D. (ed.): *Perspectives in Experimental Linguistics. Papers from the University of Alberta Conference on Experimental Linguistics, Edmonton, 13-14 Oct. 1978*. 1979.
11. BROGYANYI, Bela (ed.): *Studies in Diachronic, Synchronic, and Typological Linguistics: Festschrift for Oswald Szemérenyi on the Occasion of his 65th Birthday*. 1979.
12. FISIAK, Jacek (ed.): *Theoretical Issues in Contrastive Linguistics*. 1981. Out of print
13. MAHER, J. Peter, Allan R. BOMHARD & Konrad KOERNER (eds): *Papers from the Third International Conference on Historical Linguistics, Hamburg, August 22-26 1977*. 1982.
14. TRAUGOTT, Elizabeth C., Rebecca LaBRUM & Susan SHEPHERD (eds): *Papers from the Fourth International Conference on Historical Linguistics, Stanford, March 26-30 1979*. 1980.
15. ANDERSON, John (ed.): *Language Form and Linguistic Variation. Papers dedicated to Angus McIntosh*. 1982.
16. ARBEITMAN, Yoël L. & Allan R. BOMHARD (eds): *Bono Homini Donum: Essays in Historical Linguistics, in Memory of J.Alexander Kerns*. 1981.
17. LIEB, Hans-Heinrich: *Integrational Linguistics. 6 volumes. Vol. II-VI n.y.p.* 1984/93.
18. IZZO, Herbert J. (ed.): *Italic and Romance. Linguistic Studies in Honor of Ernst Pulgram*. 1980.
19. RAMAT, Paolo et al. (eds): *Linguistic Reconstruction and Indo-European Syntax. Proceedings of the Colloquium of the 'Indogermanischhe Gesellschaft'. University of Pavia, 6-7 September 1979*. 1980.
20. NORRICK, Neal R.: *Semiotic Principles in Semantic Theory*. 1981.
21. AHLQVIST, Anders (ed.): *Papers from the Fifth International Conference on Historical Linguistics, Galway, April 6-10 1981*. 1982.
22. UNTERMANN, Jürgen & Bela BROGYANYI (eds): *Das Germanische und die Rekonstruktion der Indogermanischen Grundsprache. Akten des Freiburger Kolloquiums der Indogermanischen Gesellschaft, Freiburg, 26-27 Februar 1981*. 1984.

23. DANIELSEN, Niels: *Papers in Theoretical Linguistics. Edited by Per Baerentzen.* 1992.
24. LEHMANN, Winfred P. & Yakov MALKIEL (eds): *Perspectives on Historical Linguistics. Papers from a conference held at the meeting of the Language Theory Division, Modern Language Assn., San Francisco, 27-30 December 1979.* 1982.
25. ANDERSEN, Paul Kent: *Word Order Typology and Comparative Constructions.* 1983.
26. BALDI, Philip (ed.): *Papers from the XIIth Linguistic Symposium on Romance Languages, Univ. Park, April 1-3, 1982.* 1984.
27. BOMHARD, Alan R.: *Toward Proto-Nostratic. A New Approach to the Comparison of Proto-Indo-European and Proto-Afroasiatic. Foreword by Paul J. Hopper.* 1984.
28. BYNON, James (ed.): *Current Progress in Afro-Asiatic Linguistics: Papers of the Third International Hamito-Semitic Congress, London, 1978.* 1984.
29. PAPROTTÉ, Wolf & René DIRVEN (eds): *The Ubiquity of Metaphor: Metaphor in language and thought.* 1985 (publ. 1986).
30. HALL, Robert A. Jr.: *Proto-Romance Morphology. = Comparative Romance Grammar, vol. III.* 1984.
31. GUILLAUME, Gustave: *Foundations for a Science of Language.*
32. COPELAND, James E. (ed.): *New Directions in Linguistics and Semiotics.* Co-edition with Rice University Press who hold exclusive rights for US and Canada. 1984.
33. VERSTEEGH, Kees: *Pidginization and Creolization. The Case of Arabic.* 1984.
34. FISIAK, Jacek (ed.): *Papers from the VIth International Conference on Historical Linguistics, Poznan, 22-26 August. 1983.* 1985.
35. COLLINGE, N.E.: *The Laws of Indo-European.* 1985.
36. KING, Larry D. & Catherine A. MALEY (eds): *Selected papers from the XIIIth Linguistic Symposium on Romance Languages, Chapel Hill, N.C., 24-26 March 1983.* 1985.
37. GRIFFEN, T.D.: *Aspects of Dynamic Phonology.* 1985.
38. BROGYANYI, Bela & Thomas KRÖMMELBEIN (eds): *Germanic Dialects:Linguistic and Philological Investigations.* 1986.
39. BENSON, James D., Michael J. CUMMINGS, & William S. GREAVES (eds): *Linguistics in a Systemic Perspective.* 1988.
40. FRIES, Peter Howard (ed.) in collaboration with Nancy M. Fries: *Toward an Understanding of Language: Charles C. Fries in Perspective.* 1985.
41. EATON, Roger, et al. (eds): *Papers from the 4th International Conference on English Historical Linguistics, April 10-13, 1985.* 1985.
42. MAKKAI, Adam & Alan K. MELBY (eds): *Linguistics and Philosophy. Festschrift for Rulon S. Wells.* 1985 (publ. 1986).
43. AKAMATSU, Tsutomu: *The Theory of Neutralization and the Archiphoneme in Functional Phonology.* 1988.
44. JUNGRAITHMAYR, Herrmann & Walter W. MUELLER (eds): *Proceedings of the Fourth International Hamito-Semitic Congress.* 1987.
45. KOOPMAN, W.F., F.C. Van der LEEK , O. FISCHER & R. EATON (eds): *Explanation and Linguistic Change.* 1986
46. PRIDEAUX, Gary D. & William J. BAKER: *Strategies and Structures: The processing of relative clauses.* 1987.
47. LEHMANN, Winfred P. (ed.): *Language Typology 1985. Papers from the Linguistic Typology Symposium, Moscow, 9-13 Dec. 1985.* 1986.
48. RAMAT, Anna G., Onofrio CARRUBA and Giuliano BERNINI (eds): *Papers from the 7th International Conference on Historical Linguistics.* 1987.
49. WAUGH, Linda R. and Stephen RUDY (eds): *New Vistas in Grammar: Invariance and Variation. Proceedings of the Second International Roman Jakobson Conference, New York University, Nov.5-8, 1985.* 1991.
50. RUDZKA-OSTYN, Brygida (ed.): *Topics in Cognitive Linguistics.* 1988.

51. CHATTERJEE, Ranjit: *Aspect and Meaning in Slavic and Indic. With a foreword by Paul Friedrich.* 1989.
52. FASOLD, Ralph W. & Deborah SCHIFFRIN (eds): *Language Change and Variation.* 1989.
53. SANKOFF, David: *Diversity and Diachrony.* 1986.
54. WEIDERT, Alfons: *Tibeto-Burman Tonology. A comparative analysis.* 1987
55. HALL, Robert A. Jr.: *Linguistics and Pseudo-Linguistics.* 1987.
56. HOCKETT, Charles F.: *Refurbishing our Foundations. Elementary linguistics from an advanced point of view.* 1987.
57. BUBENIK, Vít: *Hellenistic and Roman Greece as a Sociolinguistic Area.* 1989.
58. ARBEITMAN, Yoël. L. (ed.): *Fucus: A Semitic/Afrasian Gathering in Remembrance of Albert Ehrman.* 1988.
59. VAN VOORST, Jan: *Event Structure.* 1988.
60. KIRSCHNER, Carl & Janet DECESARIS (eds): *Studies in Romance Linguistics. Selected Proceedings from the XVII Linguistic Symposium on Romance Languages.* 1989.
61. CORRIGAN, Roberta L., Fred ECKMAN & Michael NOONAN (eds): *Linguistic Categorization. Proceedings of an International Symposium in Milwaukee, Wisconsin, April 10-11, 1987.* 1989.
62. FRAJZYNGIER, Zygmunt (ed.): *Current Progress in Chadic Linguistics. Proceedings of the International Symposium on Chadic Linguistics, Boulder, Colorado, 1-2 May 1987.* 1989.
63. EID, Mushira (ed.): *Perspectives on Arabic Linguistics I. Papers from the First Annual Symposium on Arabic Linguistics.* 1990.
64. BROGYANYI, Bela (ed.): *Prehistory, History and Historiography of Language, Speech, and Linguistic Theory. Papers in honor of Oswald Szemerényi I.* 1992.
65. ADAMSON, Sylvia, Vivien A. LAW, Nigel VINCENT and Susan WRIGHT (eds): *Papers from the 5th International Conference on English Historical Linguistics.* 1990.
66. ANDERSEN, Henning and Konrad KOERNER (eds): *Historical Linguistics 1987. Papers from the 8th International Conference on Historical Linguistics, Lille, August 30-Sept., 1987.* 1990.
67. LEHMANN, Winfred P. (ed.): *Language Typology 1987. Systematic Balance in Language. Papers from the Linguistic Typology Symposium, Berkeley, 1-3 Dec 1987.* 1990.
68. BALL, Martin, James FIFE, Erich POPPE &Jenny ROWLAND (eds): *Celtic Linguistics/ Ieithyddiaeth Geltaidd. Readings in the Brythonic Languages. Festschrift for T. Arwyn Watkins.* 1990.
69. WANNER, Dieter and Douglas A. KIBBEE (eds): *New Analyses in Romance Linguistics. Selected papers from the Linguistic Symposium on Romance Languages XVIIII, Urbana-Champaign, April 7-9, 1988.* 1991.
70. JENSEN, John T.: *Morphology. Word structure in generative grammar.* 1990.
71. O'GRADY, William: *Categories and Case. The sentence structure of Korean.* 1991.
72. EID, Mushira and John MCCARTHY (eds): *Perspectives on Arabic Linguistics II. Papers from the Second Annual Symposium on Arabic Linguistics.* 1990.
73. STAMENOV, Maxim (ed.): *Current Advances in Semantic Theory.* 1991.
74. LAEUFER, Christiane and Terrell A. MORGAN (eds): *Theoretical Analyses in Romance Linguistics.* 1991.
75. DROSTE, Flip G. and John E. JOSEPH (eds): *Linguistic Theory and Grammatical Description. Nine Current Approaches.* 1991.
76. WICKENS, Mark A.: *Grammatical Number in English Nouns. An empirical and theoretical account.* 1992.
77. BOLTZ, William G. and Michael C. SHAPIRO (eds): *Studies in the Historical Phonology of Asian Languages.* 1991.
78. KAC, Michael: *Grammars and Grammaticality.* 1992.

79. ANTONSEN, Elmer H. and Hans Henrich HOCK (eds): *STAEF-CRAEFT: Studies in Germanic Linguistics*. Select papers from the First and Second Symposium on Germanic Linguistics, University of Chicago, 24 April 1985, and Univ. of Illinois at Urbana-Champaign, 3-4 Oct. 1986. 1991.
80. COMRIE, Bernard and Mushira EID (eds): *Perspectives on Arabic Linguistics III*. Papers from the Third Annual Symposium on Arabic Linguistics. 1991.
81. LEHMANN, Winfred P. and H.J. HEWITT (eds): *Language Typology 1988. Typological Models in the Service of Reconstruction*. 1991.
82. VAN VALIN, Robert D. (ed.): *Advances in Role and Reference Grammar*. 1992.
83. FIFE, James and Erich POPPE (eds): *Studies in Brythonic Word Order*. 1991.
84. DAVIS, Garry W. and Gregory K. IVERSON (eds): *Explanation in Historical Linguistics*. 1992.
85. BROSELOW, Ellen, Mushira EID and John McCARTHY (eds): *Perspectives on Arabic Linguistics IV*. Papers from the Annual Symposium on Arabic Linguistics. 1992.
86. KESS, Joseph F.: *Psycholinguistics. Psychology, linguistics, and the study of natural language*. 1992.
87. BROGYANYI, Bela and Reiner LIPP (eds): *Historical Philology: Greek, Latin, and Romance*. Papers in honor of Oswald Szemerényi II. 1992.
88. SHIELDS, Kenneth: *A History of Indo-European Verb Morphology*. 1992.
89. BURRIDGE, Kate: *Syntactic Change in Germanic. A study of some aspects of language change in Germanic with particular reference to Middle Dutch*. 1992.
90. KING, Larry D.: *The Semantic Structure of Spanish. Meaning and grammatical form*. 1992.
91. HIRSCHBÜHLER, Paul and Konrad KOERNER (eds): *Romance Languages and Modern Linguistic Theory*. Selected papers from the XX Linguistic Symposium on Romance Languages, University of Ottawa, April 10-14, 1990. 1992.
92. POYATOS, Fernando: *Paralanguage: A linguistic and interdisciplinary approach to interactive speech and sounds*. 1992.
93. LIPPI-GREEN, Rosina (ed.): *Recent Developments in Germanic Linguistics*. 1992.
94. HAGÈGE, Claude: *The Language Builder. An essay on the human signature in linguistic morphogenesis*. 1992.
95. MILLER, D. Gary: *Complex Verb Formation*. 1992.
96. LIEB, Hans-Heinrich (ed.): *Prospects for a New Structuralism*. 1992.
97. BROGYANYI, Bela & Reiner LIPP (eds): *Comparative-Historical Linguistics: Indo-European and Finno-Ugric*. Papers in honor of Oswald Szemerényi III. 1992.
98. EID, Mushira & Gregory K. IVERSON: *Principles and Prediction: The analysis of natural language*. 1993.
99. JENSEN, John T.: *English Phonology*. 1993.
100. MUFWENE, Salikoko S. and Lioba MOSHI (eds): *Topics in African Linguistics*. Papers from the XXI Annual Conference on African Linguistics, University of Georgia, April 1990. 1993.
101. EID, Mushira & Clive HOLES (eds): *Perspectives on Arabic Linguistics V*. Papers from the Fifth Annual Symposium on Arabic Linguistics. 1993.
102. DAVIS, Philip W. (ed.): *Alternative Linguistics. Descriptive and theoretical Modes*. 1995.
103. ASHBY, William J., Marianne MITHUN, Giorgio PERISSINOTTO and Eduardo RAPOSO: *Linguistic Perspectives on Romance Languages*. Selected papers from the XXI Linguistic Symposium on Romance Languages, Santa Barbara, February 21-24, 1991. 1993.
104. KURZOVÁ, Helena: *From Indo-European to Latin. The evolution of a morphosyntactic type*. 1993.
105. HUALDE, José Ignacio and Jon ORTIZ DE URBANA (eds): *Generative Studies in Basque Linguistics*. 1993.
106. AERTSEN, Henk and Robert J. JEFFERS (eds): *Historical Linguistics 1989. Papers from the 9th International Conference on Historical Linguistics, New Brunswick, 14-18 August 1989*. 1993.

107. MARLE, Jaap van (ed.): *Historical Linguistics 1991. Papers from the 10th International Conference on Historical Linguistics, Amsterdam, August 12-16, 1991.* 1993.
108. LIEB, Hans-Heinrich: *Linguistic Variables. Towards a unified theory of linguistic variation.* 1993.
109. PAGLIUCA, William (ed.): *Perspectives on Grammaticalization.* 1994.
110. SIMONE, Raffaele (ed.): *Iconicity in Language.* 1995.
111. TOBIN, Yishai: *Invariance, Markedness and Distinctive Feature Analysis. A contrastive study of sign systems in English and Hebrew.* 1994.
112. CULIOLI, Antoine: *Cognition and Representation in Linguistic Theory. Translated, edited and introduced by Michel Liddle.* 1995.
113. FERNÁNDEZ, Francisco, Miguel FUSTER and Juan Jose CALVO (eds): *English Historical Linguistics 1992. Papers from the 7th International Conference on English Historical Linguistics, Valencia, 22-26 September 1992.*1994.
114. EGLI, U., P. PAUSE, Chr. SCHWARZE, A. von STECHOW, G. WIENOLD (eds): *Lexical Knowledge in the Organisation of Language.* 1995.
115. EID, Mushira, Vincente CANTARINO and Keith WALTERS (eds): *Perspectives on Arabic Linguistics. Vol. VI. Papers from the Sixth Annual Symposium on Arabic Linguistics.* 1994.
116. MILLER, D. Gary: *Ancient Scripts and Phonological Knowledge.* 1994.
117. PHILIPPAKI-WARBURTON, I., K. NICOLAIDIS and M. SIFIANOU (eds): *Themes in Greek Linguistics. Papers from the first International Conference on Greek Linguistics, Reading, September 1993.* 1994.
118. HASAN, Ruqaiya and Peter H. FRIES (eds): *On Subject and Theme. A discourse functional perspective.* 1995.
119. LIPPI-GREEN, Rosina: *Language Ideology and Language Change in Early Modern German. A sociolinguistic study of the consonantal system of Nuremberg.* 1994.
120. STONHAM, John T. : *Combinatorial Morphology.* 1994.
121. HASAN, Ruqaiya, Carmel CLORAN and David BUTT (eds): *Functional Descriptions. Theorie in practice.* 1996.
122. SMITH, John Charles and Martin MAIDEN (eds): *Linguistic Theory and the Romance Languages.* 1995.
123. AMASTAE, Jon, Grant GOODALL, Mario MONTALBETTI and Marianne PHINNEY: *Contemporary Research in Romance Linguistics. Papers from the XXII Linguistic Symposium on Romance Languages, El Paso//Juárez, February 22-24, 1994.* 1995.
124. ANDERSEN, Henning: *Historical Linguistics 1993. Selected papers from the 11th International Conference on Historical Linguistics, Los Angeles, 16-20 August 1993.* 1995.
125. SINGH, Rajendra (ed.): *Towards a Critical Sociolinguistics.* 1996.
126. MATRAS, Yaron (ed.): *Romani in Contact. The history, structure and sociology of a language.* 1995.
127. GUY, Gregory R., Crawford FEAGIN, Deborah SCHIFFRIN and John BAUGH (eds): *Towards a Social Science of Language. Papers in honor of William Labov. Volume 1: Variation and change in language and society.* 1996.
128. GUY, Gregory R., Crawford FEAGIN, Deborah SCHIFFRIN and John BAUGH (eds): *Towards a Social Science of Language. Papers in honor of William Labov. Volume 2: Social interaction and discourse structures.* 1997.
129. LEVIN, Saul: *Semitic and Indo-European: The Principal Etymologies. With observations on Afro-Asiatic.* 1995.
130. EID, Mushira (ed.) *Perspectives on Arabic Linguistics. Vol. VII. Papers from the Seventh Annual Symposium on Arabic Linguistics.* 1995.
131. HUALDE, Jose Ignacio, Joseba A. LAKARRA and R.L. Trask (eds): *Towards a History of the Basque Language.* 1995.
132. HERSCHENSOHN, Julia: *Case Suspension and Binary Complement Structure in French.* 1996.

133. ZAGONA, Karen (ed.): *Grammatical Theory and Romance Languages. Selected papers from the 25th Linguistic Symposium on Romance Languages (LSRL XXV) Seattle, 2-4 March 1995.* 1996.
134. EID, Mushira (ed.): *Perspectives on Arabic Linguistics Vol. VIII. Papers from the Eighth Annual Symposium on Arabic Linguistics.* 1996.
135. BRITTON Derek (ed.): *Papers from the 8th International Conference on English Historical Linguistics.* 1996.
136. MITKOV, Ruslan and Nicolas NICOLOV (eds): *Recent Advances in Natural Language Processing.* 1997.
137. LIPPI-GREEN, Rosina and Joseph C. SALMONS (eds): *Germanic Linguistics. Syntactic and diachronic.* 1996.
138. SACKMANN, Robin (ed.): *Theoretical Linguistics and Grammatical Description.* 1996.
139. BLACK, James R. and Virginia MOTAPANYANE (eds): *Microparametric Syntax and Dialect Variation.* 1996.
140. BLACK, James R. and Virginia MOTAPANYANE (eds): *Clitics, Pronouns and Movement.* 1997.
141. EID, Mushira and Dilworth PARKINSON (eds): *Perspectives on Arabic Linguistics Vol. IX. Papers from the Ninth Annual Symposium on Arabic Linguistics, Georgetown University, Washington D.C., 1995.* 1996.
142. JOSEPH, Brian D. and Joseph C. SALMONS (eds): *Nostratic. Sifting the evidence.* 1998.
143. ATHANASIADOU, Angeliki and René DIRVEN (eds): *On Conditionals Again.* 1997.
144. SINGH, Rajendra (ed): *Trubetzkoy's Orphan. Proceedings of the Montréal Roundtable "Morphophonology: contemporary responses (Montréal, October 1994).* 1996.
145. HEWSON, John and Vit BUBENIK: *Tense and Aspect in Indo-European Languages. Theory, typology, diachrony.* 1997.
146. HINSKENS, Frans, Roeland VAN HOUT and W. Leo WETZELS (eds): *Variation, Change, and Phonological Theory.* 1997.
147. HEWSON, John: *The Cognitive System of the French Verb.* 1997.
148. WOLF, George and Nigel LOVE (eds): *Linguistics Inside Out. Roy Harris and his critics.* 1997.
149. HALL, T. Alan: *The Phonology of Coronals.* 1997.
150. VERSPOOR, Marjolijn, Kee Dong LEE and Eve SWEETSER (eds): *Lexical and Syntactical Constructions and the Construction of Meaning. Proceedings of the Bi-annual ICLA meeting in Albuquerque, July 1995.* 1997.
151. LIEBERT, Wolf-Andreas, Gisela REDEKER and Linda WAUGH (eds): *Discourse and Perspectives in Cognitive Linguistics.* 1997.
152. HIRAGA, Masako, Chris SINHA and Sherman WILCOX (eds): *Cultural, Psychological and Typological Issues in Cognitive Linguistics.* 1999.
153. EID, Mushira and Robert R. RATCLIFFE (eds): *Perspectives on Arabic Linguistics Vol. X. Papers from the Tenth Annual Symposium on Arabic Linguistics, Salt Lake City, 1996.* 1997.
154. SIMON-VANDENBERGEN, Anne-Marie, Kristin DAVIDSE and Dirk NOËL (eds): *Reconnecting Language. Morphology and Syntax in Functional Perspectives.* 1997.
155. FORGET, Danielle, Paul HIRSCHBÜHLER, France MARTINEAU and María-Luisa RIVERO (eds): *Negation and Polarity. Syntax and semantics. Selected papers from the Colloquium Negation: Syntax and Semantics. Ottawa, 11-13 May 1995.* 1997.
156. MATRAS, Yaron, Peter BAKKER and Hristo KYUCHUKOV (eds): *The Typology and Dialectology of Romani.* 1997.
157. LEMA, José and Esthela TREVIÑO (eds): *Theoretical Analyses on Romance Languages. Selected papers from the 26th Linguistic Symposium on Romance Languages (LSRL XXVI), Mexico City, 28-30 March, 1996.* 1998.

158. SÁNCHEZ MACARRO, Antonia and Ronald CARTER (eds): *Linguistic Choice across Genres. Variation in spoken and written English.* 1998.
159. JOSEPH, Brian D., Geoffrey C. HORROCKS and Irene PHILIPPAKI-WARBURTON (eds): *Themes in Greek Linguistics II.* 1998.
160. SCHWEGLER, Armin, Bernard TRANEL and Myriam URIBE-ETXEBARRIA (eds): *Romance Linguistics: Theoretical Perspectives. Selected papers from the 27th Linguistic Symposium on Romance Languages (LSRL XXVII), Irvine, 20-22 February, 1997.* 1998.
161. SMITH, John Charles and Delia BENTLEY (eds): *Historical Linguistics 1995. Volume 1: Romance and general linguistics.* 1999.
162. HOGG, Richard M. and Linda van BERGEN (eds): *Historical Linguistics 1995. Volume 2: Germanic linguistics.Selected papers from the 12th International Conference on Historical Linguistics, Manchester, August 1995.* 1998.
163. LOCKWOOD, David G., Peter H. FRIES and James E. COPELAND (eds): *Functional Approaches to Language, Culture and Cognition.* 2000.
164. SCHMID, Monika, Jennifer R. AUSTIN and Dieter STEIN (eds): *Historical Linguistics 1997. Selected papers from the 13th International Conference on Historical Linguistics, Düsseldorf, 10-17 August 1997.* 1998.
165. BUBENÍK, Vit: *A Historical Syntax of Late Middle Indo-Aryan (Apabhramśa).* 1998.
166. LEMMENS, Maarten: *Lexical Perspectives on Transitivity and Ergativity. Causative constructions in English.* 1998.
167. BENMAMOUN, Elabbas, Mushira EID and Niloofar HAERI (eds): *Perspectives on Arabic Linguistics Vol. XI. Papers from the Eleventh Annual Symposium on Arabic Linguistics, Atlanta, 1997.* 1998.
168. RATCLIFFE, Robert R.: *The "Broken" Plural Problem in Arabic and Comparative Semitic. Allomorphy and analogy in non-concatenative morphology.* 1998.
169. GHADESSY, Mohsen (ed.): *Text and Context in Functional Linguistics.* 1999.
170. LAMB, Sydney M.: *Pathways of the Brain. The neurocognitive basis of language.* 1999.
171. WEIGAND, Edda (ed.): *Contrastive Lexical Semantics.* 1998.
172. DIMITROVA-VULCHANOVA, Mila and Lars HELLAN (eds): *Topics in South Slavic Syntax and Semantics.* 1999.
173. TREVIÑO, Esthela and José LEMA (eds): *Semantic Issues in Romance Syntax.* 1999.
174. HALL, T. Alan and Ursula KLEINHENZ (eds): *Studies on the Phonological Word.* 1999.
175. GIBBS, Ray W. and Gerard J. STEEN (eds): *Metaphor in Cognitive Linguistics. Selected papers from the 5th International Cognitive Linguistics Conference, Amsterdam, 1997.* 1999.
176. VAN HOEK, Karen, Andrej KIBRIK and Leo NOORDMAN (eds): *Discourse in Cognitive Linguistics. Selected papers from the International Cognitive Linguistics Conference, Amsterdam, July 1997.* 1999.
177. CUYCKENS, Hubert and Britta ZAWADA (eds): *Polysemy in Cognitive Linguistics. Selected papers from the International Cognitive Linguistics Conference, Amsterdam, 1997.* n.y.p.
178. FOOLEN, Ad and Frederike van der LEEK (eds): *Constructions in Cognitive Linguistics. Selected papers from the International Cognitive Linguistic Conference, Amsterdam, 1997.* n.y.p.
179. RINI, Joel: *Exploring the Role of Morphology in the Evolution of Spanish.* 1999.
180. MEREU, Lunella (ed.): *Boundaries of Morphology and Syntax.* 1999.
181. MOHAMMAD, Mohammad A.: *Word Order, Agreement and Pronominalization in Standard and Palestinian Arabic.* n.y.p.
182. KENESEI, István (ed.): *Theoretical Issues in Eastern European Languages. Selected papers from the Conference on Linguistic Theory in Eastern European Languages (CLITE), Szeged, April 1998.* 1999.

183. CONTINI-MORAVA, Ellen and Yishai TOBIN (eds): *Between Grammar and Lexicon.* n.y.p.
184. SAGART, Laurent: *The Roots of Old Chinese.* 1999.
185. AUTHIER, J.-Marc, Barbara E. BULLOCK, Lisa A. REED (eds): *Formal Perspectives on Romance Linguistics. Selected papers from the 28th Linguistic Symposium on Romance Languages (LSRL XXVIII), University Park, 16-19 April 1998.* 1999.
186. MIŠESKA TOMIĆ, Olga and Milorad RADOVANOVIĆ (eds): *History and Perspectives of Language Study.* n.y.p.
187. FRANCO, Jon, Alazne LANDA and Juan MARTÍN (eds): *Grammatical Analyses in Basque and Romance Linguistics.* 1999.
188. VanNESS SIMMONS, Richard: *Chinese Dialect Classification. A comparative approach to Harngjou, Old Jintrn, and Common Northern Wu.* 1999.
189. NICHOLOV, Nicolas and Ruslan MITKOV (eds): *Recent Advances in Natural Language Processing II. Selected papers from RANLP '97.* 1999.
190. BENMAMOUN, Elabbas (ed.): *Perspectives on Arabic Linguistics Vol. XII. Papers from the Twelfth Annual Symposium on Arabic Linguistics.* 1999.
191. SIHLER, Andrew L.: *Language Change. A brief introduction for students of ancient languages and language history.* 2000.
192. ALEXANDROVA, Galia, Olga ARNAUDOVA and Michele FOLEY (eds): *The Minimalist Parameter. Selected papers from the Open Linguistics Forum, Ottawa, 21-23 March 1997.* n.y.p.
193. KLAUSENBURGER, Jurgen: *Grammaticalization. Studies in Latin and Romance morphosyntax.* n.y.p.
194. COLEMAN, Julie and Christian J. KAY (eds): *Lexicology, Semantics and Lexicography. Selected papers from the Fourth G. L. Brook Symposium, Manchester, August 1998.* n.y.p.
195. HERRING, Susan C., Pieter van REENEN and Lene SCHØSLER (eds): *Textual Parameters in Older Languages.* n.y.p.
196. HANNAHS, S. J. and Mike DAVENPORT (eds): *Issues in Phonological Structure. Papers from the International Workshop on Phonological Structure, University of Durham, September 1994.* 1999.
197. COOPMANS, Peter, Martin EVERAERT and Jane GRIMSHAW (eds): *Lexical Specification and Insertion.* 2000.
198. NIEMEIER, Susanne and René DIRVEN (eds): *Evidence in Linguistic Relativity.* n.y.p.
199. VERSPOOR, Marjolijn H. and Martin PÜTZ (eds): *Explorations in Linguistic Relativity.* n.y.p.
200. In preparation.
201. PÖCHTRAGER, Markus, Wolfgang U. DRESSLER, Oskar E. PFEIFFER and John R. RENNISON (eds.): *Morphologica 1996.* n.y.p.
202. LECARME, Jacqueline, Jean LOWENSTAMM and Ur SHLONSKY (eds.): *Research in Afroasiatic Grammar. Papers from the Third conference on Afroasiatic Languages, Sophia Antipolis, 1996.* n.y.p.